PORTRAIT OF THE MIDWEST

Douglas Waitley

# PORTRAIT OF
# THE MIDWEST

From the Ice Age to the Industrial Era

Abelard-Schuman

London   New York   Toronto

To Mary:
Wife, sweetheart, and buddy

Library of Congress Catalogue Card Number 63-16298

| LONDON | NEW YORK | TORONTO |
|---|---|---|
| Abelard-Schuman | Abelard-Schuman | Abelard-Schuman |
| Limited | Limited | Canada Limited |
| 8 King Street | 6 West 57th Street | 896 Queen Street W. |

Printed in the United States of America

# Preface

As a person who was born in the Midwest and has spent most of his life in the Midwest, it has been very disturbing to find so few books written with this region specifically in mind. Midwestern schools teach little local history, and for the person of average curiosity there is almost no way to learn about locales of historical or scenic interest.

Between 1959 and 1961 the author took a series of trips around the Midwest, during which time he made it his business to seek out every place that would appeal to the layman. These trips, and the subsequent research, form the basis for PORTRAIT OF THE MIDWEST.

It has been a labor of love, an adventure, actually. It is hoped that the reader will visit many of the sites described in the Vagabond Section, and will enjoy them as much as did the author.

I am in debt to the scores of kind persons who gave me aid, directions and information during my travels and research. Many state and local historical societies have received my question-filled letters and have been kind enough to answer them. Space limits my acknowledgements of these kindnesses, but I must mention the invaluable help received from Mrs. Edgar Lee Masters, from the historical societies in New Ulm, Dubuque, Cincinnati, Greenfield, Chicago, Saugatuck, St. Louis, Ludington, Menominee (although I couldn't use their information), Cleveland, and especially Clyde, where Mr. Thaddeus B. Hurd furnished me with facts concerning Sherwood Anderson which I would not have obtained anywhere else.

I owe a great debt to my wife for encouragement when the going was slow, for gaiety and interest on our innumerable trips, for proof reading and improving my manuscript, and for aid in correcting my spelling, which I know is abominable.

DOUGLAS WAITLEY

# ACKNOWLEDGEMENTS

I am grateful to the following publishers and individuals for permission to reprint from their publications:

To The Viking Press, Inc. for the quotations from *Winesburg, Ohio* by Sherwood Anderson on page 152.

To Vanguard Press for the quotations from *Studs Lonigan* by James T. Farrell on pages 154 and 155.

To Holt, Rinehart & Winston, Inc. for the quotations from *Chicago Poems* by Carl Sandburg on pages 149 and 150.

To Harcourt, Brace & World, Inc. for the quotation from *Memoirs* by Sherwood Anderson on page 151.

To Mrs. Edgar Lee Masters for the quotations from *Spoon River Anthology* by Edgar Lee Masters on pages 146, 147 and 150.

The quotation on page 143 is from *Newspaper Days* by Theodore Dreiser (Horace Liveright, 1922) and that on page 144 from *Sister Carrie* by Theodore Dreiser (Doubleday, Page & Co., 1927).

I would like to thank the Chicago Historical Society for the use of the photographs that appear on pages 44, 80, 115, 129 and 163. Those that appear on pages 34, 66, 99 and 171 were reproduced by permission of the Ohio State Archaeological and Historical Society, the Indiana Department of Conservation, the State Historical Society of Wisconsin and the Ford Motor Company respectively.

The photograph on page 166 was taken by the author.

# Contents

# Illustrations

# CHAPTER ONE

# Progress along the diagonal

*Midwest characteristics: glaciers, black soil and corn, moundbuilders and Algonquins, French, Northwest Ordinance, economic contributions, writers, rivers, lakes, cities, seasonal changes*
*Frontier towns: Hudson, Ohio; Cairo, Illinois; Kansas City, Missouri; Council Bluffs, Iowa; Sault Ste. Marie, Michigan.*

*Not long ago* a young Englishman was touring the United States. A graduate of Oxford and a staff member of the London *Times*, he visited every section of our country. When he was through, he wrote down his impressions in a popular book entitled *As I Saw the U.S.A.* In it he divided the country into several sections. The East he found to be "mellowed," the South "melancholy," the West "vivid." But when he came to the Midwest, he was stumped, for as he states, "nobody knows quite what the Middle West is."

Actually, this confusion as to what characterizes the Midwest does not belong solely to this author, James Morris, and his fellow foreign travelers. Americans themselves have a tendency to be evasive when asked just what they consider to be the Midwest. Probably

11

the cause of this uncertainty is the fact that the Midwest is regarded as so very typically American that it seems to have few distinct or peculiar characteristics setting it apart from the nation as a whole.

Amorphous as it may seem, the present eight-states area comprising the Midwest is geologically a unit unto itself, separate from the rest of the country. These states — Illinois, Indiana, Iowa, Michigan, Minnesota, Ohio, Wisconsin, and northern Missouri — were subjected to the effects of four glaciations which demolished the Midwestern mountains, formed the landscape into rolling hills of glacial debris, and pushed the Ohio and Missouri rivers into their present positions. The southernmost boundaries of the glaciers correspond almost exactly to the boundaries of the Midwest.

Not only did the glaciers give the Midwest a distinctive land contour, but the gravel they laid down gradually combined with decomposed grass and leaves to produce a soil of black richness, which in itself sets the region off from the stony soil of New England and the Pacific Coast and the red soil of the South.

This black soil has made possible the fabulous corn belt which begins in Ohio, crosses Indiana, and reaches a fruitful climax on the prairies of Illinois and Iowa. Anyone who drives through the Midwest cannot help but he impressed with the mile after mile of corn that forms a huge green sea as summer comes on. No region anywhere can match the corn belt's fantastic fertility. Even if the Midwest had no other distinctions, its acres of boundless corn would quickly set it off from the dreary cotton fields, the oven-hot wheat fields, or the rock-bound truck gardens which border it to the south, west, and east.

In the prehistoric Indian world, the Midwest was likewise separate. There developed along the northern banks of the Ohio and its tributaries a unique race of mound builders called Hopewellians. Their ancient forts, animal effigies and burial mounds bespoke a culture far different from the southern pyramid builders or the southwestern pueblo builders. And after the mound builders had passed, the Algonquin-speaking tribes were to be found in their place, at constant warfare with the alien Sioux and Iroquois who raided them from the west and east.

During the seventeenth century, while English settlers were turning the Atlantic coast into an appendage of Britain, hardy Frenchmen were guiding their canoes through the waters of Midwestern rivers. For the almost one hundred years that the area belonged to the French, the Appalachians were a definite frontier — as real as the Alps or the Pyrenees. This French heritage has left the region with scores of French place names, among which are the cities of the sainted Louis IX (St. Louis) and Ville d'Etroit (Detroit).

After the British had won the Midwest from the French, they too recognized it as being separate from the coastal colonies and attached it to the Canadian government at Quebec. The American colonists were forbidden to migrate into this Indian wilderness.

The role of the Midwest in the Revolutionary War again demonstrates its distinctiveness. The desire of the colonists for this land forbidden them by the British was a main cause of the war; for George Washington, Benjamin Franklin, and a large percentage of the Founding Fathers had heavy investments in Midwestern land which would bring them no returns unless it was open to migration.

Immediately after the Revolution, before the Federal government itself was created, the Continental Congress gave the Midwest formal recognition by passing the famous Ordinance of 1785 which created the Northwest Territory from all the land between the Ohio, the Mississippi, and the Great Lakes. This same ordinance, by decreeing that the section lines of this new territory should be laid out in straight north-south, east-west lines, further set the region off from the coastal areas where the lines followed the irregular contours of the land. This compass-true direction of Midwestern section lines is quite startling to the modern air tourist who cannot help but see that he is entering a new region when he leaves the patchwork of eastern fields and comes upon the arrow lines of the trans-Appalachian Midwest.

The Continental Congress passed an even more important law two years later. The Ordinance of 1787 proclaimed that slavery should be prohibited in the Northwest Territory. This meant independent farmers, rather than an aristocracy of plantation owners, would form the social system of the new region. The absence of slavery was a tremendous incentive to immigration, for it meant that the land was open to millions of small farmers, not restricted to a few large plantation owners. Soon great waves of north Europeans were added to the migrating Easterners. Both groups were favorably impressed by the remoteness of the mid-continental region and combined to make the Midwest the most isolationist of American sections.

The part played by the Midwest in the Civil War was decisive. The nation just prior to the war was not split into two parts, as is commonly believed, but into three. There was the East, the South, and the Midwest — or simply the West, as it was known as then. For many years the South and the West had been closely drawn to each other both by lines of trade which ran down the Mississippi and by a common dislike for the high tariff policies of the Eastern manufacturers. It was only when the slavery issue drove the West into the Eastern camp that the South found itself a lone third and decided to make the break. And when the war came it was Midwesterners, not Easterners, who led the North to victory — it was Abraham Lincoln, from Illinois, who kept the nation steady while Grant and Sherman, both Ohio born, drove their Western armies through the Southern lines.

We have thus far recounted some of the Midwest's differences from the rest of the country — geographical, geological, pre-historical, and historical: its Hopewellian and Algonquin Indians, its French heritage, its particular immigration pattern, its isolationist tendencies, its role in the Revolutionary and Civil Wars. Moreover, the contributions of Midwesterners to modern national life have been just as distinct.

Politically, this nation has been ruled since the days of Lincoln by more presidents of Midwestern origin than from all other regions combined. Economically, the Midwest has had more than its share of inventors and business tycoons. There was Thomas Edison from Milan, Ohio, who turned his native genius toward the field of electricity, revolutionizing the world's lighting industry; John D. Rockefeller, who formed the Standard Oil trust in Cleveland and soon controlled ninety percent of the nation's petroleum; Henry Ford, who set his practical Midwestern mind toward mass production and erected an automotive empire; Elbert Gary, early chairman of United States Steel, the goliath of American industry; George Pullman who built and ran a town on Chicago's south side in which was manufactured the sleeping car which so altered railroad travel. These and many more Midwesterners began economic enterprises which have affected almost every phase of American life.

About the same time the Midwest was finding its place politically and economically, its authors were aiding in the creation of a new type of American literature. It was Mark Twain from Hannibal, Missouri, who more than any other person brought the ordinary, everyday American, not some romanticized image, into fiction. The Hoosier, Theodore Dreiser, provided the entire nation with a new and frank outlook on morality in fiction. Sinclair Lewis, seeing the hypocrisies of the entire country in the microcosm of his little Minnesota home town, broke upon the nation like a prairie thunderstorm. And from the grasslands of Illinois, Edgar Lee Masters and Carl Sandburg began writing a new type of verse that quickly became a model for poets everywhere.

But for me Midwestern distinctiveness is more than remembrances of deeds past. There is an everyday beauty to be found here. No region anywhere can boast, for example, of such wonderful rivers as the Midwest. There is the grand Mississippi, born in the murmuring rushes of Lake Itasca, wending its way shyly through the prairies and forests of northern Minnesota, cascading past Minneapolis, rushing down the spectacular canyon it has cut through the limestone of Wisconsin and Iowa, merging with the turbid Missouri a few miles above St. Louis, sweeping past Hannibal, a city still wearing its memories of the steamboat era, meandering at last past Cairo where it melts in the magnolia lands of the South.

And then there are the two main tributaries of the Mississippi: the Ohio and the Missouri — the one having its source in the rolling Appalachians, once a highway for the pioneering settlers who drifted down its forested shores to the frontier towns of Marietta and Cincinnati; the other having its source in the jagged Rockies, once a highway for rough-and-tumble fur traders, who laboriously made their way up the thick current to posts on the scorched plains and plateaus of the Far West. The two rivers, so very different in their texture, their shoreline, their destination, demonstrate the tremendous geographical breadth of the parent Mississippi.

And, there are other rivers, small and friendly: the Fox, a playful little creek at the point where Father Marquette found the Indian path that led him to the Mississippi system; the Rock, a placid mirror in the summer, saturated at all times with memories of tragic Blackhawk; the Maumee, sluggish and clay-embanked, along whose shores "Mad" Anthony Wayne led an inspired American army and from whose cliffs the ill-fated Tecumseh later watched his dream of an Indian federation die an ignoble death.

There is a beauty in the Midwestern lakes, too. Who can forget the exotic Sahara of sand that forms the eastern coast of Lake Michigan, reaching its climax at the huge dune called Sleeping Bear; the pale blue of Lake Erie one sees during a boat trip to the Perry Monument on South Bass Island; or the rusty, ore-colored water of Lake Superior seen from the volcanic-formed bluffs above Duluth?

And there are smaller lakes that have their own special enchantment. There is Cormorant Lake lost amid the morainic hills of western Minnesota, whose rocks still show holes made by Vikings who were massacred there a hundred years before Columbus. There is Lake Peoria where one can see the rocky ledge upon which the fort of the unfortunate La Salle once stood. There are even little lily ponds, like the one at Amana, Iowa, where the delicate flowers remind one of the seventy-eight-year experiment in communal living.

The cities, too, have a beauty not commonly appreciated: Chicago, the unofficial Midwestern capital, whose gigantic skyscrapers stand on land where Potawatomis once lurked to massacre the garrison of little Fort Dearborn, and whose grassy Grant Park forms a restful glade against the turquoise of Lake Michigan; Cleveland, caught in the velvet haze of the Cuyahoga valley, whose New England city square helps one recall the days when northern Ohio was merely a wilderness colony of distant Connecticut; Detroit, astride the Huron-Erie Strait, drinking down the lake-born commerce that brings the mountains of materials for her humming automotive factories, little remembering the days when Antoine Cadillac doffed his feathered cap to claim the land for the empire of France.

There is St. Louis, crowding over a low mound beside the Mississippi, boasting relics of the days when she was the world's leading fur port; and boisterous Kansas City, gazing westward from the Missouri bluffs, or St. Paul gazing southward from the Mississippi bluffs.

There is Milwaukee pulsating to the rhythm of the countless trains which make the Menomonee canyon a sea of freight cars; or Indianapolis, an alien, bustling city oddly out of place in the dreamy Hoosier-land of James Whitcomb Riley.

There is also a particular beauty in the seasons of this region where each month carries within it souvenirs of the preceding season and harbingers of the season to come. In winter huge drifts cover Mackinac Island until it looks like a mountain of snow; Lake Erie freezes over so firmly that cars can be driven across its western end; and along Main Street in Sauk Centre, Minnesota, the fresh white begins to turn gray as the snow-bound citizens watch hopefully for the thaw that seems so far away.

Yet even while the snow is falling in the north, chartreuse shoots of new life begin to pierce the soggy soil in hill-clad Brown County, Indiana. Soon the spring tide waxes full, and the countryside is alive with the bubbling brooks that seem to have sprung from nowhere to eat hungrily at the tired snow. Before long the Japanese crab apples are in fragrant bloom around the George Rogers Clark monument in Vincennes, and the exotic Golden Rain trees at New Harmony blossom forth on another year the millenial-minded Rappites were sure would never come. Then, as the season moves northward, the tulips at Holland, Michigan, burst forth, enchanting the many visitors who come to enjoy the annual Tulip Festival. And at last Upper Michigan is touched. Wild mustard covers the land, crowding against the paths Hiawatha once trod until it seems as if the world was about to be engulfed by an ocean of liquid butter.

Sometime in June spring imperceptibly turns into summer. Then the prairies where Abe Lincoln rode the circuit as a country lawyer begin to bristle with the first shoots of corn—the great god Mondamin to the Algonquin Indian tribes. The warm south wind drifts down streets in a thousand Midwestern towns where children just released from the rigors of school seek adventure as modern Tom Sawyers. By the time the rockets of July Fourth light the sky summer has reached its most pleasant stage. The symbolic flower garden at Zoar, Ohio, is at its fullest bloom; the weeping willows at Marietta, Ohio, dangle in the mild water of the Muskingum at the place where the first American settlers landed in the Midwest; and multicolored hollyhocks bloom along the National Road, their petals looking like sunbonnets of the hardy women who made the hard trek west and whose countenances are so clearly seen in the Madonna of the Trail monuments.

Then summer makes its inspiring finale in the hills of Iowa where foot-high blossoms of wild vervain grow in gigantic purple clusters in every field; where bouquets of wild bergamot powder every rise with soft lavender, lending a spicy scent to the hot, sluggish air.

Autumn moves sideways into summer, mingling and merging with it until September becomes a beautiful halfbreed. Gradually, in fields from Ohio to Illinois spikes of goldenrod begin to take the place of the yellow and white sweet clover. Before long, purple petals of wild aster and the yellow discs of the sunflower begin to cover the roadsides. Then one begins to notice a nip in the evening air and, if he is in Minnesota, he will see groups of ducks congregating in the ponds around which the leaves of the scarlet maple have just begun to turn color. By the time the flocks of ducks and geese begin to migrate down the Mississippi flyway, the oaks at Wyalusing, Marquette's vantage point of the Great River, are dropping their acorns, and sycamores at the Serpent Mound in Ohio are sending their nuts bouncing down the hillside. Rooters of the Big Ten football teams begin to fill the stadiums in the college towns now. Along Ohio roadsides college boys offer tourists low prices on apple cider, while about them orange and gold maple leaves cascade like confetti.

At last autumn grows weary and, as she begins to slumber, winter steals again upon the scene. Midwestern attics are then ransacked for skis and ice skates and last year's overcoats. Thanksgiving fades into the joys of Yuletide, and the year is complete.

Yes, the Midwest is in many ways a region unto itself. Yet sometimes it is easiest to understand the characteristics of the region by viewing the frontier towns—towns which display the vivid differences between the Midwest and the regions bordering it. There is in eastern Ohio, for instance, the town of Hudson. Founded as early as 1799 by David Hudson of Connecticut, the town, with its white frame houses and village green, is typically New England. As one walks down the hillside streets, he would see quite clearly that Hudson was not Midwestern, except geographically.

Or there is Cairo, located at the extreme southern tip of Illinois.

Farther south than Richmond, Virginia, it has a flavor entirely different from the hurry of northern Illinois. Life is easy in Cairo as the citizens sit on their wide verandas beneath magnolia trees that are green all winter. The weather is always warm from the winds that drift up from the former slave-lands across the Ohio. The citizens speak with a Southern drawl that quickly distinguishes them from other Midwesterners.

On the western borderlands the difference is likewise clear. The very flatness of the Great Plains as seen from Rainbow Drive at Council Bluffs, Iowa, tell the viewer he is leaving the soft, glaciated Midwestern hills. And at Kansas City, Missouri, the scene from Lookout Point is even more telling — the wide Missouri gracefully curving northward into the lands where the buffalo and Sioux were once supreme, the Kansas River disappearing westward into the distant horizon, outlining in gray the first portions of the Santa Fe and Oregon Trails, jumping-off points for three generations of traders and settlers. Wheat and cattle are words on the tongues and in the minds of these westerners, not the corn and the dairy cows of the true Midwesterner.

And in the north the transition is just as obvious. Those who stand on the observation platform of the MacArthur lock at Sault Ste. Marie in Upper Michigan will look over the international boundary toward the forests and lakes nestling in the hollows of a world of glistening granite. The great glaciers, which scraped away the Canadian top soil and redeposited it as the Midwestern moraines, left this part of Canada a sterile place in contrast to the lush fertility of the Midwest.

No matter how you view it the Midwest is a distinct region — and this is for the best. There is a tendency in America toward standardization which is breaking down the regional diversity. Yet this very separateness is needed if the United States is to take advantage of the creative energies of her people. Regionalism is a necessity for, as Frederick Jackson Turner, one of America's foremost historians, has written:

> (The regions) are fields for experiment in the growth of different types of society, political institutions, and ideals. They constitute an impelling force for progress along the diagonal of contending varieties . . . they promote that reasonable competition and cooperation which is the way of a richer life.

# CHAPTER TWO

# In the beginning

*Birth of the earth*
*Silurian lime deposits*
*Illinois coal forests*
*Michigan Basin*
*Formation of Appalachian Mountains*
*Glacial Period: moraines, kames and*
*kettles, pre-glacial rivers, birth of the*
*Great Lakes*
*Formation of soil*

WHERE does one begin when he wishes to paint the portrait of a region? Does he go back to the first pioneers who laboriously made their way into the virgin forests and prairies? No, for before the pioneers there were the bands of Indian tribes who filtered through the wilderness like bronze shadows. They were the first Midwesterners. But one must go back even earlier than the Indians, for before them there was the Land. Men may come and go, nations rise and fall, but the land will remain: the hills will still stand in immovable outline against the sky, the rivers will still flow down their limestone valleys, the lakes will still rustle against the sand and nudge the cattails that grow in the marshes. The land — earth, rocks, and sand — is truly the building block of the world, and the portrait of any region must begin with it.

Yet there was a time when even the land did not exist. Geologists estimate that the earth is about three billion years old and that during the greater part of two billion years it was a mass of molten gasses, a flaming miniature sun in which the seeds of billowing trees, of circling hawks, and of man himself were yet to come. Gradually portions of the burning crust began to cool and, as they solidified, became island-continents of granite floating on the still molten basalt beneath. Then, after the ocean basins had cooled, steam, which had enveloped the earth in dense clouds, began to fall as rain into those wide depressions — the oceans had been formed at last.

But the water did not lie dormant in its wide basins. Slowly it rose, until it began inundating the continental masses. The Midwest, a low area in the center of the North American land block, began to experience the first of many oceanic floodings. Up from the Gulf of Mexico the water came until it covered the Midwest and much of North America. About 500,000,000 B.C. the invading ocean carried something new in its warm depths — Life. Thus, strangely, the first living creatures in the Midwest, a region now remote from the ocean, were born of the sea.

The animals that lived in these ancient oceans may seem to have little relation to the current Midwest, but the fact is quite the contrary. Imagine, if you will, how the waters of these inland oceans must have once appeared. Corals grew in large clumps, covering the rocks with towering castles of red and pink, around which the first primeval fish swam like knights errant. Huge cephalopods crawled slowly along the ocean floor, only their quivering tentacles protruding from their beautiful, curled shells. Small trilobites scuttled everywhere like armor-encased centipedes. And, most striking of all, the graceful animals called Sea Lilies swayed on body-stalks which often reached ten feet in height and which ended in a wreath of five to forty delicate arms. With their brilliant colors of yellow, red, white, green, and brown, they were like bright bizarre flowers in bloom.

As the endless years passed, each animal of this ocean of the Silurian period lived its allotted time, then died, its scaly body settling into the sludge already mounting on the ocean bottom. Gradually the accumulated shells compressed into hard limestone rock. After the Silurian Sea receded, this limestone remained — often hundreds of feet in thickness — to form some day in the distant future the basin of Lake Michigan, the white cliffs of Wisconsin's beautiful Door Peninsula, the high bluffs of Mackinac Island, and the barrier over which the waters of the upper four Great Lakes cascade at Niagara. Thus much of the Midwest is built on the bodies of countless sea animals that lived 300 million years ago. Where, the limestone is exposed, the observer stands in an ancient graveyard.

After the Silurian Sea had retreated to the Gulf, the earth began a series of contortions that seem almost unbelievable to us who think of the land as being so stable. The earth beneath Cincinnati slowly rose in a broad dome. About the same time the land in northern Wisconsin swelled upward. Then a long, narrow arch spread across Illinois and Indiana connecting the two domes. Another arch crossed northward from Cincinnati, beyond Detroit into Canada.

The rise of the domes and arches caused other areas to sink — an event of utmost importance to future Midwestern development. Central and southern Illinois, the territory west of the arch, dropped into a low, ill-drained depression that soon became a vast swamp. In this mucky, yet extremely fertile area, thick forests took root. But they were forests quite unlike any to be seen today. There were no fragrant pines, no gnarled oaks, no autumn-gold maples — evolution had not proceeded that far. Instead, the roof of the forest trembled with the filigree foliage of huge fern trees — some of which rose to one hundred feet. And, covering the forest floor, was a thick undergrowth of fern bushes, each leaf as delicate and as gracefully formed as finest lace. Large, multi-winged insects, many with wingspans over two feet, buzzed from plant to plant; but otherwise the forest was completely silent, for the germ of the first bird lay hidden yet within the cells of those reptiles whose snouts protruded above the stagnant swamp water. It would be a strange scene for those used to the treeless prairielands of modern Illinois.

As the giant ferns died, they toppled into the still water where they gradually decomposed into peat — millions of years later to change into coal. The presence of this coal brought the steel industry to Chicago and Gary and was basic in establishing the Midwest as an industrial region. Much of this coal was found so close to the surface that it was profitable to mine it by scraping off the fifty feet of gravel which covered it and dig it out with huge steam shovels. This open-pit method left the land a jumbled complex of gravel and clay. It reaches its most unusual form around Braidwood, Illinois, where long rows of treeless earth have been piled up to form a lunar landscape. It is an eerie experience to drive down some of the county roads and find flakes of coal in which there is the firm imprint of a delicate fern leaf that is over 225 million years old.

Between the arches which ran through Chicago to Wisconsin and through Detroit to Canada, another wide and very deep depression developed. Known as the Michigan Basin, it has played an essential part in the development of the Midwest; for, as the area sunk, it forced the Silurian limestone on its outer edges upward like the rim of a saucer. The rain that over a period of millions of years washed down the sides of the saucer gradually formed deep valleys between the upward curve of the limestone and the debris that it had washed part way down. These drainage patterns set the stage for the later emergence of Lake Michigan and Lake Huron.

The period after the formation of the Illinois coal fields and the Michigan Basin was important for events which happened in the east and west. The area between Ohio and the Atlantic had been a flat, swampy place similar in most respects to the bogs of Illinois. However, the land was slowly compressed and, under tremendous pressure, folded upward in long ridges which became the Appalachian Mountains. When, 100 million years later, the Rockies were thrust up in the west, the Midwest was formally framed. Now, cut off from the sea, it would develop inward on itself, relatively aloof from maritime influences.

But, while the Appalachians and the Rockies were being created on its borders, the Midwest remained a sleepy region where endless erosion had leveled all landmarks into obscurity. The barriers that once held the blue lakes had been worn away, and the water had drained off. The hills had dissolved into sand and clay — only the low humps of such minor ranges as the Mesabi and Baraboo serve as souvenirs of once grand mountains. There were no waterfalls, no cataracts with rainbow-colored mist, no foaming rapids; the rivers had long since eaten away all obstructions and now meandered over the flatness in sluggish, horseshoe-shaped courses. The region was tired and worn out.

Then, suddenly, everything began to change. About one million years ago there appeared on the distant northern horizon a long line of gray — low at first, then growing higher as it approached year by year. This was the first of the four glaciers that would sweep across the Midwest and completely alter the landscape.

There is something extremely dramatic about the advent of the glaciers. They came and left with a rapidity that is startling — in the geological sense. It took over fifty million years for the Silurian Seas to rise and fall; it took even longer for the Appalachian Mountains to be formed. Yet in less than a million years four separate torrents of ice moved across the Midwest changing the courses of the rivers, grinding out the Great Lakes, piling countless billions of tons of gravel over the eight-state area, erecting thousands of new lake beds, and leaving the Midwest a changed place in almost every way — all in a mere flick of time, a spark in the fires of infinity.

Imagine how it began. A change in certain meteorological conditions made the snow in Canada pile up faster in winter than it could melt in summer. As the drifts increased in size, the thickly-packed snow at the bottom turned into ice. When the accumulation had reached a tremendous height, perhaps three miles, the sheer weight forced the bottom ice to be squeezed out at the edges like putty. The portion that oozed from the main glacial mountain was probably a full quarter-mile high.

As the glacier moved down upon the Midwest, it made its presence felt long before it actually appeared. At first it was only that the winters became a little longer and colder. Then the oaks and maples began to die, to be replaced by pines and spruces. Soon thereafter the rivers turned into roaring torrents from spring to fall — so different from their previous sluggish condition — and their waters would be milky-white from the ground stone of the glaciers.

Finally the glacier itself would appear in the north and the frigid wind which blew across its thousand icy miles would hold the Midwest in a winter grip the year around. By the time the wall of ice had approached, the pines themselves would be stunted, gasping for life, and all the wild animals would long since have left this snow-choked land.

The glaciers bulldozed onward until they covered all but the extreme southern portions of Ohio, Indiana, Illinois, and Missouri and a pie-shaped piece of land in southwestern Wisconsin known as the Driftless Area. The life of each glacier was not long, however — only about one hundred thousand years — and, as it melted, it deposited the rocks and boulders it had picked up moving across Canada in the form of gravel. The Nebraskan Glacier, which opened the Ice Age about 1,000,000 B.C., was followed by the Kansan about 715,000 B.C. The remains of these two overlay southern Iowa and northern Missouri. The third, the Illinoian, occurred about 300,000 B.C. and is most obvious in Illinois (except around Lake Michigan), southern Indiana, and southern Ohio. The last, the Wisconsin, occurred about 70,000 B.C. and covered all or most of Minnesota, Wisconsin, Michigan, Indiana, and Ohio.

Thus it is that the surface of Iowa, formed by the Kansan Glacier is 400,000 years older than that of neighboring Illinois; and Illinois is in turn 230,000 years older than Wisconsin.

The debris that was caught in the foot of the moving glaciers was distributed across the Midwest to an average depth of about fifty feet. Where it was laid flat or in gently rolling mounds, it is known as a ground moraine; where piled into high ridges, it is known as a terminal moraine. These terminal moraines indicate the location where the southernmost foot of the glacier melted as fast as the ice flowed down from the north, thus releasing at this point a tremendous amount of gravel. Almost all of Minnesota's celebrated ten thousand lakes are cradled in hollows of these moraines and the curved lobes of the ice sheets may be easily traced by noting the pattern of the lake groupings. A high terminal moraine (known as the Valparaiso Moraine) circles the shores of Lake Michigan and may be seen most vividly at Milwaukee where the Menomonee River cuts through it in a wide valley; or at Willow Springs, just west of Chicago, where the Des Plaines River has eroded a deep gorge. The Shelbyville Moraine is festooned across the lower Midwest with its rounded ridge conspicuous as its course proceeds from Rockford, Illinois, south to Decatur and from there eastward across the rest of Illinois, through Indiana just south of Bloomington, and northeast through Ohio to Lake Erie. This moraine marks the extreme southern penetration of the Wisconsin glacier.

In addition to the ground and terminal moraines, the glacial drift has been fashioned into other formations. Two of the strangest are known as kames and kettles. Kames are low, conical hills that are composed of gravel which had once been washed into the bottom of small ponds on the surface of the glacier and were laid on the land when the ice melted. Kettles are circular depressions in the drift that were once occupied by blocks of ice which melted slower than the surrounding glacier. These kames and kettles are found throughout the Midwest but may be seen at their best along the Kettle Moraine Drive in eastern Wisconsin.

Even those portions of the Midwest that the ice did not reach bear indelible imprints of its nearby presence. The turbulent meltwater coursed through unglaciated flat lands in southern Indiana and Ohio, carving the bedrock into the beautiful hills that so entrance the visitors to Indiana's Brown County State Park or into the charming caves and weird canyons that visitors see in Ohio's Hocking State Park.

Not only did the glaciers change the land contours of the Midwest, they also radically altered the river system. The main Midwestern river once was the gigantic Teays, which began in Kentucky, flowed north through Ohio, then turned west across Indiana where it passed through the valley of what was later the Wabash, and continued into Illinois as far as Beardstown where it turned southward along a channel later adopted by the Illinois River. But the Teays, flowing directly into the path of the glaciers, was doomed. The waters of this mightiest river were stilled and its wide valley so completely covered with gravel that only geologists probing for the bedrock are aware of its existence.

Other pre-glacial rivers fared better. One million years ago the Missouri began, then as now, in the northern Rockies. But instead of turning sharply southward in the Dakotas, it continued straight across Minnesota where it joined the Mississippi. When the glaciers began encroaching on the Missouri, it curved around the lobes until it eventually joined the Mississippi at St. Louis — almost 600 miles south of its original channel.

The pre-glacial Ohio was a minor stream separated into several sections. One made its way northeast from Marietta to the St. Lawrence — exactly opposite of its present direction. Another began near Clifty Falls, Indiana, skirted to the north of Cincinnati (leaving the modern riverfront completely dry) and joined the Teays.

In northern Ohio a river flowed to the Atlantic along a deep channel which the glaciers would widen into the bed of Lake Erie. Another river flowed along the side of the Michigan Basin where its channel would become enlarged into Lake Michigan.

Even the mighty Mississippi was changed. Whereas it once arched across Illinois to join the Teays near Spring Valley, the glaciers rearranged its course westward to its present bed. During the disintegration of the ice sheet, the Mississippi was one of the main carriers of the meltwater and this served to greatly widen and deepen its channel. There are few spectacles anywhere to match the majesty of the limestone canyon of the Mississippi between Cairo in Illinois and St. Paul. Those who take the Great River Route can only wonder at the gigantic torrents of water which once careened down from the north, carving out the wide bluffs which now cut across the Midwest like a deep, white wound. No man can claim to have seen the United States until he has driven through the valley of the upper Mississippi.

As the glaciers began retreating, it soon became apparent that, not only had they changed the contours of the land and altered the courses of the rivers, they had also scraped out the beds of five huge inland seas which would give the region a coastline and permit it a vast shipborn trade even though it was a half-thousand miles from the Atlantic. These Great Lakes began emerging as soon as the ice had melted beyond their southern tips. At first only a tiny portion of Lakes Michigan and Erie appeared. They were at flood stage and their waters quickly broke through the surrounding moraines. Ancestral Lake Michigan swirled down the Chicago River and through the Valparaiso Moraine to turn the Illinois River into a raging tide. Lake Erie rammed through the moraine at Fort Wayne and sent its waters dashing down the Wabash.

When the southern portion of Lake Huron was freed a few thousand years later, its excess water spread across central Michigan along the Grand River, reaching Lake Michigan near Grand Haven. This one-time connecting strait is marked by the ridge of the former beach, which is most noticeable just north of Benton Harbor.

One of the strangest events in the birth of the Great Lakes occurred when the ice had retreated just beyond the Lakes' northern borders. The tremendous weight of the ice forced the land to tilt downward to the north, causing in turn the waters of Lake Huron to flow in that direction. This completely dried up the southern portion of the lake including the link leading to Lake Erie at Detroit. When the glacier retreated still further, the land in the north began to rise again; and it is still rising to this very day—so short has been the time since the Wisconsin glacier has been gone. Geologists have measured the rate of rise at Duluth and have found that the city is now five inches higher than it was when it was founded a little over a hundred years ago.

After the last of the glaciers departed, the land was completely changed. Huge piles of gravel lay over the once flat countryside, rejuvenated rivers rushed through deep meltwater canyons, and the newly formed Great Lakes tossed in their stony beds. An entirely new world had been born, radically different from the red clay hills to the south, the granite wilderness to the north, the mountainous regions to the east and west.

Then the first seeds drifted over the barren landscape. Landing on the cold stones, their life was hard and short. But as they died, their decomposed structures mingled with the gravel to provide the soil which would nourish the plants that were to follow. Soon a clump of tough grass grew here, a sprout of cottonwood grew there. Gradually Iowa, Illinois and northern Missouri became covered with a lush growth of prairie grass. In the east, deep forests of oak and maple turned the sunlight into jade as it filtered through their thick canopy of leaves; while in Michigan, Wisconsin, and Minnesota, fragrant forests of pine sang in the cool breezes. And, as the grass, oak, and pine turned into humus, a soil of unbelievable richness was built. The country became bespangled with an endless array of brilliant wild flowers. New animal life came to the land: gigantic flocks of pigeons, cranes, and geese; thundering herds of buffalo, furtive bands of deer; the muskrat, the beaver, the raccoon.

Now the creation was complete. The land was alive again. The scene was set for the advent of the first men.

# Like withered leaves

*The night* was bitter cold, and the star-chips which pierced the brittle air outlined a small group of men, women, and children who sat huddled close to their sputtering fire. No one spoke, for all the decisions had already been made. Tomorrow they would break camp and begin moving southward along the shores of the wide bay. Now and then someone would raise his eyes, gaze wistfully at the towering spruce caught in the amber firelight or at the rolling hills outlined against the stars, utter a sigh, then stare again into the dwindling fire. There was a sadness among them too deep to be expressed. Yet no one doubted the necessity of the move. Year by year the ocean was reaching farther up the land, causing the meadows to become swamps where the game animals rarely ventured.

And so the next morning the tribe gathered together their sacred objects, looked at their homeland one last, long time, and began trooping dejectedly along the frosty shoreline. As they moved southward, they unknowingly were crossing into a new world. Someday the Arctic Ocean would entirely cover the land they were now leaving, and it would become the Bering Strait. These migrating peoples were about to isolate their race for five hundred long centuries.

The tribe continued to move south until they found good hunting land. Then they built their crude wigwams and would have been content to remain except that other tribes migrating from the north began to encroach on them. As century followed century, the tribe moved on many times, sometimes a few miles south, sometimes a few miles east. And as they and other tribes hesitatingly filtered into the deserted continent, they began changing both physically and culturally from their Asiatic brethren. Their language began altering first, then their cultural tools, and finally even their body structure itself. Thus, slowly, mysteriously, a new race was created: the American Indian.

The ages continued to roll on — twenty thousand years, thirty thousand, forty thousand — a series of millenia. Yet for the Indians, without the slightest concept of Time, it was as nothing. They had no past, no future, only the vital present. There was no such thing as history, only the beautiful legends that were sung around the campfire. Of their former life in Asia or of their ancient trek across the Bering land bridge, they had not the slightest remembrance. Though the bones of a million ancestors were strewn across half the continent, the tribal memory reached back no farther than the recollections of its oldest living member.

No one will ever know what the first Indians must have felt when they entered the Midwest; but one can imagine the interest, and perhaps superstitious awe, with which they looked upon a land that seemed as if it had just been created. Everything was different from what they had been used to, for the glaciers had barely gone. There were huge piles of stones rising like great fortresses out of the almost barren surface; flooded rivers swirling down long canyons; huge, rounded boulders lying carelessly over the countryside; low hills, so different from the jagged peaks to the west; and most startling of all, wide inland seas, whose water was not salty, jutting into the prairies.

Everything was new to them as they moved into the virgin land: the first camp in the Midwest, the first fire, the first buffalo killed. And later on there would be the first baby to be born and the grave of the first elder to die.

Yet they did not have time to appreciate the novelty of their situation. Life was hard, and there were always little mouths wailing for food. So the warriors hunted the giant cats that lurked in the thick underbrush, or the great sloths that reached up to their shoulders, or the miniature horses that were soon to become extinct. But these were tame sports compared with bringing down the huge, hairy elephants that roamed the frozen northlands where the glaciers still held sway. These mammoths would provide meat for many days and it was to hunt them that a group of these early Indians headed northward around the year 10,000 B.C.

In the band was a teen-age girl who must have skipped gaily along with her parents, thrilled at the joy of the chase, relishing the carefree future that seemed to be spread before her. As the band made its way across a treacherous stream near glacial Lake Agassiz in Minnesota, the girl's happy chatter was suddenly changed to a scream. She may have slipped on a mossy stone or stumbled over a submerged log, but before the terrified eyes of her mother and father she was swept beneath the icy current never to be seen alive again. The tribe probably paused while the parents lamented their dead child, then marched onward into the mists of time. But the body of the girl, wedged beneath the gravel at the river bottom, was found ten thousand years later by a startled crew excavating for a road — to become the most ancient evidence of the existence of humans in the Midwest. It was a strange destiny for one so young.

As age merged into age, the Indian tribes wandered up and down the continent sometimes following the herds of wild animals, sometimes pursuing, sometimes pursued by hereditary enemies. Having no written history, they could never know the magic that was occurring before their eyes — the drying up of southern Lake Huron, the draining of Lake Agassiz, the gorging of the Mississippi canyon. They were unaware that the mammoths, sloths, camels, and horses were, as species, becoming extinct. And, because they were in contact with no other race, they could never imagine the civilizations that were rising in distant Egypt, Babylonia, and China. The Indians were perfectly content in their savage freedom, not knowing they were terribly alone, cut off from all other races; not realizing until it was too late the awful price they were to pay for their splendid isolation.

But around the year 800 A.D., the tribes along the Ohio River began experiencing a strange awakening. With eyes opened wide, as if for the first time, they discovered the miraculous cycle of the seed: place it in the earth, see that it gets water, protect it from weeds and — behold! — in the summer it will blossom forth with tender fruits. If the harvest is dried, it will provide food enough to satisfy more than everyone during the entire year. And with this new knowledge certain tribes began raising a new grain — maize it was called. Soon their gardens began dotting the bottomlands, and they gave up the wandering life. Year by year the proud farmers watched the sure food supply increase the numbers of their tribe and saw their villages grow into towns. Because not everyone was now needed to hunt for food, certain individuals were freed from this task and given special duties — as ceremonial chiefs, priests, weavers, pottery makers, singers of songs. Gradually these peoples, called Hopewellians by modern archeologists, raised themselves to a cultural level far above that of the more primitive tribes that surrounded them.

The Hopewellians left behind many remembrances. From a shard of pottery we see pretty dancing girls swaying to the music of reed instruments. From a pipestone carving we see a graceful bird about to spread its wings. From an opened tomb we see necklaces of multicolored pearls, figurines hammered from delicate leaves of copper, exquisite clay statuettes embroidered with semi-precious stones. Out of these fragments we are able to visualize the Hopewellian culture as it was in the days of its splendor—and it is an appealing vision.

The afterlife was an ever-present concern to them. They erected large mounds around the more illustrious of their dead, laying beside them the implements they would need in their reincarnation. Throughout the lower Midwest these mounds mark the sites of Hopewellian towns. Sometimes they were built in the form of the animals they worshipped, such as the magnificent serpent in southern Ohio.

Other times the mounds were merely oblongs or low cones. Once in a while, at some sacred location, the earth was thrown up in the form of embankments around the crest of a hill. The masterpiece of this type of mound was constructed in eastern Ohio: three and a half miles of walls which reach up to twenty-three feet in height. Known presently as Fort Ancient, it is more probable that the Hopewellians used it for massive religious gatherings.

Burial mounds erected about 800 A.D. by the Hopewellians near what is now Marietta, Ohio. Drawing was made in the late nineteenth century.

But by the thirteenth century the Hopewellian culture was on the decline. No one will ever know what caused the loss of vigor that once was theirs. Perhaps too intensive cultivation destroyed the fertility of the corn fields. Perhaps centuries of peace made their warriors effete. Or perhaps, most tragically of all, the end of their cultural capabilities had been reached — everything new had been discovered, the world became an old, tired place, without a challenge, without the joy of being able to do something better or make something more beautiful and meaningful. The later Hopewellians no longer had the energy to ward off the savage tribes which longed for their riches, no longer cared to stop the erosion that was washing away their grand, earthen monuments, no longer were concerned if mothers and fathers refused to provide for babies they did not want. These were sad, gray days when, little by little, the Hopewellians left their declining towns and resumed the wandering, primitive life that their ancestors had once so proudly given up. Soon they had merged with savage tribes, their descendants often living in miserable villages at the foot of magnificent mounds whose significance they did not know.

Not long after the Midwestern Indians had regressed to barbarism, another, superior group made its way into their midst. These Indians were not natives, as the Hopewellians had been, but came up the Great River from the south, and so have been called Mississippians. The Mississippians were true pioneers who, leading their women and children into this northern frontier, must have been exposed to the same perils of attack and bloodshed as the white race who would someday invade the Midwest from the east. And how unusual the Mississippians must have appeared to the Midwestern savages who probably gasped at the huge, earthen pyramids these foreigners were erecting — so different were they from the low burial mounds left by the Hopewellians. Especially at Cahokia, Illinois, did the strangers construct a towering pyramid which, tier upon tier, rose one hundred feet. On the very peak was a temple from which a gaudily dressed priest held conferences with the gods of sun and rain.

Not only were the Mississippians culturally far above the decadent Midwesterners, but they were also linked by trade or even by blood with the mighty Aztecs of Mexico. This tie must have given them a haughty disdain for the crude ways of the local tribes. Viewing themselves as an elite race of conquerors, they reached out in many directions for more territory. One battalion was sent into the hinterlands of southern Wisconsin where they built a strongly fortified town on the Crawfish River. From this fortress, currently called Aztalan, the warriors fanned out over the neighborhood, terrorizing the natives with their cannibalism. Finally, however, the Mississippians were overwhelmed in what must have been one of the most savage battles in prehistoric America. Aztalan was left in smoldering ruins.

During the fifteenth century the Mississippian culture passed its zenith. By the time Father Marquette floated by the Grand Pyramid of Cahokia in 1673, only the ghosts of this once mighty race were there to watch him from the crumbling ruins. Both Hopewellian and now Mississippian culture melted into the surrounding savagery with scarcely a ripple remaining. Indians whose ancestors had once painted dancing figures on pottery masterpieces or had ruled the sun from a towering pyramid now grovelled in the ground for roots. The Indian had gone as far as he could, for he had not the luck of the European to be exposed to the civilizing effects of energetic peoples from distant lands. In this Indian world of sameness there were no new ideals to stir the tribes into political alliances for their own betterment. No tribe was safe from the lightning attack of one of its neighbors, and glory was won, not by statesmanship or intellectual achievement, but by the number of scalps one could accumulate.

Yet even within this chaos, there was a feeling of kinship among the tribes — memories, perhaps, of the bygone Hopewellian and Mississippian days. Throughout the Midwest and the Great Plains there was the legend of Gitche Manito, the Master of Life, descending from his sky home to the great Pipestone Quarry in Minnesota. Here, as carefully retold by Henry Wadsworth Longfellow, he called all the warriors together:

> And they stood there on the meadow,
> With their weapons and their war-gear,
> Painted like the leaves of Autumn,
> Painted like the sky of morning.

Then the Mighty One commanded them to respect the sacred pipe:

> Therefore be at peace henceforward,
> And as brothers live together

From that day the Great Pipestone Quarry was a place of peace. No Indian would attack another, even his most hated enemy, while he was digging the soft reddish stone that he would fashion into the bowl of the peacepipe. And smoking the pipe would become an integral part of every Indian ceremony, a tradition of deepest respect for every tribe.

Worship of maize was another custom that brought the Indians closer together. Even though a tribe might wander far and wide after game, they planted the mysterious grain on plots to which they returned after the hunt was over. So greatly did their winter supply of food depend upon maize, that they regarded its discovery as a miracle to be told and retold to the young of every tribe. Invariably the Corn Spirit was a handsome young person, sometimes a man, sometimes a maiden, who had appeared before a legendary tribal hero as part of a vision:

> Tall and beautiful he stood there,
> In his garments green and yellow;
> To and fro his plumes above him
> Waved and nodded with his breathing . . .

Then the Spirit permitted itself to be conquered by the worthy Indian and, after its body was placed with proper ritual into the earth, the miracle of rebirth occurred:

> Til at length a small green feather
> From the earth shot slowly upward.
> Then another and another,
> And before the Summer ended
> Stood the maize in all its beauty.

But, although the Indians had many of the same gods, myths, and legends, there was little sense of unity. The Algonquin-speaking tribes that ruled the Midwest were at constant war with each other, little dreaming that the dialect they spoke revealed the tribes had been brothers at a time in the not-too-distant past. The members of the Algonquin family would have done well to have presented a united front, for they were harrassed on two sides by ferocious enemies — the Iroquois on the east and the Sioux on the west. Yet, due to age-old feuds, they could never form themselves into a confederation as firm as that of their enemies.

The Algonquin world just prior to the arrival of the white man was one of indefinite and everchanging boundaries. In Upper Michigan and slowly moving into eastern Minnesota were the Chippewa. The warriors of this tribe were pre-eminent among the Algonquins, for they were the only ones ever to beat both the Iroquois and the Sioux in pitched battles. They were canoemen "par excellence" whose frail birchbarks were to be found shooting the rapids at Sault Ste. Marie or skimming the placid waters of the beautiful Tahquamenon. Their storytellers would liven many an evening with the adventures of their legendary hero, Hiawatha: his fight with the Evil One, Pau-Puk-Keewis, his wooing of the Sioux maiden, Minnehaha, his conquest of the Maize Spirit, Mondamin. They were the aristocrats of the Algonquins — proud, bold, handsome — and their 5,000 seasoned warriors were a force that few other tribes could withstand.

In the wigwams of the Chippewa were often found contingents of their cousins, the Ottawa. Bound to the Chippewa by blood and having split from them not many years earlier, the Ottawa roamed lower Michigan where they controlled the important Detroit Straits. The Ottawa, with grotesque tattoos and boasts of cannibalism, were in no way the equivalent of the Chippewa. Yet their very love of war and their more strategic location led them to take a far greater part in Indian affairs.

The Chippewa were often visited by groups of Potawatomi with whom they were likewise closely related. The Potawatomi were not as numerous as the Chippewa nor as warlike as the Ottawa, so they had a tendency to be harassed by more aggressive tribes. Up and down the western shore of Lake Michigan they wandered watching anxiously for signs of Fox, Sioux, or Iroquois. For a time they made their headquarters around the important portage at the Chicago River where they straddled the trade route between the Great Lakes and the Mississippi.

In the dark coniferous forests of central Wisconsin dwelt one of the strangest Algonquin tribes, the savage Fox. Sullen, vengeful, excitable, they were at war with almost every tribe which bordered them. Fox warriors were, man for man, probably the best fighters in the Midwest and they maintained a successful contest against the powerful Chippewa even though their numbers were only a third as great. They were a flamboyant tribe with their headdress of red-dyed animal bristles and a brilliant white hand painted on their shoulder. Their bitterness and hatred for their brethren brought them into alliance with the Iroquois and Sioux — the only Algonquin tribe ever to have such an onerous arrangement.

Nearly as quarrelsome were the Sauk, constant allies of the Fox. The Sauk ranged along the eastern shores of the Mississippi as far south as Illinois. Surrounded by numerous enemies, the Fox and the Sauk stood by each other in constant comradeship. And together theirs was the poison that ultimately spelled the doom of the Algonquins.

On the billowing prairies south of the Sauk and Fox lived the six luckless tribes of the Illini confederation. Far from the lush lakes and rippling streams of the north, the Illini never learned the craft of the birchbark canoe. Instead, they were forced to depend on clumsy dugouts for travel down the wide Illinois River. Trembling at strange noises, fearful of cloud shadows, the Illini lived a precarious existence in a land once the center of the powerful Mississippian Moundbuilders. Possibly these decadent Indians were even descendants of those noble warriors.

The fuse in the Algonquin powderkeg was the Shawnee of Ohio. A wandering tribe, they drifted like Arabs from the Atlantic coast, to the Gulf, to the Midwest. They were will-'o-the-wisps, first here, then there, moving like sparks in a blustery wind, igniting each territory into which they moved. Linguistically they were very close to the Sauk and Fox, but their alliances usually tended toward the Delawares of the Atlantic seaboard. Their fierce hatred of the Iroquois made them a bulwark against any movement into the Midwest. They constantly stirred the more sluggish Algonquin tribes into hostilities, and seldom was a large war party formed that did not have a Shawnee as one of its leaders.

On the flanks of the Midwestern Algonquins were two large nations with which they were seldom at peace. To the east were the mighty Iroquois. There never has been a tribe that yielded such power in relation to its numbers. The political goals of the Iroquois were truly imperial and during the sixteenth century it appeared that they were about to forge an Indian empire which would extend from their home in New York as far as the Mississippi. Legions of the terrible Iroquois appeared everywhere in the Midwest defeating the Ottawa, devastating the Illini, scattering the Shawnee, and even penetrating into the distant lands of the isolated Chippewa. They came within a whisper of becoming the Romans of the New World.

West of the Mississippi lay the treeless lands of the Sioux. Stalwart as fighters, the Sioux had little of the political idealism of the Iroquois. They claimed most of Minnesota and Iowa, and their war parties were a constant menace to the forest-dwelling Algonquins east of the Mississippi. Yet the Great River was a natural boundary between the two linguistic groups, for the Sioux were horse Indians not used to the river and lakes where a birchbark ruled supreme.

Thus 50,000 years after the first Indians had migrated over the Bering land bridge, the tribes were still living in a bloody chaos. The Hopewellian and Mississippian cultures had matured and for a time seemed to offer hope that the Indians could rise above their primitive stone age conditions. But they had been ephemeral, stunted flowers growing in infertile soil. None of their wise men had remained to warn the tribes that an aggressive race was landing on their shores, that they must stop killing their strongest braves in useless inter-tribal wars, that they must organize a mighty red army that would sweep the bearded ones back into the sea. So the Indians whooped gleefully over their enemy's scalp, burned his villages, destroyed his corn fields — and all the while the white invaders gathered on the edge of the Indian world, slowly increasing in numbers, patiently waiting for the day when they would fulfill the prophesy of the mournful Hiawatha:

> "I beheld, too, in that vision
> All the secrets of the future . . .
> I beheld our nation scattered,
> All forgetful of my counsels,
> Weakened, warring with each other;
> Saw the remnants of our people
> Sweeping westward, wild and woeful,
> Like the cloud-rack of a tempest,
> Like the withered leaves of Autumn!"

# Tous du long de la riviere

*The year 1634* broke upon the Midwest the same as every year since 50,000 B.C. A Shawnee woman knelt beside the Ohio River wearily cleaning the carcass of a large deer her husband had killed; an Illini warrior stood on the uppermost pinnacle of a bluff over the Mississippi scanning the prairies for signs of any invader; a Sioux boy laughed gleefully seeing a buzzard riding the back of a dead buffalo as it floated down the Missouri. As far as each tribe could tell, everything was just as it had always been; just as it would always be. True, there had been vague rumors about a strange race landing on the St. Lawrence River, but hardly a single Algonquin or Sioux had ever seen these strangers in person. For almost two generations fanciful stories had been told about the men with bleached skins — told and

41

retold so often that they were only half believed.

But the year 1634 was important for the Midwest because at that time the first white man penetrated into its interior. With his arrival the endless prehistoric days were over and history began in the Midwest.

That this first Midwestern explorer was a Frenchman rather than an Englishman was no accident. When the English began their settlements along the eastern seaboard, they found that the Appalachian Mountains separated them from the interior. The French, however, not only founded Quebec on the St. Lawrence in 1610—a decade before the Pilgrims landed at Plymouth — but quickly discovered that the wide valley of the river led them automatically into the region of the Great Lakes.

Yet, though the energetic French leader, Samuel de Champlain, sent his young men ever deeper into the wilderness, the French were never quite certain where they were. Basing their information on Indian tales and an inaccurate knowledge of geographic distance, they believed that the Pacific Ocean lay not far to the west and that an undiscovered waterway, a Northwest Passage, would lead them across the narrow block of land which supposedly separated the St. Lawrence from the Pacific and the fabulous splendors of China.

In 1634 Champlain sent Jean Nicolet in search of the elusive Northwest Passage. Nicolet, setting out from Montreal with seven eastern Indians as guides, pointed his canoe into the dreamy, fable-enshrouded western land where at any moment the spires of Cathay might tower above the pines of Michigan, or where a golden gondola of the mighty Khan might appear beyond the next cape of Lake Huron. When Nicolet passed through the churning Straits of Mackinac and entered Lake Michigan, he must have felt an elation, a sense of accomplishment. Never before had the limitless miles of blue water and sandy shore been seen by a white man. Thousands would pass this way after him, but never again would the landscape present the virgin freshness that it did now.

As he proceeded down Green Bay, the savages he found on the shore confirmed his hopes that he was approaching a new race. They were called the People of the Great Water or the "Sea," as Nicolet translated the Algonquin. If this was true, it meant that the long sought passage to the Pacific could not be very far distant. Nicolet sent word to the strangers that he was coming, and with trembling hands put on a formal robe of Chinese silk strewn with flowers of many colors. But when he stepped from his canoe, he found the "Chinese" were only another tribe of Indians, the Winnebagoes — Siouan aliens in Algonquin territory.

After Nicolet's failure, almost forty years passed before the officials at Quebec sent the next adventurers into the mysterious unknown that still clung like an inpenetrable mist over the western end of their narrow empire. In 1673 Louis Joliet and Jacques Marquette set out in two birchbark canoes with five French paddlers to try to solve the enigma of the Great Water that the Indians had been mentioning ever since Nicolet had discovered the Midwest.

They were an unusual pair. Joliet was a merchant in search of trade routes and cared little for the Indian except as a gatherer of beaver pelts. Marquette, a Jesuit missionary, was searching for souls to save and cared not the slightest for wealth in furs. Joliet was a sturdy man destined to spend many more years in the wilderness, while Marquette was a frail person who, though he had lived among the savages at the missions he had established at Sault Ste. Marie and St. Ignace, was physically unfit for the frontier and would be in his grave within two years.

Yet fate played a strange trick on these two men. When Joliet's journal was lost in the rapids above Montreal, Marquette's little diary was all that remained of their epic journey. Thus Marquette, who cared little for personal glory, is remembered; and Joliet, who was the actual leader of the expedition, is all but forgotten.

It was no easy task the governor asked of the two men. The territory beyond Green Bay was completely unknown. It was only from the Indians that they could gain any information at all and this was usually inaccurate, always confusing, and at times actually untrue. When the two were told that bloodthirsty tribes were waiting to ambush them on the upper Mississippi, or that giant river monsters often gulped down entire canoes, or that the heat along the lower Mississippi was so stifling that they would all die — when they heard these stories told to them in most earnest seriousness, they had to weigh all the facts and fancies carefully. They could all be true or they could all be false, and the explorers had no way of knowing until they found the mysterious Mississippi, or Father-of-Waters, that the red man had told them about.

"Father Marquette Sets Out to Discover the Mississippi River." Chromolithograph by an unknown artist. The landscape is similar to that found along the upper Illinois River.

And so in the spring of 1673 the seven men left the mission which had been recently established near the foot of Green Bay, paddled up the ever-diminishing Fox River, portaged along a well-marked Indian path, and found themselves on the banks of the wide Wisconsin River. Down the westward-flowing water they went, drinking in the perfume of June, watching the blue hump of the Baraboo Range pass before them, skirting the many islands around Tower Hill. At long last they reached the gray bluffs of the Mississippi, and, as a wave of excitement swept over them, they scrambled up the Wyalusing Bluffs to gain a better view of this, the Big Water that had been a legend since the founding of Quebec over half a century earlier. On the summit, standing amid scores of Indian burial mounds, they looked upon the scene spread before them. The long canyon extended north and south as far as their eyes could see. On their right was the sandy channel of the Wisconsin. To the west were low hills melting into the crimson lands of the sunset. There was a feeling of awe among the men, for there was not the slightest sign of human habitation — only swaying green trees, flickering, dun-colored water, and a purple horizon that seemed to reach into infinity.

Returning to their canoes, the explorers eagerly began to descend the Mississippi. They found themselves passing through a lush land where immense herds of buffalo came to the water's edge to drink, where huge flocks of birds darkened the sky, where plump fish leaped from the river to disappear among the fragrant water lilies. A few days later, when they entered the prairieland of the Illini, they were startled to see a hideous bird-god painted in stark red, black, and green on the side of the canyon. At the mouth of the Missouri their canoes careened dangerously as they crossed the turbulent merging current. When they passed the forest-cloaked Ohio, the "Beautiful River" of the Iroquois, they found the weather growing ever warmer and more sultry. By the time they had traveled as far south as the mouth of the Arkansas, they reluctantly decided that the Mississippi did not flow into the Pacific but into the Spanish lands that bordered the Gulf of Mexico. Fearing that they would fall into the hands of the hostile Spaniards if they continued, they began their journey back up the river.

By September they were in Green Bay. The trees that were just budding when they left were now shedding their leaves in a blaze of amber. In the brief span of one growing season the geography of North America had been radically changed; the "Big Water" of the Indians was a river, not an ocean, and it flowed south, not west. There was no easy route to China. The Midwest was a region unto itself.

Joliet returned to Montreal but Marquette, burning with a zeal that hardly suited his wan body, left Green Bay the following October for

the lands of the Illini. Spending the winter in a miserable hut surrounded by the swamp that would one day be part of Chicago, the
Jesuit continued in the spring to the village of the Kaskaskia Illini
on the Illinois River. There, in a few weeks of brief glory, Father Marquette told the eager Indians the wonders of the Savior and the Holy
Virgin. Such was his marvelous reputation that at one time a circle
of five hundred chiefs and old men crowded around him, behind
which stood fifteen hundred warriors all anxious to learn the secret
of the white men's power.

But by the time Easter arrived, Marquette knew his days were
numbered. His body could not take the punishment that his spirit
cast upon it. As he grew weaker, he resolved to return to his old mission at St. Ignace. Finally, with two companions, he embarked along
the southern coast of Lake Michigan. The canoemen made their way
through the choppy water, watching with no pleasure the shimmering hills of shifting sand that seemed to stretch forever northward.
At last Marquette realized he could go no further. On the eighteenth
of May, 1675, he feebly asked his men to put to shore. That night
amid the forlorn dunes of Michigan the gallant Father breathed his
last. He was buried beneath the drifting sand close to the lake he
had loved — alone in the savage wilderness for which he so willingly
gave his life.

Four years after the death of Marquette another Frenchman stood
among the Michigan dunes. But this was not a man of the kindly,
self-denying mold of Marquette. This was proud Robert Cavelier,
Sieur de la Salle — a man of haughty bearing, who recently had received a five-year monopoly for Midwestern trade directly from the
Sun King, Louis XIV, himself. Tall, broad-shouldered, as strong as
the hardiest of his men, LaSalle was a born leader — even though his
harshness and lack of feeling for his men left him with many bitter
enemies. This austere, ofttimes tyrannic, personality dreamed
dreams as grandiose as Alexander's or Caesar's — dreams that sounded like insanity to his earthbound companions. Not content to be a
mere explorer like Joliet or a saver of souls like Marquette, LaSalle
saw himself as an emperor who ruled over a territory more extensive
than any European country. It was LaSalle's plan to create an Indian

kingdom in the Midwest, whose source of wealth would be fur, whose limits would be the huge basin of the Mississippi and its tributaries, and whose port would be a major metropolis at the mouth of the Mississippi. Could he but succeed, the continental heartland would be French and Indian forever.

As LaSalle stood on the bank of the St. Joseph River in November 1679, he must have reflected how near he was to success. On the bluffs behind him rose the first step of his Midwestern empire, Fort Miami, which would be his supply base on Lake Michigan. Any day now his faithful lieutenant, Henri Tonty, would arrive with the reinforcements which would enable him to set forth for the territory of the Illini whose central location he had chosen for his capital. And the "Griffon," the first sailing craft ever to ply the waters of the Great Lakes — a boat LaSalle and his men had built with their own hands — was even then returning from his fort on Lake Erie with the anchors, rigging, and other materials which would enable him to build a ship on the Illinois to take him down the Mississippi, through the Gulf of Mexico, and across the Atlantic to France. Once the mouth of the Mississippi had been discovered, the Midwest would be open for French goods without the difficult and costly portage at Montreal.

Soon Tonty arrived and, even though the "Griffon" had not arrived, the party of thirty-five began making its way up the St. Joseph. At the point where the river made a sharp south bend they portaged to that branch of the Illinois known as the Kankakee. From there they floated into the grasslands of the Illini where, on the shores of Lake Peoria, a wide place in the Illinois, LaSalle found their principal village. The Indians swarmed out to meet him, their hostility turning to friendship when they learned the French would aid them in an impending invasion by the Iroquois. LaSalle immediately set his men to building a strong fort on a bluff overlooking the lake. The stockade was called Fort Creve Coeur after a French bastion in Europe, but its translated name, "Broken heart," proved prophetic.

During the next few months LaSalle grew continually more uneasy. The beauty of the scene was lost on him — the wide valley over which his fort frowned like a medieval castle, the rippling waters of the azure lake, the pencil-thin lines of smoke which curled up from the turtle-backed wigwams. Taciturn with his subordinates, reserved

with Tonty, his only friend, LaSalle was a lonely man whose invert-
ed personality would not permit him to tell anyone the anguish he
felt at receiving no word from the "Griffon." Finally, knowing the
erection of his kingdom depended upon his discovering the mouth of
the Mississippi and establishing a trade route across the ocean to
France, LaSalle left the fort in charge of Tonty and marched across
a thousand miles of partially spring-flooded country to Montreal —
where he discovered that the boat with his essential supplies had
been mysteriously lost. No word, then or even today, was ever to be
heard of it. This was a blow from which LaSalle never fully recovered.

Yet LaSalle was like a statue cast in iron. Unflinching, he collected twenty-five more recruits. With them he immediately set out to
rejoin his men at Fort Creve Coeur. Yet as the men approached the Illini country, they saw ominous signs that the Iroquois had been there
before them. First they found deserted Iroquois campsites, then bits
of feathers and emptied palettes of vermilion war paint, and finally
fresh tracks. By the time they were in the once smiling Illinois valley,
LaSalle's most dreaded fears were confirmed. Where there were once
densely populated Illini towns, there now was complete devastation.
The wigwams were nothing more than mounds of ashes with rotting
human skulls stuck on the lodge poles. The ground was strewn with
mangled corpses around which wolves and buzzards gathered. Fort
Creve Coeur was burned to the ground and all its men gone. With a
feeling of shock and dismay, LaSalle turned from the nightmarish
scene and sadly made his way back to the fort which he had built
at the mouth of the St. Joseph with such high hopes but a year earlier.

Yet LaSalle soon learned that Tonty was safe; and after his friend
rejoined him, LaSalle resumed efforts to create his Indian empire. Accordingly, on December 21, 1681, he set out with Tonty and fifty-
three French and Indians on his much deferred voyage to discover
the mouth of the Mississippi. As the party left the winter-bleak valley
of the Illinois and entered the bursting springtime greenery of the
lower Mississippi, their spirits began to soar. Yet for LaSalle, moody
and silent as always, there was little joy in the expedition which
would carry his name to posterity, for his cherished dream of sailing on an ocean-going vessel through the mouth of the river and
back to France had vanished with the demise of the "Griffon." None-

theless, on April 9, 1682, he landed at the turbid, island-choked mouth, erected a column bearing the arms of France, and proclaimed by right of discovery all the land drained by the Great River for the King of France. Thus on that day France received, in the words of the historian Francis Parkman, "the vast basin of the Mississippi . . from the woody ridges of the Alleghenies to the bare peaks of the Rocky Mountains . . all by virtue of a feeble human voice, inaudible at half a mile."

After LaSalle returned to the Illinois country, he began constructing a new fortress — this one on a virtually impregnable rocky tower, since named Starved Rock. The word went out among the Algonquins that here was a man so little afraid of the Iroquois that he dared to rebuild his capital in the very territory they had recently devastated. And so Algonquin tribes from all over the Midwest gathered at Starved Rock, building a huge Indian town that contained twenty thousand tribesmen and their families.

It was a spectacular success for LaSalle; but the very mass of Indians demanded that he quickly establish a port in order to ship them French goods in exchange for the furs they were gathering. For this reason LaSalle left Tonty in charge and made the long journey back to France where he pleaded his case so effectively that the king allowed him four large ships, a hundred soldiers, scores of laborers, and a goodly number of girls of marriageable age with which to begin his Mississippi port. With this imposing company LaSalle returned to the New World.

But just when success seemed the closest, misfortune rode the gulf winds and the ships overshot the Mississippi. The colonists disembarked by mistake on Galveston Bay and near there in 1687, after a year of dissension and utter destitution, LaSalle was murdered by some of his discouraged followers — a doubly tragic end both for the man, who might have become great, and for his country, that might have erected a strong colony in one of the world's richest regions.

With the death of LaSalle, the French momentarily ceased their penetration of the Midwest. However, by 1700 it was clear that they had to forcibly occupy it if they were to prevent the British from flooding over the Appalachians. Therefore to control the rivers, which were the only highways, they began an active policy of fortress building. The strategic Mackinac Straits were guarded by a garrison stationed at Michilimackinac; the Detroit Straits were plugged with a garrison brought there by the dashing Antoine de la Mothe Cadillac; the Wabash was dominated by blockhouses at Vincennes, Ouiatenon, and Fort Wayne; the Fox was controlled by the village and fort at Green Bay. The Mississippi was uncontestably French, with towns and forts dotting its shores from Prairie du Chien at the mouth of the Wisconsin to the tri-centers of French power at Cahokia, Fort Chartres, and Kaskaskia in Illinois. Even on the unexplored Missouri, Fort Orleans was established far out among the wild plains Indians.

Yet even so, the Midwest could not properly be called a part of the French empire. It was more an exclusive French trade area — where the garrison towns were inconspicuous amid the vast sea of trees and prairies. The French government at Quebec actually had very little control over the activities of its nationals in the Midwestern area, and much of the trading was done by nominal outlaws called *coureurs de bois,* or forest runners, whose trading activities were carried out with complete disregard for the law which forbade anyone but agents of the crown from this form of business.

The *coureurs de bois* were strange creatures who joyously renounced the luxuries of civilization to wander with the savage tribes through the rugged majesty of the wilderness. They were recruited from the young Frenchmen who had migrated from their native France to seek freedom and adventure in the New World. When these men arrived at Quebec or Montreal, they found all about them the forest with its caverns of arched trees, its waterfalls of rainbow-splintered colors, its rushing streams dashing past from places unknown. In this wilderness there was excitement, beauty, and, perhaps, a wealth in fur. The temptation was too great, and the sturdy young men who could have stayed to raise families left for the woods — thereby keeping New France an under-populated region only a small fraction the size of its rival, New England.

The *coureurs de bois* made their headquarters at Michilimackinac. From there their canoes spread out down Lake Michigan to the Fox, Illinois, or St. Joseph waterways or across Lake Superior to the piney northlands around the Pigeon River and the Lake of the Woods.

Drifting with their adopted tribes, they lived a rowdy life, drinking brandy in wild orgies with the chiefs and sleeping with the princesses whom they took to wife for the season. Then when the excitement was over, they would relax for a while in the sleepy, riverside villages — at Cahokia where the Illini embraced them as brothers, at Prairie du Chien where Sioux and Sauk vied for their friendship, or at Vincennes where Shawnee and Miami entertained them with throbbing dances.

The Midwest during these days was a happy place where every day broke with a scarlet intensity, where emotions were untamed, but comradeship was without bounds. Wherever the *coureurs de bois* went there was singing, whether they were paddling down the calm waters of the Wabash, shooting the rapids at the Sault, or coasting the sandy shore of Lake Michigan. Most of the songs they had learned in their native France, and the singing of them provided both rhythm for the oar strokes and fond memories of maidens they had loved, and possibly lost, sometime long ago. One of their favorite songs went:

> *Tous du long de la rivière,*
> *Légèrement ma bergère,*
> *Légèrement, légèrement.*
>
> (All along the river,
> Swiftly my love,
> Swiftly, swiftly.)

Scores of verses accompanied this chorus — many of them made up impromptu as the fur-laden canoe sped over Midwestern rivers.

But there was in this earthly paradise a tribe in which the singing Frenchmen were not welcome. The warriors of the Fox nation crept like murderous shadows through the forest killing without mercy any enemies they found — be they red or white.

The trouble began in 1712 when a band of one thousand Fox came to Detroit to receive the presents the French commander, Cadillac, had promised them. However, the commander had been changed and the policy altered. When the belligerent Fox could not be induced to leave without their gifts, the French encouraged a large group of Ottawa and Potawatomi to attack their hereditary enemies. This was done and, after a long siege, all but a few of the Fox were massacred. Those who managed to escape brought back the tale of French trickery, and for twenty years not only was the Wisconsin River closed to French traffic, but Fox war parties raided posts as far south as Fort Chartres in Illinois. The Chippewa eventually joined the coalition against the Fox, yet even so the war did not end until tremendous losses had been suffered on both sides. The Fox, finally overwhelmed by sheer numbers, were all but annihilated — the pitifully few survivors taking refuge with their Sauk friends.

By the year 1754 the French Midwestern empire, while appearing on maps as a huge monolith, was in reality a hollow shell guarded by tiny garrisons that were spaced hundreds of miles apart and were maintained precariously in the midst of a fickle Indian population. The British had begun to infiltrate through the Appalachians, and in that year the two New World powers began active warfare, to determine which would control the continent. Almost none of the fighting took place in the Midwest, though Algonquins as far away as the Chippewa aided the French in the rout of General Braddock in western Pennsylvania. But the French lacked the manpower for a long war, and the tide soon turned. By the time the Treaty of Paris was signed in 1763 the British had not only taken Quebec and Montreal but had forced the French to cede them the entire Midwestern area east of the Mississippi.

The British moved slowly to occupy the far-flung realm of the French, and not until 1765 did a detachment arrive on the distant Mississippi. It was at Fort Chartres, once France's main bastion, that the *fleur de lis* was sadly lowered for the last time. And, as the white banner fluttered down the mast, an era had passed. The days of the happy-go-lucky *coureurs de bois* were over, for even those that remained were now to be merely employees of the large, impersonal British fur companies. Though they would still sing their songs, there was a melancholy which none of them could deny. The primeval joy had been drained from the region, to be replaced by the seriousness of the Anglo-Saxon invader. All too soon the land would be cleared, farms would break up and dot the boundless prairies and forests, and *"Tous du long de la rivière"* would be heard no more.

# CHAPTER FIVE

# The big knives

*Introduction: the Ohio River; the Revolutionary War*
*George Rogers Clark's march on Kaskaskia*
*The fall of Vincennes, 1779*

*It was spring* in the year 1778. The sun shining through the new greenery of the forest tinted everything a delicate aqua — as if the landscape were under the sea. George Rogers Clark and his little army of 176 drifted down a wide, arching river, watching the vines of wild grape that swung in the warm breeze, then the brilliant clumps of flowers that clung like coral to the banks. Birds flew by, dipping and soaring in the invisible currents of air flowing around and over the men. Each bend of the river brought a new vision of beauty, a hypnotic symphony of green, making even the untutored frontiersmen gasp in wonderment. Oh-hi-o — "Beautiful River" — the Indians called it.

Yet the men were not deluded by the peace that seemed to surround them. They knew they were boating down the frontier line of the fierce Shawnee, and even while the pastel light dazzled their eyes, a thousand savages might be preparing to ambush them.

As the boats slowly went down the Ohio, the men felt another concern. They knew they were on a mission of war — Clark had a commission direct from Patrick Henry, Governor of Virginia — but they had thought they were going into Kentucky (recently made a county of the Old Dominion) in order to aid the settlers there who were suffering depredations from the British-allied Indians north of the Ohio. Yet the Kentucky settlements were being left far behind them as they glided deeper and deeper into the unknown. The men then realized that Clark was on a secret mission — another of the daring ventures that were occurring throughout the country during these dangerous days of the revolution against Great Britain.

While the men watched the surging river rush through the arched forest, their thoughts turned to the terror the "Revolution" had produced on the frontier. General Henry Hamilton, Lieutenant Governor of Detroit, had turned the Algonquin tribes into British auxiliaries, sending them on murderous sorties into Kentucky. Word had spread that Hamilton was even paying his red allies up to fifty dollars for every white scalp brought him. The attacks of "Hair Buyer" Hamilton had threatened to force the Americans back over the Appalachians. It was to meet this threat that Clark had been authorized to raise this army.

Fifteen days after leaving the outpost at Fort Pitt, the men landed at an island near the Falls of the Ohio opposite modern Louisville. Then Clark gathered them about him and explained what there secret mission was to be. The best way to defend Kentucky was not by waiting for Hamilton's raiders to strike at any of a score of widely scattered places, but by taking the fight into the British lands north of the Ohio. If they could conquer the populous French towns in the Illinois country and on the Wabash, Hamilton would be forced to turn westward to counterattack, thus relieving Kentucky. Therefore their goal was to be Kaskaskia.

The men listened to Clark's explanation in disbelief. Illinois was a land on the very rim of the world. The only Americans who had been there were traders who brought back strange descriptions of boundless prairies and of a wondrous river, the Mississippi, the grandest of the continent. Under normal circumstances the adventure of visiting new places would appeal to the frontiersmen, but now they knew they would be entering a land under British rule, a land swarming with hostile Indian tribes, a land of Frenchmen who had long been enemies of the Americans. The men agreed that Clark had no right to ask them to join such a dangerous expedition in which they would be leaving their native country to attack a place where they would be outnumbered a thousand to one. They murmured dissatisfaction, some whispered of desertion. Yet as their discontented gazes fell upon their leader, the muttering stopped.

The man before them was someone to inspire confidence. Six feet tall, muscular, his red hair flashing in the sunlight, George Rogers Clark spoke with authority, even though he was but twenty-five. The men knew that he had been a leader in Kentucky despite his youth — even representing that newly settled country before the Virginia Assembly in 1776. Daring and audacious, nonetheless he seldom acted without thorough preparation. And when he told them that he had already learned the vulnerable state of the Kaskaskia garrison from two spies he had sent out one year earlier, the army knew that this was no scatterbrain scheme but a well-conceived plan with more than a good chance of success. From that point on, they were with him.

On June 24, 1778, after three weeks training, the little army again set their boats in the Ohio and began the difficult passage through the Falls — in reality a series of rapids. As they skimmed the churning water, they were engulfed in the copper light of a solar eclipse. It was surely an omen, many thought, as the foaming water broke in an odd iridescence. Then they emerged on the calm water below. At the same moment bright sunlight again flooded the countryside, and the men were left to ponder whether the eclipse had meant good or evil.

A few days later they landed several miles above an abandoned French post, Fort Massac.

Now the crucial stage of the expedition began. One hundred miles northwest lay Kaskaskia, the largest of the French river towns. The British had recently turned the command over to a loyal French nobleman, Rastel de Rocheblave. From a group of hunters recently

Kaskaskia, the old French capital of Illinois.

returned from the town, Clark learned that Rocheblave and his French townspeople were violently anti-American, referring to them by the Indian term "the Big Knives," believing them to be savages even more fierce than the Indians. For this reason, the hunters said, the Kaskaskia militia, almost twice as numerous as Clark's army, would resist the Americans with great fury.

It was thus clear to Clark that the success of his plan demanded that he surprise the town before the militia could muster. Once in possession, he felt he could bring the French over to the American side, since not only did they hate the British, but France had recently signed an alliance with the United States.

After engaging one of the hunters as a guide, Clark and his men set out for Kaskaskia along an old military road that ran between Fort Massac and the town. For about fifty miles they made their way through a region of steep hills and dense forests — but the difficulty of the march was considerably lightened by the luscious patches of wild blackberries which seemed to grow everywhere. Soon, however, they broke out upon the prairie. This was a most dangerous obstacle, for in that vast, treeless space, the army stood out in stark relief. White or Indian bands could spot them many miles away; and if they did, the alarm would be quickly spread. The situation called for a most rapid movement. But it was just at this moment that the old French road became obliterated by the grass, and a short while later the guide became lost.

Clark was in no mood for delays. The prairie stretched all the way to Kaskaskia and he had no time to waste. With his red hair bristling in anger, he wrathfully threatened the guide with execution if he could not find the trail by evening. The frightened man, knowing Clark would certainly be as good as his threat, frantically searched for the path. Within two hours the army was again on the march. On the evening of July 4 Clark was at Kaskaskia.

The army peered over the hill to look at the town. Everything was peaceful, so peaceful in fact that Clark suspected an ambush. But when scouts reported that there was no sign that the citizens suspected anything, Clark divided his force into three divisions and made ready to attack. One division under his personal leadership was to surprise the fort which guarded the town from a bluff above it. The other two would encircle the town and, at a prearranged signal, would burst into it from all directions.

Ever so quietly the two divisions crept toward the town while Clark and his men made their way up the hill toward the fort. The success of the plan required that he gain control of the fort without rousing the townfolk and their militia. Under the guidance of a captured French farmer, they stealthily crept up to the very walls of the fort, expecting the challenge of a sentry at any moment. Then they opened a rear gate, which the farmer had told them would be unguarded, and warily entered the fort grounds, knives drawn, each man tense and alert. To their astonishment the fort was devoid of sentries, the sound of music indicating that every man had left his post to watch what they later learned was an officers' ball. The Americans moved through the fort with cat-like silence, stationing themselves at all strategic locations. When Clark saw that everything was in readiness, he audaciously walked into the dancehall and leaned against the door watching the dancers. For a while no one noticed him. Then an Indian, suddenly recognizing the trappings of an American, uttered a wild cry of surprise.

The music instantly stopped while panic seized everyone. When the screams of the women and the shouts of the men finally quieted, the youthful frontiersman, without moving a muscle or raising his voice, informed them that their town had just passed under the authority of the state of Virginia. At that he motioned his men into the room and the officers and men were placed under arrest. The fort had been taken without the loss of a single man or the firing of a single shot!

Then at the signal, the rest of Clark's army dashed into the sleeping town shouting at the top of their lungs, making such a clamor that the startled French mistook them for a force far larger than they actually were. Orders were given that no Frenchman should come from his house until so ordered by Clark. In this way the militia was prevented from forming and, when morning broke, Kaskaskia was firmly in American hands.

But Clark realized his victory had placed him in an extremely hazardous position. Now that his presence was known, he no longer had the element of surprise on his side — far from it. At any moment the citizens of nearby Cahokia, supported by a thousand of their Indian allies, might descend upon him. Clark, with no hope of reinforcements, with no source of supplies, and with no place of refuge, would be completely at their mercy. Therefore, in order to win the French to his side, he made certain his troops behaved with exemplary courtesy to the conquered Kaskaskians. At the same time he strove to impress the French that the American government thought highly of them and would respect their nationality. The Kaskaskians were utterly won when their priest, Pierre Gibault, informed them that the Americans would permit them to practice their Catholic religion with complete freedom.

Word of Clark quickly reached Cahokia, but the alarm evaporated upon learning of his friendly treatment of the Kaskaskians. Cahokia, long discontented with British rule, then switched allegiance with enthusiasm. Father Gibault further advanced the American cause by making a long trip to Vincennes on the Wabash at which time he described Clark so favorably that that town, too, deserted the British. Thus during the summer of 1778 the most populous portion of the Midwest slipped from the British without even a token sign of resistance. Clark was the hero of the year.

But in the late fall the tide began to turn. While Clark saw enlistment terminations take away almost half of his already scarcely adequate force, General Henry Hamilton, the notorious "Hair Buyer," was making frantic preparations to avenge the loss of the French towns. The war belt was instantly sent out among the lake tribes, and soon hundreds of canoes lined the Detroit strait, each filled with painted Chippewa, Ottawa, and Potawatomi braves. Taking the field in person, Hamilton and his mixed force of five hundred British regulars, Detroit militia, and Indians hastened down the Wabash and in December were before the gates of Vincennes.

At the appearance of such an overwhelming force, the Vincennes militia deserted the American cause with even greater rapidity than they had joined it. Captain Leonard Helm, whom Clark had left in charge of an American garrison of three men, had no choice but to surrender. The British flag again flew over the French town.

Hamilton then settled into winter quarters in Fort Sackville, the small stockade which dominated the town. Seeing that it would be impossible to feed such a large number of men during the winter months, Hamilton permitted the Detroit militia and Indians to disperse, ordering them to rejoin him in the spring when they would sweep Clark from Kaskaskia.

When word reached Clark's camp that Hamilton had retaken Vincennes with half a thousand men, the Americans were filled with dismay. Retreat, if not actual disaster, seemed inevitable. Yet when Francis Vigo, an Italian trader who had recently been in Vincennes, gave Clark the invaluable information that Hamilton had gone into winter quarters with only eighty men, Clark immediately decided to attack. There was no use dissuading him by reports that the countryside around Vincennes was impassably flooded by unseasonable thaws or that Hamilton's force could be quickly increased by the Vincennes militia of two hundred and fifty, or by the large groups of Indians who were encamped nearby. On the seventh of February, 1779, with a force of 170 Big Knives and adventurous young men from Kaskaskia and Cahokia, Clark began the 185-mile trek to Vincennes — a march which was to become an epic in American history.

The first week was bad enough: a freezing rain almost continuously falling made the soaked prairie a swampy morass. The men sloshed through the dreary countryside, their shoes and clothing always wet, the nights spent sleeping tentless on the damp earth, exposed to the chill rain and the bitter wind. Rifles began to rust, and moist gunpowder became useless. Yet during the first week morale did not falter, for Clark made certain that each evening was enlivened with a feast of deer or buffalo and that the nights were gay with Indian dances performed by each company in competition with the others. There was constant laughing and joking between the Americans and the French. They were all young and this first portion of the journey, hard though it was, seemed almost like a frolic. But on February 13 they reached the banks of the Little Wabash, and the frolic was over.

The Little Wabash and a tributary, now known as Muddy Creek, flowed side by side across their path. The distance between them, about three miles, was completely flooded with water, in some places four feet deep. To wade through this icy, breast-high lake was more than the men had bargained for. Both Americans and French hesitated at the river bank, directing black glances at Clark who urged them to cross. An impasse had been reached where the slightest, most trivial excuse would send the army scurrying back to the warm shelter of Kaskaskia.

Then, just when the grumbling was becoming most ominous, the small, fourteen-year-old drummer boy suddenly laughed at the men. By silly antics and the telling of jokes, he diverted their discontent into good humor. Clark then was able to lead them into the water, while the boy kept up their spirits by sitting on his drum and gleefully demanding to be pushed since the water was nearly over his head. The drummer won Clark's admiration and might very well have been the determining factor in the decision of the men to continue.

For four days after crossing the Little Wabash the going was not difficult. Then on the seventeenth the Embarrass River was reached. Vincennes now lay six miles to the west — only a half day's march. But to everyone's dismay the Embarrass was flooded, and it was necessary to detour twelve miles south to the Wabash ford. To add to their troubles, Clark now issued an order forbidding the shooting of game due to their closeness to the fort. Since their reserve supply of food had already been consumed, this meant they must go hungry until they reached Vincennes!

When the rain-soaked army came to the Wabash a day later, another even gloomier scene was before them. In the semi-twilight of the almost perpetual drizzle they could discern that the Wabash had overflowed until it was over six miles wide. All landmarks, paths, and campsites had been obliterated. No land remained above water except low mounds of saturated mud which protruded here and there like bodies of dead sea animals. The valley of the Wabash was a forbidding desolation, a lead-gray swamp of muck and slime.

Clark kept his hungry army on the western shore for two days while scouts hurriedly scoured the area for enough boats to carry them up the river to Vincennes. When but two boats could be found, Clark's only choice was to march his men through the flooded mire. Accordingly, on the twenty-first, the boats began ferrying the army across the deep channel of the Wabash and that evening, after a short march, they made their camp on a low hill on the east side of the river known as the Upper Mamell.

The following morning, before the dismal march was to begin, Clark made a reconnaissance in one of the boats. The goal of the day was to be a low hill called Sugar Camp after the grove of sugar maples on it. Clark found that the water was up to six feet deep in places, which meant that many of his non-swimming men would have a difficult time making the crossing, even with the aid of driftwood floats. To make matters even worse, the chill of the night had frozen the surface of the water nearly an inch thick.

When Clark returned to camp with the disheartening news, a howl of discontent went up. The men, cold, wet, and weak from hunger, felt the end of the trail had come. There was serious talk of abandoning the enterprise and not even the playful drummer boy could lure them on. But just at this moment, when all seemed lost, Clark displayed the daring that made him a great leader of men. Quickly blackening his face with gunpowder, he gave a series of stirring Indian war whoops and dashed into the frigid water, taunting the men to follow him. The theatrical display worked, and the entire army tramped after their captain.

That day was the most discouraging of any. The troops were barely able to stumble to Sugar Camp, only a half-dozen miles from Upper Mamell. At sunset they heard the evening gun at Hamilton's fort, just as they had for the past five days. It seemed to mock them for their slow progress and miserable condition.

The next morning, with their goal so near, the men utterly gave out. Having gone without food for five days, they were half starved. Their clothes were in rags; their arms and legs ached with the cold; their faces were raw from the wind and rain. When Clark saw that even his antics could not inspire them, he played his last desperate card. Posting twenty-five loyal men in the rear, he ordered the men to follow him or be shot. There was no humor in his command. The weary men had no choice but to trudge once more into the swamp. It was the eighteenth weary day of marching.

By one o'clock that afternoon they had made their way to Warrior's Island — a small copse of trees within sight of Vincennes two miles distant. The plain around the island, usually dry, was flooded, and Frenchmen from the town were on horseback shooting at huge flocks of ducks resting on the water. One of the Kaskaskians decoyed a hunter to the island where he was astonished to find himself surrounded by Clark's bearded, gaunt, rag-clad army. Clark learned from him that there were up to six hundred men in Vincennes, including a large number of hostile Indians. Knowing that without trickery his little force could never hope to take the town, Clark told the hunter that the men he saw were but a tiny portion of the number that would soon join him. Then he sent the man back to Vincennes with a bold message warning the French that he would soon attack the British with a huge army of Big Knives and that, unless they wished to be treated as enemies, they should remain in their homes until the fighting was over.

Clark anxiously watched the man through his spyglass as he returned to his people. He saw the hunters gallop to town and then noticed a tremendous wave of excitement sweep over Vincennes as the message was related to the townsfolk. Then men and women hurried to the edge of the swamp to try and see the mighty American army which was gathering on the hidden side of Warrior's Island. Clark then turned his glass toward the fort, but to his surprise there was no sign of activity. From this he guessed that the garrison had been forewarned and had already prepared him a warm reception. But there was no turning back now. Gathering his bedraggled army together, he brazenly marched out into the shallow water in full view of the watching population several miles away.

Now Clark performed one of the most skillful maneuvers in American military history. Carefully taking his line of march so that low rises hid the men entirely from the British fort, he let portions of the army appear momentarily to the French and Indians. Those onlookers saw legion upon legion of rugged soldiers marching out from behind Warrior's Island. And when a company was hidden behind one of the many rises, colorful battalion strands on high poles indicated where they were. Twelve companies in all — one thousand men — were counted by the French and Indians. Believing resistance to be hopeless against such a mighty host, the French quickly retired to their homes while the Indians slunk northward out of town. By marching and countermarching Clark had peacefully vanquished Hamilton's entire auxiliary force!

On the evening of February 23, as Clark and his men were silently occupying the town, General Henry Hamilton sat in a comfortable room in Fort Sackville playing cards, certain no American army could penetrate the vast swamp that surrounded him. The people of Vincennes were sure that the huge American force would conquer the British and so, fearing that the victors would punish any informer, they had not warned Hamilton. The British commander, tall, handsome, of a genial disposition, enjoyed the game, while he drank frequent cups of sweet apple toddy. Hamilton's thoughts concentrated on the flavor of the toddy, the pleasure of the warm fire, the enjoyment of the game of cards. And perhaps he even allowed himself the luxury of dreaming of the coming spring campaign when he would drive Colonel Clark from the Illinois country.

Meanwhile, the Americans had surrounded the fort. When at a signal the firing began, Hamilton barely took notice. Indians or French were always shooting their guns; it was nothing unusual. A few more shots and still Hamilton sat at his game. Suddenly a volley roared from every side and the General jumped to his feet. Cursing the noise, he stomped out to the parade grounds, irritated that the natives should be disturbing him, still unable to believe he was actually being fired upon. He found his men just as confused as himself. Flashes of light were exploding in the moonlit darkness, but they thought it was only the Indians indulging in their bizarre amusements. Then a sergeant gasped and fell. With that the unbelievable truth dawned. They were actually being attacked!

Utter confusion reigned within the fort as the redcoats dashed to their posts. When they reached the gun ports and peered into the night, they found the moonlight playing strange tricks on them. Each dancing, half-illuminated shadow became an attacker — yet when they shot at it, it melted away. Then from another section came golden bursts of flame that like the momentary glow of a fire-fly did not last long enough to cast any lingering light. Hamilton's soldiers bravely exposed themselves at the gun ports, but could see nothing to fire at except the phantom shadows.

Clark used more ruses to magnify the numbers of his force. While most of his men kept up a blazing fire, others dashed back to the town to laugh and hoot as if they were a large force of reserves eager to be called into action. Hamilton's men cast anxious looks at one another, believing themselves to be hopelessly outnumbered. Even Hamilton, experienced soldier that he was, began to doubt his ability to withstand for long the onslaught of such an army.

Yet ironically, it was not Hamilton, but Clark, who was in trouble. He had no cannons with which to batter down the stout walls of the fort. A protracted siege was out of the question, for the nearby Indian tribes would be on him as soon as the smallness of his force was discovered. And even at that moment Clark's scouts reported that a flotilla of British supply boats — apparently unknown to Hamilton — was proceeding down the Wabash to reinforce him. Unless Hamilton could be induced to surrender within twenty-four hours, the game would be up.

The firing continued all night and into the early morning. At nine o'clock Clark sent Hamilton a demand to surrender, proclaiming severe consequences if it became necessary to storm the walls. This message had the desired effect of working on the fears of Hamilton's men who dreaded a general massacre from the ferocious Big Knives. Yet Hamilton refused to be swayed by their demonstrations and proclaimed that the fort would not be surrendered. Clark's men therefore resumed their firing with renewed vigor.

At noon Hamilton asked for a three-day truce during which time he and Clark could discuss possible surrender terms. It was an obvious stall and Clark saw immediately that the British general must be desperate to mention the word surrender. But even as negotiations were proceeding, an event occurred which brought terror to the garrison and gave Hamilton no choice but to meet Clark's every demand.

A band of fifteen Ottawa Indians appeared from the east, marching in triumphant procession toward the town. Sent out by Hamilton to attack the American settlements in Kentucky, they had done their job well and were returning with many scalps. Seeing the British flag flying over the fort and hearing no firing, they walked unsuspectingly into Clark's hands. When the savages found their mistake, they tried to escape, but the furious Americans killed most of those who fled and took nine others as prisoners. Then, while the defenders of the fort looked on in horror, the Americans tomahawked each of the helpless Indians — thus revenging their slain Kentucky comrades.

With his frightened men now on the verge of outright mutiny, Hamilton agreed to begin talks with Clark for immediate surrender. As Hamilton walked out of the fort, Clark met him, his hands and clothing still dripping with the blood of the slain Indians. Together they walked to the little French church just east of the fort where, after a great deal of blustering by Clark, Hamilton reluctantly agreed to surrender the fort and his entire garrison.

At ten o'clock the next morning, February 26, Hamilton and his troops marched out of Fort Sackville and laid down their arms. Only after Hamilton saw Clark's entire army drawn up did he realize just how few men Clark actually had. He stared in disbelief. He, an experienced officer, the Lieutenant Governor of Detroit, the scourge of the frontier, he, General Henry Hamilton, had been duped by a crude frontiersman. The surrender had been unnecessary! Hamilton turned his head and it is reported there were tears in his eyes.

No one knows what Clark did the evening of the surrender. He probably partook in the victory celebration of his men. He certainly had a long interview with Hamilton. Possibly later in the evening he left the camp of his boisterous soldiers and walked the short distance to the banks of the Wabash. The dark water would have been flecked with moonlight and would have made a low rustle as it brushed the tree trunks at flood tide. He may have watched the restless water for a while and then turned to let his mind's eye pass over the shattered palisades of the fort, over the hundred houses of Vin-

George Rogers Clark receives the sword of surrender from General Henry Hamilton at Fort Sackville in Vincennes. Painting by Frederick C. Yohn.

cennes, and over the horizon itself to the frontier settlements he knew so well in Kentucky, western Virginia, and Pennsylvania. His easy journey down the Ohio had shown him what a natural highway the river would be for eastern pioneers. As soon as the war was over, America would expand even more rapidly than ever. He may have swelled a little with pride, knowing that the capture of Kaskaskia and Vincennes had given his countrymen claim to the gigantic area north of the Ohio. Someday, he was certain, the scattered Indian wigwams would be gone and the prairies would be dotted with prosperous farmhouses. Perhaps even the French towns would lose their Gallic flavor to become part of the great American commonwealth. Then Clark may have turned northward, looking up the moonlit Wabash. This was the route to Detroit. The new land he had opened up would never be secure until the British were driven from that place. Clark may have clenched his fist as he vowed to conquer Detroit; then turned to walk back to camp.

Yet history had an unfortunate future marked out for the redheaded daredevil. Although it was mainly due to Clark's dramatic conquests that the United States was awarded the Midwest at the close of the Revolutionary War, Clark himself was never again to play a prominent role in the development of the region. His dream of marching on Detroit did not reach fulfillment, and as the years moved on his negotiations with the Spanish at New Orleans brought a cloud of possible treason around him. Bad drinking habits caused him to lose his position as Indian Commissioner. At last, hounded by creditors, he lived his declining years in near poverty in a cabin he built at Clarksville, Indiana, overlooking his beloved Ohio. This cabin, a simple two-story affair, was at the foot of the Falls, the very same rapids he had shot so many years earlier when he was a young man. And there in the twilight of life a great man awaited merciful death, hearing, perhaps, a tattoo played by a little drummer boy and the muffled laughs of his hardy Big Knives.

# CHAPTER SIX

# The blacksnake

Introduction: the valley of the Maumee
"Mad" Anthony Wayne
Fort Greenville
Fort Defiance
Battle of Fallen Timbers, 1794

*The valley of the Maumee* is a lonely place. The river, saffron with mud, flows listlessly through vine-choked banks, oozes through dissolving islands of clay, and at last, wearily disgorges into Lake Erie. During its entire 110-mile course there is hardly a city worthy of the name between Fort Wayne, where it sleepily begins, and Toledo, where it drowsily ends.

The Maumee is more a soggy, weed-encrusted drainage ditch than a river, and for most of its life it was lost in the dismal Black Swamp, an undrained area that remained when the waters of glacial Lake Erie receded. Covering most of the region from Detroit to Lima, Ohio, the Black Swamp was a dark place infested with snakes, spiders, and other animals of similar undesirability. For thousands of years the

68

only sound was that of the lost and lonely wind intermingled with the splash of decaying vegetation.

But gradually the swampy waters began draining down the emerging Maumee. Then such tribes as the Shawnee, Miami, and Wyandotte found the sluggish river an ideal link between their homes near Lake Erie and the trade routes down the Wabash. Yet the valley itself still festered with murky remains of the Black Swamp and was deemed unhealthy and unfit for habitation.

This region, bespeaking death and decay, would hardly seem the place to seek military glory. Yet in the summer of 1794, a bent, graying man led an army of weary American soldiers into this hole of mud, slime, and evil smells. He himself was dying, as he well knew, yet he was here to vindicate his past, and neither the rigors of the march nor his own failing constitution would deter him. This man was "Mad" Anthony Wayne, a Homeric, forgotten figure whose heroic saga should be fondly remembered by every Midwesterner. Now hear his story.

It is the year 1793. Something of a crescendo has been reached in the Northwest Territory. The Indian tribes, strongly supported by the British, have decided it is time to make a stand. They have seen their favorite hunting grounds grabbed from them to become the State of Kentucky. But now they draw the line at the Ohio River — all territory north will be Indian forever. Death to the settlers!

When General Josiah Harmar, commander of all the armies of the West, sets out to chastise them, he himself is chastised! And when General Arthur St. Clair, personal friend of President Washington and Governor of the Northwest Territory, sets out to chastise the chastisers, he is ambushed and his army massacred! It is a war of extermination and the Indians are making good their threat — a thousand grinning skulls of broken American armies bear ample testimony to their resolution.

The two settlements on the Ohio are in panic. Rufus Putnam at Marietta predicts the colony will be abandoned unless the Indian menace is quelled, and the people at little Cincinnati fear to go out at night for the woods are filled with vengeful Indians. It is clear to everyone concerned — the Indians, the British, the Americans — that the hour of decision has come. Would the Midwest be an Indian protectorate of Great Britain or would it be American?

George Washington, both discouraged and irritated, began to lose faith in American commanders. He searched frantically for a new general but, when his first choice, Light Horse Harry Lee, wisely refused the empty honor, the President, more in desperation than admiration, chose an old revolutionary comrade, Anthony Wayne. There were grave doubts in Washington's mind concerning Wayne's capabilities. He had earned the nickname "Mad" due to his reckless daring in battle, but this quality hardly recommended him, for the ease with which the Indians ambushed both Harmar and St. Clair called instead for a man of extreme caution. Yet experienced American generals were hard to find — so Wayne was given the dubious distinction of leading the third army into the graveyard lair of the Shawnee.

"Mad" Anthony, however, was not the impetuous person he had been in his youth. After the glories of the Revolution he settled down to civilian life, but a less-than-acute business sense had left him in serious financial straits. To make matters worse, an ill-advised venture into the harsh world of Georgia politics had besmirched his wartime reputation. Under ordinary conditions such a disastrous civilian career would serve to hasten one's response to the call of military patriotism. But Wayne, now approaching old age, did not look forward to the severe hardships that wilderness campaigns entail — to say nothing of the personal danger. Indeed, gout had so crippled him that the pain in his leg often made it torture just to mount a horse.

Yet, this was Wayne's chance to prove himself. With new fire in his veins, he made his way over the Alleghenies to join his army at Pittsburgh. But all the while he was assailed with doubt: could he succeed where Harmar and St. Clair had failed? If he didn't, he would never be given another opportunity.

When he arrived at Pittsburgh, Wayne could see that the cards were stacked against him. It was bad enough to receive word that Washington had so little faith in him that he had sent diplomats into Indian land to beg the warriors for peace. An even harder blow was the motley group of men that had been assigned to him as an army. Some were castoffs from the demoralized force of St. Clair; some were recruits gathered from the gutters and jails of the East; and others were just plain misfits and ne'er-do-wells. His rag-tag force was, in other words, a typical militia of the eighteenth century. The people of Pittsburgh laughed at them: they were a sideshow, not an army. One can only imagine Wayne's feeling of hopelessness. He had asked for a force of battle-hardened regulars. Instead he had been given these!

In the meantime Washington's diplomats had met no success. They hurried from tribe to tribe, pleading with the haughty chiefs to state their terms — anything but total surrender would be acceptable! But the chiefs, possibly relishing the joy of meeting another American army, and secure with promises of British aid, proudly announced that the Americans, one and all, must retreat south of the Ohio. And, as if to emphasize this point, two of the American ambassadors were murdered by an anonymous band of young Indians.

The diplomats, with fear for their lives as well as for the future of their country, hurried with the bad news to Washington. It was then, after all other alternatives had been exhausted, that the President gave "Mad" Anthony his orders to march.

But when Wayne sailed down the Ohio for Cincinnati and the front, it was not with the same motley horde that had been given him at Pittsburgh. While the diplomats had been busy begging, Wayne had been busy building. He had become an iron drillmaster and disciplinarian. For three quarters of a year he had worked on his men until he had finally made an army out of the disorganized, demoralized, liquor-soaked, unruly mob that had gathered at Pittsburgh. And when they landed at Cincinnati, the people were impressed. These were not shifty-eyed rabble, but true soldiers. Wayne had formed the men into battalions modeled on the legions of Caesar; each with its own colors. The men were proud of their Legion of the United States, as it was called. They were proud also of their commander. But most important, they were proud of themselves. Each man was now a tough, disciplined warrior ready for the hardships which lay ahead

On September 11, 1793, the Legion moved out of Cincinnati. As they left the shelter of the village, their confidence, while not exactly dwindling, took on a more realistic coloring. Tramping up the haunted trail left by Harmar and St. Clair, they found the forest engulfing them in a semi-twilight, and although they were passing through the scarlet and gold of flaming autumn, their thoughts were not on the beauty but on the danger. The marching column was no longer a compact, well-formed army, but had been turned by the forest into a long string of twenty-five hundred travelers — an ideal object for ambush!

But Wayne was not to be taken off guard. Indian spies who constantly watched the advancing army sent word back to their leaders that this army was not like the others. The soldiers were alert, there were no stragglers or deserters, sentries and scouts were always on duty. As day by day Wayne came closer to the Miami and Shawnee towns, the chiefs began to take alarm. Finally even their cocky leader, Little Turtle, realized this time he would have a real fight on his hands. And so he called for reinforcements. His runners began dashing through the forests and prairies, summoning the warriors of their many allied tribes. "The Americans are now led by a chief who never sleeps," Little Turtle's message read. "He is like a deadly Blacksnake. Let us meet in the valley of the Maumee."

But Wayne, waging a war of nerves, did not attack that autumn. Instead, he went into winter quarters in a fort which he called Greenville after his old comrade-in-arms, Nathanael Greene. Then, when the Indians relaxed, he sent a flying column on Christmas Eve twenty-three miles north to build a fort on the site of St. Clair's dismal defeat. Fort Recovery it was named, and as such represented a loss of face to the Indians, who could not hold that which they had once taken.

When spring came, the tribesmen were ready. At the junction of the Maumee and the Auglaize the largest meeting of warriors ever held in the Midwest commenced. The Shawnee and Miami were there, of course, as were their allies, the Delaware and Wyandotte. From the west came more distant tribes: the fierce Ottawa still burning with the hatred that Chief Pontiac had left with them; the crafty Potawatomi who soon would earn a notoriety for their massacre of the garrison at Chicago; and the Chippewa whose mighty men were the only Indians ever to beat the wild Sioux of the plains. It was a rally of over two thousand — and it was believed their number would be further augmented by a contingent from the terrible Iroquois.

Yet Wayne had even more to contend with. The British, always alert for empire building, had seen the embryo of an emerging Indian nation and had sent their blessing in the form of guns and other military supplies. In addition, they were even at that very moment constructing a strong fort fifty miles down the Maumee.

When Wayne led his men out of Fort Greenville, there was little laughing or joking. They were headed for battle against a powerful adversary who would neither ask nor give any quarter. Scarcely a day passed that supply trains were not attacked, and small bands of Indians constantly harrassed any group of soldiers that became detached from the main army. As the Legionaires moved down the Auglaize, they felt themselves surrounded by an invisible enemy. No one knew when an arrow would sing and a comrade stagger and fall. Yet when the soldiers dashed into the woods to find their attackers, there was no one there!

These were the tactics that had disrupted many an American army, but they did not work with Wayne's trained men. Just as important, the Indians were unwittingly schooling the very men who in the coming years would break the back of their race. There was William Henry Harrison, young, handsome, ambitious, who as Wayne's aide-de-camp was watching the progress of the army with sharp eyes. Only twenty-two now, in six years he would be given the governorship of the gigantic Indiana Territory, in seventeen years would thrash the Indians at Tippecanoe, and in forty-six years would be elected president of the United States.

There was Meriwether Lewis, two years younger than Harrison, who saw the Indians with the wise wonder of youth and would one day be visiting with tribes so distant they were then little more than legends. And in 1807 his close friend, President Thomas Jefferson, would make him governor of the newly acquired Lousiana Territory — an empire which stretched from the Mississippi all the way to the Rockies.

And there was William Clark, younger brother of the famous George Rogers Clark, victor at Vincennes. He himself would be just as famous when he returned from his epic overland trip to the Pacific with Meriwether Lewis in 1806. Clark would eventually become governor of the Missouri Territory and would negotiate away millions of acres from the plains Indians. And he would live to see the defeated tribes he was about to fight harshly herded across the Missouri where their fate was one of near annihilation.

Yes, these were the days when such men rode through the Ohio forests to keep their appointments with destiny.

Early in August 1794, Wayne reached the Maumee. This was a long awaited moment, and one can imagine the pride with which the old commander began the construction of Fort Defiance at the junction of the Auglaize: "I defy the English, the Indians, and all the devils in hell to take it!" But the Indians did not hear his pugnacious challenge; they had moved down the valley, preferring to give battle closer to the protection of the British fort.

From Fort Defiance Wayne sent the Indians a final offer of peace. When the red chiefs would not give a definite answer, Wayne began his fateful fifty-mile march toward the waiting Indians. As the army moved down the Maumee, the men enjoyed fresh vegetables and ears of roasted sweet corn from the fields the Indians had cleared. Yet, though it may have reminded them of a picnic, they were under no illusion. They knew they were on the very rim of the civilized world; that they depended entirely on their own resources; that a defeat would not only spell the end of the Northwest Territory, but would bring their own doom just as certainly. It was no picnic.

When Wayne's scouts reported that he was five miles from the enemy, he had his men strip for action. All unnecessary gear was placed in an area named Fort Deposit. Then the long awaited order was given to advance in battle formation!

The army moved down the north bank of the Maumee, the cavalry riding on the right flank and the infantry marching in two parallel lines beside them. As the men tramped quietly through the trees, they heard the taunts of hidden Indian spies. Then, far down the shore they saw a thick line of overturned trees behind which a horde of Indians was confidently entrenched. Two miles further on stood the earthen wall and the pointed palisades of the British Fort Miami. Wayne stopped his men opposite the battlement of fallen timbers, the river at his back. He looked around him to see that the Legionaires were all in position. He slowly raised his arm, and a hush fell over both the soldiers and the Indians. Then, the signal was given, the bugles sounded; the battle was begun.

Wayne sent his cavalry at the Indians first. They spurred their horses furiously toward the timber battlement, leaped over it, and fell upon the Indians with their broad swords. But before they hurdled the trees, Indian fire had emptied more than a dozen saddles.

No sooner had the horsemen made contact with the enemy than Wayne signaled for the first of two waves of infantry to charge. Their orders were to trail their guns, stocks in the grass, in the hope that this disdain of firearms would make the Indians leave their cover and meet them in the open. Now it was the turn of the soldiers to call out taunts to the barricaded Indians. Wayne's plan worked, though only the many months of drill kept the men from holding fire.

As the Indians came out the Legionaires met them head on with bayonets. For a moment there was confusion while man met man in a fight to the death. But then, at first slowly, the Indians began retreating. And when they turned to regroup, the cavalry in their rear sent them reeling. Suddenly, panic seized the undisciplined ranks of the Indians. It was every man for himself. Even before the second wave of infantry had reached the battle, the tribesmen were in full retreat!

Almost two years' preparation was over in forty minutes. "Mad" Anthony Wayne, an old man with less than twenty-four months to live, a second-choice commander, had broken the Indian menace that had held the frontier in a grip of terror for over a decade. More than that: his complete victory at Fallen Timbers had dispelled the possibility that the Midwest would be taken from the United States by the British. The portrait of the Midwest would from that time on be American, not British nor Indian.

One hundred and thirty-five belated years later a statue of General Wayne was placed on the bluff overlooking the site of Fallen Timbers. It is a lonely statue, as lonely as the unusual man who led his valiant Legion into the hinterlands of the old Northwest Territory. This Yorktown of the Midwest is as little remembered as is the tired but dogged man who brought this great victory to his country. Could the Midwest — could the very nation itself as we know it — have survived without Anthony Wayne and the Battle of Fallen Tim-

bers? It is, perhaps, too great a presumption to answer an unequivo-
cal "No," but the fates of nations and peoples have ridden on lesser
events — a blow by Brutus, a shot at Sarajevo. What Washington was
to the thirteen colonies, what Lee was to the South, what Sam Hous-
ton was to Texas, so was Wayne, though in a lesser degree, to the
Midwest. Let him be thus remembered.

# CHAPTER SEVEN

# The huntsman
# and Crouching Panther

*Introduction: Old Piqua*
*Tecumseh*
*William Henry Harrison*
*The Battle of Tippecanoe, 1811*
*The War of 1812*
*Seige of Fort Meigs*
*Battle of Lake Erie*
*Battle of the Thames*

*Old Piqua* was a fine village — the pride of the Shawnee nation. It consisted of almost a thousand lodges scattered along the western bluffs of the Mad River in Central Ohio. There was constant activity in Old Piqua: braves returning heavily laden with meat from the hunt, women going to and from the river as they washed clothes or drew cooking water, children laughing as they dashed through camp in the garb of warriors. The river banks had long been worn smooth by thousands of feet and there was almost always a fleet of half a dozen or more canoes on the water, sometimes carrying fishermen or hunters, other times filled with men bedecked in war paint. On ceremonial days the air around Old Piqua throbbed to tom toms and the chants of warriors. During the evenings spiraling campfire smoke cast a warm blanket of light over the scene as the clans gathered to tell and retell the wondrous stories of Shawnee heros, real and legendary.

The Shawnees had been a wandering nation, but now they had found a permanent home at last, and they were happy.

But gradually clouds began to appear on their horizon. A strange race of white men was seen in the region called "Kentucky," the favorite hunting ground of the tribe. Of course, the Shawnees had long been used to French and English traders, but these newcomers were different — they brought their women and children with them and planted crops. They were an aggressive, hostile people who drove away the game animals and who, from their timbered forts that frowned upon the once smiling countryside, barred the red hunter from a region that had long been his. Word of these ruthless invaders traveled through the Shawnee nation; soon war drums began to call the braves together.

It was in 1768, during those early days when the first Americans appeared to the south, that a baby was born in Old Piqua. His mother, a Creek woman who had migrated from the area of Alabama with her Shawnee husband, named the little one Tecumseh, varously translated as "Crouching Panther" or "Shooting Star." She was proud of her little baby, as all mothers are, and probably dreamed the usual dreams that her son would one day become a great warrior. Yet in the case of Crouching Panther even the aspirations of the mother could scarcely envisage the meteoric career of her newborn child.

Tecumseh grew up during years filled with excitement. Old Piqua was a rendezvous for the constant parties of warriors who marched southward to harass the invaders; and when the braves returned, the excitement became even more intense. Victory processions were formed, wild celebrations were held, and the white captives were put on display. There was always a man or two to be tortured and the lodges of the favored clans would receive white women and children whom they would adopt into their family as slaves, wives, or brothers, as the case might be. From the time he was four until he was sixteen Tecumseh had a white boy captive as his companion. Then, when he was ten, he made friends with the great Daniel Boone, who had been taken prisoner but who soon escaped.

But the growing youth did not always witness the victories of war.

Sometimes the tide went against the Shawnees, as in 1780 when George Rogers Clark, fresh from his capture of Vincennes, led a vengeful army on a retaliatory raid which left Old Piqua in shambles. And even worse was the fate of a group of Delaware Indians, close relatives of the Shawnee.

Most of the Ohio tribesmen had been watching the Delawares with a mixture of contempt and envy. They had become Christians under the guidance of David Zeisberger, a minister from the province of Moravia in Germany. Zeisberger had taught the Delawares to renounce war and to live in pacifistic harmony in three permanent towns along the Tuscarawas River. He thought their example would inspire the other tribes to take up Christianity and would thus enable them to gain respect and tolerance from the encroaching Americans. The Americans, however, did not trust the Indians, whether they were Christian or not, and when a band of Shawnees raided a white outpost during the winter of 1782 and brutally murdered a white woman, the Big Knives rode angrily into Gnadenhutten, one of the Delaware towns. Refusing to believe that the Moravian Indians had no part in the massacre, they tomahawked and scalped the entire village of ninety persons — mostly women and children.

The Gnadenhutten disaster sunk deep in Tecumseh's mind, even though he was only fourteen. He could see that the Americans were not merely at war with the Indian braves, but were fighting against the entire red population — it was in fact a war of extermination. Eight years later he eagerly took up the hatchet to join with the redmen in their impressive victories over Harmar and St. Clair. In 1794 he joined Little Turtle behind the barricade at Fallen Timbers and saw the Indians beaten by Anthony Wayne and betrayed by the British at Fort Miami.

During the humiliating negotiations at Fort Greenville, Tecumseh, attending as one of the younger, minor chiefs, watched in disgust as the leaders bartered away thousands of acres of land. He felt a bitter sadness when he realized that Old Piqua fell within the Fort Greenville line. It had all happened so quickly — one generation ago Old Piqua was the center of a powerful Indian confederacy; now it was deep in a region reserved for the white man alone.

So Tecumseh turned from Greenville with a firm resolution in his

Signing of the Treaty of Fort Greenville, 1795. Included in the painting, believed to have been done by an officer on General Anthony Wayne's staff, are General Wayne, William Henry Harrison and Chief Little Turtle. Greenville Creek is in the background. The site is now a park.

heart. The old leaders must go. Young men must take their places — men who would be dedicated to a military union of all Indian tribes. He would be their leader; he, Tecumseh, Crouching Panther, in whose veins flowed blood from the northern Algonquins and the Creeks of the Gulf Coast.

At the same Greenville conference was another young man who was to play an important part in the Midwest's history. This man was

William Henry Harrison, a thin, almost anaemic-looking officer whose sallow complexion and delicate mannerisms made him seem even younger than his twenty-two years, and whose background was such that it was incredible that he should be found at a post on the extreme frontier. His father was the illustrious Benjamin Harrison, wealthy Virginia planter, close friend of George Washington, and a signer of the Declaration of Independence. William had attended medical school in Philadelphia under the guardianship of none other than Robert Morris, known to the nation as the Financier of the Revolution and one of the richest men in the entire country.

But young William was not a youth of the common mold. He had read Charles Rollin's eight-volume masterpiece, *Ancient History,* and his mind thrilled to the military splendors of the past. Discontented with the staid life in the East, he turned with the natural instinct of a huntsman to the adventures to be found on the wild frontier. As was customary with the rich, he secured a commission in the army from a family friend — President Washington in this case — and, even though the country was reverberating with the news of Harmar's terrible defeat, he crossed the mountains. At the log fort that would one day become the city of Pittsburgh he boarded a flatboat and drifted down the Ohio to Cincinnati, arriving at the little river hamlet just in time to learn of the shocking massacre of General St. Clair's force. But the young man had a far stronger character than his slim figure seemed to indicate. When Anthony Wayne took command, he saw Harrison's energy and intelligence and appointed him his aide-de-camp. Wayne was proved right in his estimation, for at Fallen Timbers Harrison was conspicuous for his bravery.

After Wayne's departure, Harrison's career proceeded apace. Appointed commander of Fort Washington, the sleepy stockade which guarded Cincinnati, he had ample time to familiarize himself with the political situation of the Northwest Territory. He saw that second in importance to St. Clair, Governor of the Northwest Territory, was Colonel Winthrop Sargent, the Territorial Secretary. Out for success, Harrison sedulously cultivated the Colonel's friendship; and when Sargent was soon appointed Governor of the Mississippi Territory, he obligingly recommended his friend for his former job. In the spring of 1798 President Adams accordingly made Harrison Territorial Secretary — a lofty position for one only twenty-five years old.

Yet this was only the beginning. The Northwest Ordinance had decreed that when a territory had 5,000 free white male inhabitants it should be entitled to an elected assembly and a delegate in Congress. This population figure was reached about a year after Harrison became Secretary, and an assembly was duly elected. The duty of selecting the Congressional delegate was then taken up by the assembly. Governor St. Clair autocratically pushed his son forward, but when Harrison skillfully presented his candidacy as representative of the common farmer, he received the coveted appointment — though with the very slender margin of one vote. Thus it was that in the fall of 1799, young Harrison reappeared in Philadelphia, the city he had left eight years earlier, to take his place as Congressman. It was a spectacular success story.

But the dizzy spiral of fortune had not stopped. Harrison, not overawed by the distinguished gentlemen in whose company he found himself, introduced a bill which radically reduced the obstacles in the way of the ownership of public land. The bill became known as the Harrison Land Law and brought the thin young man to the attention of his co-legislators. For this reason, when Ohio was sliced from the Northwest Territory prior to becoming a full-fledged state, Harrison was seen as the logical appointee as governor for the remaining region, to be called the Indiana Territory. President Adams, who had been a friend of Benjamin Harrison and who had occasionally entertained William as a dinner guest, concurred with Congress, and the appointment was his.

As Harrison made his way to Vincennes, the capital of the Indiana Territory, he must have marveled at his amazing success. He was only twenty-seven and yet was the virtual ruler of a tremendous region which stretched from the Ohio River northward to Lake Superior — a region containing the future states of Indiana, Illinois, Michigan, Wisconsin, and part of Minnesota.

Shortly after arriving in Vincennes, Harrison began building a mansion worthy of his new position. Called Grouseland, it became the talk of the entire area — there was no home finer within a thousand miles. The mansion was modeled after his father's home in Virginia, having thirteen spacious rooms, four large chimneys, and a grand council chamber which overlooked the Wabash River. Grouseland soon became a kind of GHQ where the far-reaching plans of its energetic owner were incubated. Quick to seize opportunity, he sent his agents throughout the region calling the Indians to councils, where they were induced to barter away their tribal land for trinkets, nominal annuities, and hard liquor. It was a clever, whirlwind campaign that brought land into the government domain faster than ever before. Ambitious Harrison knew his name would be on the lips of everyone west of the Appalachians and known to many in the East.

As Harrison rapidly proceeded with his plan to rid the Indiana Territory of Indian ownership, Tecumseh began a counterattack. He and his brother, a one-eyed epileptic medicine man called the Prophet, traveled from tribe to tribe denouncing the old chiefs who were so carelessly signing away the land. Soon discontented warriors from every Midwestern tribe were flocking to the camp that the two brothers had laid out at the junction of the Wabash and the Tippecanoe Rivers. Tecumseh knew this was an excellent location from which to check Harrison's activities, for it was on a direct supply route with the British stronghold, Fort Malden, on the Detroit River, and was at the same time poised like a dagger over the head of the governor two hundred miles down the Wabash. As Tecumseh watched the army grow, he knew that Harrison must soon see the danger he was courting.

Harrison, of course, realized the danger of Prophetstown, as the Indian camp was called, and, summoning his militia to Vincennes, he sent Tecumseh an invitation to discuss the uneasy situation on the frontier. Tecumseh responded by canoeing down the Wabash with a bodyguard of 175 choice warriors. He met with Harrison in front of the Grouseland mansion in an atmosphere filled with distrust and suspicion. Both leaders were aware that they had reached a point of no retreat — Tecumseh could not disband his military camp without losing face and Harrison would not promise to refrain from land buying. The words grew heated and once it seemed as if the two men would come to actual physical combat. Seeing the futility of further discussion, Tecumseh finally announced he was leaving for the Gulf Coast to form an alliance between the southern and northern tribes.

While Tecumseh moved hopefully through Alabama and Georgia, Harrison acted to undermine the chief's fulcrum of power in the north. With absolutely no authority from President Madison, he gathered together an army of one thousand regulars and volunteers and led them up the Wabash toward Prophetstown. By trespassing on lands still owned by the Indians, he was not only committing an act of aggression, but was actually disobeying the President of the United States.

As the army made its way toward the Indian city, Harrison must have felt the awful responsibility he had assumed. Perhaps he had misgivings, for he was placing himself and his men in considerable danger — he knew full well that the armies of Harmar and St. Clair had been larger and had been destroyed by the Indians. In addition, a defeat would greatly strengthen Tecumseh's hand and expose the helpless, scattered families on the frontier to the ravages of the victorious Indians. All in all, it was a provoking and dangerous gamble.

On the evening of November 6, 1811, the small army encamped on a low knoll shaped like a flatiron about four miles from Prophetstown. The Prophet, in charge of the camp during his brother's absence, was well informed of Harrison's advance. That afternoon he had sent a delegation of braves to assure Harrison that the Indians were entirely peaceful. Yet as night settled over the army camp, Harrison, wary as usual, ordered his men to sleep with their rifles at their sides.

One can only imagine the feelings of the sentries who were posted that night. They must have stared into the silent blackness that surrounded the camp, alert and tense, listening to all the varied sounds of the wilderness so greatly intensified to their straining ears. But as the night gradually faded into pale dawn the nervous sentries could relax; no attack had come. Harrison too, rising before the rest of the men, felt relieved as he drew on his boots and told the drummer that he might soon sound reveille. Already a few men had risen to warm themselves by the rekindled fires.

Suddenly, a sentry looking through the half-light saw an Indian in the bushes. He fired his gun, but as he turned to run, a bullet brought him down. Then, from north of the camp, came the terrible Indian battle cry, and hundreds of painted warriors leapt out of the bushes and dashed pell-mell upon the startled camp, braving the bullets that whined around, believing the Prophet's promise that his magic made them invulnerable. The outer line of tents was quickly reached and furious hand to hand combat ensued. Before the first wave of attackers were forced to give ground, three soldiers lay tomahawked and scalped, a score of others were wounded. Momentary confusion prevailed as the soldiers tried to dash to their preassigned positions. A second Indian attack hit the right flank; it was only halted by the personal valor of Major Joseph Daveiss and his Kentucky troopers. Daveiss led a counter-charge but was killed before he could reach the Indian lines. Then, a third Indian attack began in the rear.

At the first firing Harrison had jumped onto his horse to direct the inexperienced militia. Almost oblivious to his own personal danger, he was an inspiration to his men, but an unmistakable target for the enemy. A bullet flashed through his hat; another grazed his skull; a third struck his horse in the neck. Yet still Harrison urged his men on. As the battle continued, Harrison saw that the Indians were not so numerous as their shooting had first made him believe — between six and seven hundred was a later estimate. He then shifted five companies to the front and ordered a charge. The men, shouting as they drove forward, were met by a deadly hail of arrows and musket fire, yet they managed to reached the partially-hidden savages in the brush. Although as many as one out of five of the Americans became casualties, they did not falter but slowly forced the Indians to break into an open retreat that was not stopped until they had reached a swampy area where Harrison's mounted support could not follow.

Three months after Harrison's hard fought victory, Tecumseh returned from his recruiting journey in the South. Although he had been largely unsuccessful, an important faction of the Creeks, one of the largest tribes, had been drawn to his side. He had received no word of the Battle of Tippecanoe, and it was only when he reached the Wabash that the terrible truth began to dawn. Just as LaSalle 131 years earlier had revisited the horror of an Iroquois attack, now Tecumseh found himself amid the desolation of a white attack. The warrior's village he had fostered with such care was abandoned, the log cabins burned, the fields of corn destroyed. But Tecumseh was as hard as iron. Making his way to the British Fort Malden, he began reinlisting the discontented tribesmen, swearing vengeance upon Harrison for the treachery at Tippecanoe.

Tecumseh did not have long to wait for his opportunity. Great Britain and the United States, long at odds concerning their interests both at sea and along the borders of the Northwest Territory, finally entered a state of war on June 18, 1812. This conflict, known as the War of 1812, became in the West a series of attempts to dislodge the British from Fort Malden, their important base on the Canadian side of the Detroit River. As early as July, an American general, William Hull, crossed into Canada, but was thrown back by the British and their Indian allies led by Tecumseh. Hull retired to Detroit where he was deceived into believing he was surrounded by a vastly superior force. On August 16, 1812, Hull, despite violent remonstrations from his officers, surrendered his 2,000 men to what he afterwards learned were but 1,300 besiegers. This, one of the most ignoble capitulations in American history, was Tecumseh's greatest hour. He had been active in planning and executing the skillful deception.

Amid the fervor caused by Hull's disaster, Harrison resigned as Governor of the Indiana Territory to accept President Madison's appointment to the chief command in the Northwest. Harrison immediately began to erect training camps in northwestern Ohio, and started work on a major outpost at the falls of the Maumee to serve as the main supply center when the army began its march to retake Detroit. When Tecumseh's spies brought him news of these new developments, he saw the danger and realized that the one way to defeat Harrison's plan was to destroy the outpost, named Fort Meigs after Ohio's governor, before it could be sufficiently manned. Therefore he boarded British transport ships with a force of 1,500 braves and 1,100 British and Canadian regulars commanded by General Henry Proctor, sailed to the mouth of the Maumee, and marched up the river nineteen miles to the fort. Tecumseh was overjoyed to learn that Harrison himself was in command with only 1,200 men.

The siege began April 26, 1813, as Tecumseh sealed off the outpost by occupying the high land to the southeast and cutting off all roads with strong war parties. In the meantime General Proctor drew his men up on the bluffs opposite Harrison and began to prepare his batteries. The plan was for the British gunners to blast away the fort's defenses, after which the warriors would carry it by assault.

Harrison, however, had not been idle. In frantic preparation for the bombardment which he knew would come, he had commanded his men to work in shifts around the clock, digging deep entrenchments in which they might find shelter from the cannon fire. It had been a race against time, but again Harrison's luck held, and when the British started firing on May 1, the exhausted Americans had constructed two deep trenches which ran the entire length of the fort. As the cannonading began, the morale of Harrison's men sagged, for the constant danger from the whistling shot was shattering to the untried troops. Red hot cannon balls splintered the wood pickets and chewed gaping holes in the earthen walls; and when the men repaired the damage, they exposed themselves to the Indian musket fire — Harrison even receiving a painful bruise on the hip from a spent bullet. They had to be ever alert to prevent an assault, yet the incessant shrieks of the Indians and the rapid trickle of rain water into the uncovered trenches made sleep impossible. Nevertheless, as the days wore on, the men became accustomed to the hardships and began to glory in their heroic resistance to the supposedly overwhelming odds.

As the siege continued, Tecumseh, seeing his Indians becoming more and more dissatisfied with the inactivity, grew anxious to bring matters to a conclusion. One day, therefore, he approached the fort and offered a taunting challenge to Harrison: "Had the Big Knives grown to be such cowards," he shouted, "that they burrowed into the earth like frightened groundhogs? Were they afraid to meet the Indians in open combat?" The chief's voice rang loud and clear across the no-man's-land. "I have with me 800 braves. You have an equal number in your hiding place. Come out with them and give me battle." Here was war in the Indian fashion, man to man. Tecumseh had thrown the gauntlet in the presence of more than 3,000 men. The two armies waited in silence for Harrison's answer.

One can imagine the tense scene there on the wind-swept bluff:

the rushing river below, the swaggering Indians just beyond musket range, the line of watching redcoats on the opposite shore, the tired men in the fort, their eyes on their dark-haired leader. Harrison was not a big man, but he was not afraid of battle. The temptation may have been great for him to throw open the gates and charge upon his adversary. For a moment or two, while the hushed lines waited, his eyes may have wandered up the Maumee valley to that distant speck called Fallen Timbers where he had fought with Anthony Wayne — almost twenty years ago. He realized that he was no longer a dashing young lieutenant, but a seasoned general, charged with the responsibility for an entire army. The time for the dashing deeds of youth had gone. He then made his decision. He would not fight Tecumseh, but would hold the fort as the springboard for the future invasion of Canada.

The cannonading was then resumed with increased fury. But on May 9th, Proctor, realizing that the walls could not be permanently breached and noting the large numbers of Indians that had already begun leaving the camp, dismounted his guns and returned to the ships. Tecumseh had no choice but to follow. Crouching Panther had caught the hunter in his lair and had not been able to take him. He was never to have another chance.

The siege of Fort Meigs brought home important conclusions to both antagonists. Tecumseh was disillusioned, for he could see that Indians were not fitted for the long sieges of a white man's war. Not only that, they were not responding to his call for warriors. This was a fight for the very survival of the Algonquin tribes, yet only the merest fraction of available men had come to the Fort Malden rendezvous. The Indian power seemed to be breaking up right before his eyes, and he realized that he would have to fight a defensive war from that point on. It was a sad prospect for a vigorous warrior to face.

But Harrison, too, had been disillusioned by the affair at Fort Meigs. He had seen the rapidity with which the British fleet transported the Indians and redcoats and knew that so long as that fleet controlled Lake Erie his supply line could be pierced almost at will. Even if he retook Detroit, the army would be exposed to severe danger if food and ammunition should fail to arrive from Ohio. It became obvious that the army he was training was useless so long as Commodore Robert Barclay and his ships sailed the lake unopposed.

And so, as the summer of 1813 wore on, all eyes turned toward the harbor of Presque Isle (now Erie, Pennsylvania) where twenty-eight-year-old Oliver Hazard Perry was feverishly completing work on an American fleet. Perry's work was slow, for not only did much of the material have to be hauled by wagon from the East, but his workers were mainly unskilled frontiersmen. Gradually nine vessels took shape; and, on August 12th, Perry sailed proudly out of the harbor — in search of Commodore Barclay. Perry moored at Put-In Bay on South Bass Island where he dared the British to come out from their safe anchorage under the guns of Fort Malden.

Early in the morning of September 10, Perry's lookouts sighted Barclay's sails. Perry immediately prepared his ships for war and by ten o'clock the fleets had approached maneuvering range.

Now began an extremely tense afternoon for Tecumseh and Harrison. Tecumseh on the Canadian shore knew that the most important battle of his life was now occurring, yet ironically it was a battle in which he could not participate. Harrison in his military camp on the Sandusky River knew that all his efforts during the past year depended upon Perry gaining control of Lake Erie. For three hours the two men listened to the dull thud of the water battle, neither being able to see the fleets which had disappeared over the horizon. Then the firing suddenly stopped. Scouts on both sides of the lake watched expectantly for the arrival of their fleet which would spell victory. While hundreds of anxious eyes scanned the quivering horizon a silence settled over the scene which was even more tense than the firing had been. At last, American observers saw sails approaching from the north. Slowly the American ships, their rigging torn, huge holes in their hulls, and with wounded and dying men littering their decks, sailed into Sandusky Bay. Perry hastily scribbled what was to become an immortal message on the back of an envelope and sent it by special messenger to Harrison twenty miles up the river. "We have met the enemy and they are ours," it read in triumph.

Now Harrison moved with great speed. Marching his army to the mouth of the Portage River, he placed them aboard Perry's ships and ferried them to Hartley's Point three miles below Fort Malden. There 4,500 soldiers swarmed ashore, each man sensing victory and eager to meet the enemy. A detachment easily took Detroit and the rest immediately marched upon the British stronghold at Malden.

When General Proctor had received the news of Barclay's defeat, he realized that the Americans would soon be on him and decided to retreat eastward up the River Thames. Tecumseh was incensed against what he regarded as British duplicity, for they had won him to their side by vowing never to abandon them as they had at Fallen Timbers. At one point the chief in a rage stormed into Proctor's tent, insisting that he and his army fulfill their agreement, and for a moment it appeared as if the British and Indians would fight among themselves. But Tecumseh, whose force had been reduced by desertion to less than one thousand, saw that without the British he was lost, and reluctantly agreed to follow them deeper into Canada.

As soon as Harrison learned that his enemies had fled, he was on their trail. For three days flying columns of American advance guards sped after the Indians and British, their trail easily marked by wagons, clothing, and even guns that had been discarded as the flight turned into a rout. At last Tecumseh could stomach no more. In a council of war he demanded that Proctor stop and fight the Americans like a man — even going so far as to threaten to shoot him if he retreated farther. It was decided to give battle on the next day, October 5, 1813.

The night before the battle Tecumseh had a premonition that he would die, and perhaps he was glad for he must have known by then that his Indian race was doomed. He was forty-five years of age, an old man in Indian terms, and, though he had fought the Big Knives with every ounce of his being, year by year he had seen them encroach steadily on Indian territory. His childhood home, Old Piqua, once the pride of the Shawnee nation, was gone. Prophetstown had been completely destroyed; the Wabash, once an Indian highway, was now filled with American flatboats. Even Fort Malden, the scene of gigantic Indian rallies, had by now fallen into the hands of the enemy. Perhaps Tecumseh even saw the ironic symbolism of the site he had chosen for what he was certain was his last battle. It was only a few miles from Moraviantown, a settlement of "Moravian" Indians who had fled the terrible massacre at Gnadenhutten into what they imagined was the safety of Canada. Now they were to witness the last, forlorn stand of the Algonquin tribes.

The next afternoon Harrison approached in battle formation. The sound of bugles rent the air and his cavalry charged. There was never any doubt of the outcome, for Tecumseh's forces were outnumbered two to one. Proctor saw the inevitable and fled before the fighting had barely commenced. Tecumseh, however, remained to spur the Indians to greater exertion. The tumult of battle roared around him, yet he stood his ground. Finally a charge pierced the Indian line, and the men of the opposing armies met in grim hand to hand combat. The power of numbers began to tell. The Indian dead began to accumulate. At last the broken redmen could stand no more, and fled in all directions. The white soldiers, brutally determined to finish the fight in Indian style, fell upon the dead and dying, scalping and mutilating them before Harrison could call them back.

Immediately after the battle Harrison searched among the fallen for Tecumseh. It was certain that he had been killed, for many men reported it, and the Indian captives themselves were bewailing his death. But neither Harrison nor any others, red or white, could identify the chief's remains from among the corpses. The body of the great Shawnee was never found. Perhaps it was there on the banks of the Thames; perhaps it was buried secretly by some of his devout followers; or perhaps the mortally wounded warrior managed to drag himself to some lonely place where he died alone. But the fact remained that Tecumseh was dead and the hopes of the Indian race died with him. Never again would the Algonquin war cry shatter the night to send fear into the hearts of a Midwestern army. The curtain had fallen on another era in Midwestern history, for the Indian was dead and but a legend, along with the singing *coureur de bois*. Military reputation was to carry Harrison eventually to the presidency, but Crouching Panther had been slain and soon his name would be all but forgotten by the white men and would be only a dim, dim memory to his own race. Hiawatha had indeed sailed, never to return, into the purple sunset.

# CHAPTER EIGHT

# O'er the hills to three frontiers

*The Farm Frontier: Cincinnati, Ohio;*
*Madison, Indiana; Shawneetown, Illi-*
*nois; The National Road; Conrad Rich-*
*ter* — The Trees, The Fields, The Town
*The Fur Frontier: St. Louis, W. C. Ken-*
*nerly* — Persimmon Hill
*The Timber Frontier: Hamlin Garland*
— Trail-makers

*At the conclusion* of the War of 1812 the Indians had largely been driven from the Midwest. The land lay open, uninhabited, and inviting. A wave of enthusiasm caught many hardy and adventuresome easterners, for they were aware of the great opportunities available on the new frontier: there would be roads to build, farmlands to clear, towns to construct; bridges would be needed to span the waterways, boats and stage coaches to transport immigrants, stores to furnish merchandise; there would be mayors, congressmen, and governors to elect. Opportunity fairly begged for takers. Rarely in any nation's history had such a gigantic region been suddenly available for immediate settlement. Eastern newspapers constantly carried

92

stories of the rich land to be found over the Appalachians, their proclamations backed by enthusiastic letters from recent settlers.

As eastern families sat around their hearthfires making plans to leave their homesteads, they began to realize that the Midwest was not one huge uniform area, but actually three separate and highly different frontiers — the farming frontier, encompassed by the dense forests of Ohio and the wide prairies of Illinois; the trading frontier, extending from St. Louis far out along the Missouri; and the timber frontier in the pine country of northern Wisconsin, Minnesota, and Michigan. Each was different, each appealed to different types of people.

The farming frontier attracted the majority of the immigrants, not only because most of them were farmers to begin with, but also because it was the closest and most accessible to them. They hitched up their wagons, loaded them high with food, tools and children, and trudged westward to Pittsburgh over the military roads Braddock and Forbes had carved more than half a century earlier. At Pittsburgh they purchased or built a flatboat, consisting merely of logs lashed together, and floated down the Ohio to the riverside towns where they would obtain a wagon to carry them to nearby homesteads.

Flatboating was an experience that held little pleasure for the pioneer family whose every possession, even the seed necessary for beginning their farming venture, was riding with them on the frail craft. Because they usually started down the river in the early spring to arrive in time for planting, the pioneers often found their flatboat caught in the violent spring tides which would carry it helter-skelter toward rocky islands, treacherous sandbars, or monstrous submerged trees. Frequent smash-ups spilled the family into the icy water and sent their prized possessions spinning down the racing river — lost forever. At other times there was the danger from outlaw ruffians who preyed upon the unsuspecting easterners. One of the most famous of these bands was located at Cave-In-Rock in Illinois. A huge sign over the cave proclaimed, "Liquor Vault and House of Entertainment," but those who docked often found their goods pirated and their very lives in danger.

The use of the Ohio as the first great highway into the Midwest meant that major junctures for commerce would soon develop along its banks. First and foremost was Cincinnati, to be known as the Queen City. Cincinnati was the logical place to land for the thousands of families who wished to follow Wayne's old military road northward into the rich lands emptied of Indians. Then, as the farmlands began filling, merchants and European immigrant peddlers sent increasingly large amounts of goods to the growing town for sale to the eager farmers. The river levee became a hive of activity, especially when, during the 1830's, the steamboats arrived to spread their wares on the wide stone landing. With the increased commercial activity the riverside district took on a new aspect, far different from the days when it was merely a vegetable patch for the little garrison at Fort Washington. Front Street became known as Rat Row, for along its bustling way squat warehouses sprung up, as did dingy saloons and cheap hotels, to receive the boatmen and drovers, and shops of all sorts to display the products in such demand by the farmers and their luxury-starved wives.

The fame of Cincinnati spread far and wide — even to distant Europe where none other than Charles Dickens decided to include it on his American tour. The English author, arriving in the city by steamboat in 1842, was much impressed by that portion of the town which extended beyond the reeking waterfront. In his *American Notes* he wrote:

> Cincinnati is a beautiful city; cheerful, thriving, and animated ... with its clean houses of red and white, its well-paved roads, and footways of bright tile ... the private residences remarkable for their elegance and neatness ... the city, lying in an amphitheatre of hills, forms a picture of remarkable beauty.

In addition to Cincinnati, other cities along the Ohio soon were thriving. Madison, Indiana, became a wealthy town where stately Greek Revival mansions began to line the river bank. James Lanier, one of the richest men in the state, constructed a home whose majestic circular staircase, thirty-foot Corinthian columns, and gently rolling acres of lawn made it a showplace of the Midwest.

Down the river from Madison was Shawneetown, once the temporary home of a portion of the Shawnee tribe and in the 1830's Illinois' first boom town. Its wealth at first stemmed from the nearby salt springs but, as the Ohio became alive with flatboats, Shawneetown found itself at the point of embarkation for pioneers scrambling into the hill country of southern Illinois or traveling on the cross-country short cut to St. Louis. Quickly stores and warehouses began to spring up along the shore, and in 1839 a certain kind of masterpiece — a massive bank — rose on the muddy earth of Shawneetown, its ponderous Doric pillars protruding above the mists of the river. So great was the fame of the Shawneetown bank that a humble delegation from the village of Chicago came to beg for money. But the imperious bank directors deemed Chicago too far from the river to amount to anything and refused the loan.

The Ohio River, though it might have seemed to be an eternal wellspring to the prosperous inhabitants of Cincinnati, Madison, and Shawneetown, had its faults as a highway. In the winter it was frozen over and completely useless; in the spring it was often flooded; and in the late summer and autumn it tended to become so low that snags and sandbars marooned both the clumsy flatboats and the erratic steamboats. It was clear that a reliable land route was needed, and immediately after the War of 1812, Congress began work on the National Road, which would run all the way from Baltimore on the Atlantic, over the Appalachians, across the Ohio River at Wheeling, and through the Midwest with the termination to be at St. Louis. The National Road, as it slowly began reaching westward, was the wonder of the nation with its magnificent sixty-six-foot roadway, its well-graded gravel surface, and its bridges of solid masonry destined to last for hundreds of years.

It was not until 1837 that the National Road was opened through all of Ohio, but even before this pioneers had used the completed portions to take them across the mountains. They had come mainly by sturdy Conestoga wagon — a sixteen-foot frame covered with a twenty-four-foot canvas top, and hauled by six horses. With the sides painted blue, the wheels red, and the canvas a shaded white, the Conestogas made a colorful sight, especially when seen, one after the other, on the Road: the fluttering leaves casting moving spots of sunlight over them; the husband, driving the horses, his deep-set eyes watching the mileposts announce his steady progress toward Wheeling or Zanesville or Springfield; the wife trudging beside the wagon, her once bright skirts covered with dust, carrying, perhaps, a young baby in her arms; the children romping in the mornings beside their mother or sitting bedraggled in the afternoons in the bumpy wagon whose iron-rimmed wheels managed to find every rock in the road. As evening fell, the family might sight the flickering light of an inn announcing a place where they could find food and a brief night's rest before continuing their seemingly unending journey.

But although the way was long and the pioneers may have experienced spells of discouragement, they were not deterred, and on their lips were songs of hope that echoed up and down the Road. One of their favorites went:

> Cheer up, brothers, as we go
> O'er the mountains westward ho,
> Where under boughs of mistletoe
> Log huts we'll rear,
> Where herds of deer and buffalo
> Furnish the cheer.

And the rousing chorus continued:

> Then o'er the hills in legions, boys,
> Fair freedom's star
> Points to the sunset regions, boys,
> Ha, ha, ha, ha!

When at long last the families reached their destination, the journey along the Road must have seemed a pleasant dream compared with the backbreaking job then before them. Since the land they had chosen for their homestead was invariably covered with dense forest, for the trees virtually smothered the countryside as far as the eye could see, the first settlers found the forest a real and deadly enemy. Their story has been told by Conrad Richter, an author who spent his childhood among neighbors of pioneer stock, in his Pulitzer Prize-winning trilogy, *The Trees, The Fields,* and *The Town.* Richter's heroine, Sayward Luckett, is a girl of fifteen when she arrives in the Ohio wilderness. Her family consists of her father, a man who loved the unrestricted life to be lived on the frontier and who, in seeking his fortune ever farther in the west, eventually deserted his family; her mother, a shriveled, dying woman, worn out at the age of thirty-three, whose one wish was to see the blue sky free from tattered leaves; and her four brothers and sisters, each of whom would experience their share of the sorrows and hardships to be encountered while growing up on the developing frontier.

Sayward's first home was a half-faced lean-to that her father built to house the family while he rambled through the autumn woods to his heart's content. Finally, as the chill fall rains began, he started work on a log cabin, the entire family helping lift the notched logs into place and then carrying white clay from the river bank to daub in between the chinks. The door was a long buckskin weighted with a log at the bottom; the floor was packed dirt over which wood mice raced and chipmunks rolled walnuts and the window was the Luckett's marriage paper, made translucent with bear's grease and plastered over an opening. Their beds were of dried leaves, the children sleeping in the low loft under the rafters, Sayward's mother and father resting on the ground in front of the fireplace. But the leaves and bed covers of furs were not enough to keep them comfortable during the winter when blasts of wind slid through the clay daubs, causing water to freeze only a few feet from the fire that was kept constantly ablaze.

The luxuries of pioneer life were simple, yet their very simplicity made them that much more meaningful; homebaked bread, so fragrant that just the thought of it made Sayward and the children shout with joy; a trip to the trading post with its exciting bolts of dressmaking material and wooden buckets of brightly colored beads; a rare visit by one of the few female neighbors when Sayward served tea and biscuits and spoke woman-talk.

As Sayward grew up she saw things change. More and more neighbors began coming in over the National Road, their farms, at first little cubbyholes in the immensity of trees, gradually merging to become open fields. Then there was the last Big Hunt when the wild things of the forest were surrounded and killed for the sheer joy of the sport: 19 wolves, 21 bear, 297 deer, and coon, fox, squirrel, and turkeys too numerous to count. Soon a mill was built on the river, the first school was opened, and merchants began turning the fields around Sayward's log cabin into a town. By that time the pioneer days were over: the forest was gone, the trading post gone, the wild animals gone, and the first settlers themselves had begun to die out. The frontier had passed westward.

The fur frontier, with its headquarters at St. Louis, boasted an older heritage than the farm frontier. The fur era had its Midwestern beginnings in the days of LaSalle, and St. Louis could claim ties dating back to the founding of Cahokia in the seventeenth century. The fur trade had continued to be in the hands of Frenchmen until Upper Louisiana, the last portion of French land, became American — the transfer being marked by a special ceremony at St. Louis in 1804.

The change of ownership brought a profound change to St. Louis. Though the town was at first still overwhelmingly French, American merchants and traders began flocking in, eager to partake in the wealth of furs that Meriwether Lewis and William Clark had discovered on their epic journey to the Pacific from 1804 to 1806. The fur horizon was further broadened the latter year when young Zebulon Pike returned from an exploration of the headwaters of the Mississippi. St. Louis, favorably situated at the confluence of the Missouri and the Mississippi, became the logical place from which to outfit the teams of traders who began to ascend both rivers in search of the Indian tribes with whom they could trade their beads, whiskey, and guns for beaver fur.

Posts and forts soon began dotting the banks of the two rivers. On the Mississippi, Prairie du Chien, located at the mouth of the Wisconsin, became a major sub-station where Hercules Dousman, head of a division of the famous American Fur Company, built a mansion that became well-known for its beauty throughout the area. Farther up the Mississippi, the Federal Government began work on a fortress to protect the river traffic in the land of the Chippewa and Sioux. This bulwark, named Fort Snelling after its commander, rose castle-like on a rocky precipice overlooking the junction of the Mississippi and Minnesota Rivers.

Villa Louis and grounds in Prairie du Chien, Wisconsin, as they appeared in the late nineteenth century. The mansion was built in 1843 by Hercules Dousman, Wisconsin's first millionaire.

Out beyond the Missouri things were different, for there the plains tribes followed the migrating buffalo herds, making it difficult for the traders to establish permanent bases of operation. The future metropolis of Kansas City was begun when François Chouteau, agent for the American Fur Company, built a trading post in 1821. Seven years later the Company opened another post at Council Bluffs, long a meeting place for the itinerant tribes. However, most of the important fur posts were further up the Missouri, out of Midwestern territory.

During the early days of the fur trade, as much of St. Louis was still a French town, the balconied mansions of the new-rich contrasted picturesquely but invidiously with the odd and ramshackle homes of the *voyageurs* or oarsmen. Charles Dickens, visiting St. Louis shortly after being in Cincinnati, caught the flavor of the *voyageur* section:

In the old French portion of the town the thoroughfares are narrow and crooked, and some of the houses are very quaint and picturesque... Some of these ancient habitations, with high garret gable-windows perking into the roofs, have a kind of French shrug about them; and, being lop-sided with age, appear to hold their heads askew, besides, as if they were grimacing in astonishment at the American Improvements.

The Americans that were making the "Improvements" mentioned by Dickens, were largely newcomers attracted by the stories of fortunes to be made in the fur trade. The son of one of these men lived until 1912, long enough to tell his daughter such vivid reminiscences of the early days that she published them in book form as *Persimmon Hill, A Narrative of Old St. Louis and the Far West*. Elizabeth Russell, in recording the observations of her father, William Clark Kennerly, has provided future generations with interesting glimpses of a time far different from today's.

Kennerly, growing up in the St. Louis of the 1820's and 30's, found himself in the midst of a kaleidoscopic world. From his home on Persimmon Hill, a low elevation five miles northwest of the waterfront, the young boy could watch the constant procession of fur boats putting into the landing where the *voyageurs* carried the precious cargo to the warehouses. Sometimes Kennerly's father would take him down to the levee where he would see steamboats in numbers so thick that most could not reach the docking area and had to tie up to the stern of another vessel. There, too, would be groups of Indians, leaving their canoes beside the huge steamboats, on their way to visit William Clark, the Indian Commissioner, their bodies proudly erect and decorated with beadwork and buffalo bones. At other times he would find himself in the midst of a long mule train that had just arrived from Santa Fe, the swarthy Mexican guards chattering rapidly in Spanish while their darting black eyes watched the movement of the city around them with interest and distrust.

Kennerly's heritage went much farther back, however. His grandparents on his mother's side had migrated from France, and in their spacious Parisian-style home, they filled him with wonderful stories of the old days when St. Louis was a creole village. It was a pleasure for the lad to walk with them through their garden, the seven-foot high wall seeming to block off the present, and to relive that day when his grandparents were young and had stood on the waterfront on a blustery March day in 1804 watching the Stars and Stripes flutter up the masthead for the very first time. Sometimes his grandparents even took him to visit the venerable Auguste Chouteau, the co-founder of St. Louis way back in 1764. Chouteau's grandson became his fast friend and companion.

Yet, though the French past appealed to Kennerly, the boy's main ties were on the American side where none other than William Clark had married his father's sister. Clark had returned to St. Louis after his memorable journey to the Pacific to become Governor of the Missouri Territory and, after Missouri had become a state in 1821, he assumed the important position of Commissioner of Indian Affairs. During Kennerly's childhood the mansion of Uncle William was almost always filled with Indian delegations, each bringing their "Redheaded Father" such valuable or unusual presents that he soon turned his Council Chamber, a hundred-foot wing attached to the southern end of his home, into a museum which became world renowned.

Kennerly often visited his Uncle William and sometimes found himself alone in the Council Chamber. He would pass before the displays, itching to play with the battle-scarred knives and blood-stained arrows. He would gaze in wonderment at the brilliant feather headdresses and the buffalo-skin shields of many colors and designs. He would find little Indian dolls peering back at him just as if he was their owner; and nearby would be papoose cradles and childrens' buckskin clothing, reminding him that the frontier was not only for men.

But Kennerly realized that the mystery of the Council Room, the hubbub of the levee, and the fragrance of old French gardens were only man-made settings for the eternal river which gave meaning and purpose to everything. The young people of St. Louis were as much enchanted by the Mississippi-Missouri as were their more business-like parents. On the first warm days of spring they would clamber up the bluffs by the Chain of Rocks where they could gain a view for many miles. On the calm nights of summer, young lovers would go on moonlight boat trips thirty miles downstream where

Kennett's Castle soared like a Rhenish chateau high above the water — there to make love while the silver water crested all around them. Even in the winter the river was part of their lives, especially during those days when it was frozen and they could skate, laughing and shouting, across its pockmarked surface all the way to Alton, Illinois.

Yet the river was sometimes like a half-tamed pet that suddenly turns on its master. Steamboats were constantly catching on snags and blowing up; or unseasonable floods would sweep across the levee, carrying off tons of valuable merchandise. At other times the river would contaminate the drinking water and terrible epidemics would follow — like the one of 1849 that forced many families to be transported to the miserable shelters on Quarantine Island, and left four thousand dead.

As Kennerly grew up, he saw the city rapidly change. Americans entered the city in ever increasing numbers — as did foreigners: stolid, beer-drinking Germans or pugnacious, fun-loving Irish. St. Louis then began to expand far beyond the waterfront, eventually crowding close around the swampy area near Persimmon Hill where Kennerly once shot wild ducks. The young man became a merchant, dealing in coffee and molasses until the coming of the Civil War closed the Mississippi. At that time he joined the Confederate forces with whom he fought with valor and returned to St. Louis when the war was ended.

But the post-bellum city was not the place it had formerly been, for the colorful riverboats had been replaced by the sooty steam trains and the romantic fur trade had given place to industrial development. At this point Kennerly's daughter ended her account of early St. Louis, realizing that an era had, indeed, passed into history.

By the late 1830's the farming frontier along the Ohio and the fur frontier along the Missouri and Mississippi were rapidly disappearing. Yet at almost the same time the third, and last, frontier opened up in the pine-lands of the North. This lumber boom began with operations in Michigan and Wisconsin. At the height of the lumber era up to 140,000 men were busy chopping, rafting, and sawing — a vast army that attacked the forest with an insatiable fury that did not subside until the last stands in upper Minnesota were felled just after the turn of the century.

The life of the lumberjack is hard to visualize, not only because he no longer exists, but, even more so, because it was so very different from anything we are accustomed to today. Lumbering was seasonal; yet unlike almost all other outdoor activities its season was in the winter — the time when the heavy logs could be towed over the snow. The world of the jack was one of forest solitudes where the boughs of the evergreens were heavy with snow, where the wind was as sharp as chilled steel, and the sky so deep a blue that it made one blink in disbelief. It was a world of brilliant sunsets when the snow absorbed the colors as a blotter absorbs liquid; it was a world of hard labor, of perspiration freezing as it trickled down one's nose, of muscles weary with the swing of the axe or the jerk of the saw; it was a world of crashing timber, of groaning horses, of mighty appetites, and of hardy laughs. It was a winter world, cold, brittle, bleak — yet invigorating as only winter can be.

In addition to the lumberjacks, there were other picturesque men on the timber frontier. Essential in the operations of the company were the timber cruisers, highly-skilled men who traveled in small groups far and wide over the forests, searching out the best lumber stands and the most convenient logging rivers. Hundreds, if not thousands, of the gem-like lakes of the North were discovered and named by these men. Then, after the lumberjacks had leveled the trees and hauled them through the snow to the river banks, the raftsmen, the most daring individuals of any frontier, lashed them into rafts and piloted them down the crashing, turbulent, spring-flooded streams to the sawmills.

The story of the timber frontier as it affected one man is told by Hamlin Garland in his book *Trail-Makers of the Middle Border*. Garland's father, Richard, migrated to Wisconsin in 1849, making his way past Stevens Point, known at that time as the "Gateway of the North," to the lumber camp which was at Mosinee Mountain. At Camp Number Three he met the dozen or so men who would be in his crew. All winter they chopped, and as they did, the forest they were killing became, in odd irony, a mother and protector, sheltering them from the savage winter winds.

There was charm in the sense of safety which the forest gave. The calm at the roots of the trees was like the quiet of deep seas.

A deep sense of camaraderie existed in the small camp, which brought a feeling of unity and good fellowship to the men— though each knew that when winter passed he would go his own private way, not to return until the following winter, if ever. The men called each other by nicknames: "Boston Charley," "Nutmegs," "Vermount." Richard was known as "Yankee Dick." They lived in a crude, log bunkhouse with a large chimney and a perpetually roaring fire. Nearby were smaller structures for the tools and for the horse teams. After a hard week's work, Dick found it a great pleasure to spend Sunday in the bunkhouse mending his clothes, listening to the other men tell tall stories, or just watching the cook attempt to make the occasion festive by baking a "plum-duff," or huge dried-apple pie. Some of the men went to the saloons, which always seemed to follow the camps, but most preferred to save their money, knowing that mothers depended upon it or that sweethearts looked upon it as assurance that the day of marriage was approaching.

The winter somehow passed quickly in the lumber camps. Before the men knew it the blows of the axe sent trickles of water, not snow, down their backs and the wind that had once been so keen and bracing became limp as a palm leaf, filling their hearts with strange languid feelings and their minds with fond thoughts of home. Then the camps began breaking up, most of the men returning to their farms to the south, a few of the more adventuresome staying to raft the logs down to the sawmills. Yankee Dick, a hardy young man of nineteen, chose to become a rafter.

The transition from lumberjack to rafter was startling and abrupt — from the serenity of drifted snow to the turbulence of foaming rapids; from the tall, swaying timber to the horizontal, shivering logs; from the majestic silence of the forest to the wild thrashing of flooded rivers. The savagery of the rivers, fairly boiling with melting snows, was a challenge to any man who dared make "The Drive." Though peril greeted them at every bend, there was a joy and an exhilaration to the job — the wind licking their cheeks with April freshness, the logs splintering the river into a million rainbow-hued chips of light, and the forested shoreline skimming past them, unraveling a constantly changing vista. There was wild joy even to be found in the dangerous places, like the Dells of the Wisconsin River where whirlpools ten feet deep spun the rafts like frail cakes of ice.

But lumbering and rafting were for young men, and, as Richard grew older, he knew he must turn to farming if he was to make a living. He married and purchased a farm that lay crumpled against the walls of Green's Coulee near La Crosse. There, amid the gray, lusterless rocks, he heared again the vibrant verses he and his fellows had sung when they came over the Appalachians: "O'er the hills in legions, boys."

Then, with eyes turned once more toward the sunset regions, he moved his family first into Iowa, then to distant Dakota, the very rim of the civilized world at that time.

In *Son of the Middle Border*, Hamlin Garland tells the sad later life of his father who returns in his old age, a defeated, worn man, to the home Hamlin built for him on the edge of Green's Coulee. The sunset trail had ended for him, as it did for so many of the legions who crossed the mountains, in defeat and discouragement.

Thus did the three frontiers gradually pass; merging imperceptibly into planned, civilized life, yet leaving a bittersweet residue of memories that would be told and retold to generation after generation as the pioneers became parents, then grandparents. The Sayward Lucketts would see again the brown and green aisles of vanquished trees; the Billy Kennerlys would stand again in Uncle William Clark's haunted Council Hall; the Dick Garlands would hear again the muffled crash of pines toppling into thick embankments of freshly fallen snow. The pioneers would leave their stories, diaries, and written recollections as a priceless heritage for the generations following them. They had found the Midwest an untamed wilderness and had left it in farms, fields, and towns. Though not all had enjoyed an equal amount of success, each had partaken in the spectacular and successful conquest of the great area of the Midwest.

# CHAPTER NINE

# Shangri-la in the Midwest

*Harmony*
*New Harmony*
*Zoar, Ceresco, Bishop Hill*
*Amana*
*The Mormons: Kirtland, Nauvoo*

*The Midwest*, which lay open and virtually unoccupied after the victories of the War of 1812, appealed to others, in addition to the individualists of the expanding fur, lumber, and farm frontiers. Idealism burned within the hearts of these other men and women, for they saw the new region as a place where they could work together in the creation of small, self-contained communities where brotherhood and good will would rule. To these groups the Midwest appeared to be one of the last remaining places in the world where they could live their lives away from strict governmental rule and the encroachments of hostile populations.

Some of the groups came from Europe where political and economic conditions made life all but intolerable. One body of Ger-

106

mans, for example, was led by a big man filled with stern confidence. They called themselves the Harmonists and believed their leader, George Rapp, when he proclaimed that the angel of the Lord had told him the Judgment Day was at hand and they should prepare for it by living clean, wholesome lives. His steel-barbed beliefs lodged in the minds of his followers like a whaler's harpoon, and almost one thousand Harmonists forsook the land of their birth to migrate with Rapp to the distant Midwest where they could live in accordance with God's wishes as revealed by Rapp.

Seldom before or since has the Ohio River — that grand highway of Midwestern migration — carried a more unique group than the Rappites who floated down it in 1814. They had none of the wonderment of the old French fur traders, none of the enthusiasm of the men of Clark or Wayne, none of the eagerness of the farm families. The future held no mystery for these serious, unsmiling Germans, and they must have gazed with sad knowingness at the spirited Americans who so wrongly believed their flatboats were carrying them toward a prosperous future. The Harmonists knew the shrill trumpet of Gabriel would soon announce the End of the World.

When they landed at their new town site on the eastern bank of the lower Wabash River, they found it a mass of river-soaked trees and overgrown swamp plants. The river, however, winding as it did through the lovely, virgin landscape, gave the place a haunting beauty that was a far cry from the tired, domesticated land of their native Germany. Rapp was happy with the site; he had chosen it on a trip made some months earlier, for he believed that the hard labor of clearing the tangled forest would occupy the thoughts of his congregation while they were waiting for the Second Coming.

Quickly the town took shape. Four large Community Houses were completed where the single men and women could live free of rent. A sturdy granary was erected to hold the bountiful produce of the fields, its four-foot stone walls enabling it to be converted into a fort if the occasion arose. Residences for the married couples began to line the streets and Rapp himself soon occupied a fine brick house. Most important of all, a grand church was erected in the center of town. Its unusual shape in the form of a Maltese Cross and lovely, hand-carved Rose Doors made it an object of beauty as well as a place for worship.

The town was named "Harmony," in accordance with Rapp's philosophy that the goal of a godly life could best be achieved by each person striving to live in perfect harmony with his neighbor. Rapp believed that harmonious living could best be accomplished when each of his followers worked for the good of the community as a whole, contributing the entire fruit of his labor to the community. The agricultural fields were therefore held in common and the crops divided among the Harmonists according to his need. Rapp also believed the institution of marriage fostered a selfishness whereby one person agreed to confer his or her affections upon one person only, to the exclusion of others in the community. Therefore, since Judgment Day was so near at hand and there was no reason to bring children into the world, Rapp decreed that there would be complete celibacy at Harmony. Perhaps nothing so demonstrates the hold Rapp had over his followers that almost without exception husbands and wives agreed to live together from that time on merely as brothers and sisters.

Now the years began slowly, uneventfully, inexorably to pass. One year went by, then two, then three. Each evening the watchman chanted: "Again a day is passed and a step made nearer the end. Our time runs away and the joys of heaven are our reward." Four years, five years, six years. Still the Harmonists waited expectantly, thrilled at daybreak when the song of a meadowlark was momentarily mistaken for Gabriel's trumpet, alert at midday when the clang of a blacksmith's anvil sounded like the opening of heaven's gates, awakened at midnight when their ears seemed to catch the voice of Eternity in the murmur of the wind. Seven years, eight years, nine years. The day must be coming soon – almost a half million dollars had been collected to provide them transportation to the Holy Land when the time finally came.

After ten years, Rapp, still never doubting that the Call would come, but feeling that the prosperity of the colony was tending to bring materialistic thoughts to the Harmonists, decided they would abandon their town and return up the Ohio to Pennsylvania where the building of a new town would reinvigorate his people. And so, in 1825, Rapp sold the land and buildings at Harmony to Robert Owen, a British idealist. Yet so certain was he that the Second Coming was near that he stipulated in the contract of sale that Owen must care for the cemetery for only twenty years — certain by that time the righteous dead would have arisen to join their comrades in the Kingdom of Heaven.

Robert Owen, the new owner of Harmony, did not share Rapp's conviction in the approaching Judgment Day, but instead believed he could create a heaven on earth. World leaders, who laughed at men like Rapp, listened to Owen, for his factory at New Lanark, Scotland, with its superior working conditions, high wages, and correspondingly high production, seemed to prove that he was a man able to combine utopian sentiments with solid business sense. His book, *The New Moral World,* was read and discussed everywhere; and when he came to the United States, he had the ear of President John Quincy Adams himself.

Owen thought he had found the secret to a perfect society. He envisaged ideal communities of about two thousand people living in towns laid out in the form of hollow squares. All the land and buildings would be held in common. Everyone would partake in the government of the town, with the smallness of the population insuring complete democracy. There would likewise be ample facilities for various cultural activities, for each town would have free schools, a university for those desiring additional education, a well-stocked library, and ballrooms and community dining rooms where everyone could get together with his neighbors. Spacious living quarters would be furnished and each apartment would be provided with the most modern conveniences.

Owen was convinced that, if people could just see the advantages of the small communes over the crowded, crime-ridden cities or the backward, poverty-stricken country villages, the entire structure of social life the world over would be altered along these new lines. For this reason, when Rapp offered his isolated town for sale, Owen purchased it as the ideal place to begin his noble experiment. It was renamed "New Harmony" and was to be a New Jerusalem from which Owen's ideas would sweep over and reinvigorate the world.

Soon the dour Rappites were replaced by more than a thousand spirited Owenites — Americans mostly, drawn from all walks of life. From his headquarters in the old Rappite Community House Number Three, Owen watched his colony grow. His happiest day came when a large group of famous scientists arrived in what was referred to as the Boatload of Knowledge. The scientists were to be in charge of education, thereby spreading the joy of knowledge among the simpler men and women who were to work in the fields. The world watched while New Harmony began the great experiment that might make that year, 1825, a turning point in history.

But Rapp and Owen were not the only ones who saw in the Midwest an opportunity for utopian colonies. In 1817 a group of Germans settled in a picturesque village in Ohio through which wound the Tuscarawas River; in 1844 a number of Americans began an idealistic colony in middle Wisconsin; and in 1847 a band of Swedes lived in hand-dug caves beside Edwards Creek in Illinois before erecting their permanent lodgings. These towns — Zoar, Ceresco, and Bishop Hill, respectively — all showed early signs of prospering. Each was formed according to beliefs that community effort must replace the atomistic individualism that was the main ingredient of the turbulent frontier.

One of the most successful and most interesting of the colonies was begun in 1854. At this time a small advance guard of a German religious society, called the Community of True Inspiration, decided that the land beside the Iowa River was the place to settle. Though the surrounding hills lay desolate beneath a matted layer of autumn-brown grass, they could see that here, lost in the immensity of the mid-Iowa prairies, was the ideally isolated site for which they had crossed a treacherous ocean and tramped more than two thousand miles to find. At last they had discovered the hidden Shangri-La where their people could live their lives close to God, far away from the doubts and temptations of civilization.

The rest of the Inspirationalists arrived during the summer of

1855 and gradually a village began to take shape. It was typically German with crooked streets, quaint brick houses, neat gardens, and a multitude of fruit trees. But it was far different from their ancient homes in Germany, nonetheless. How often they must have wished that their belief in the Divine Will being manifested through special Inspired Ones and thus, their frequent refusal to obey the orders of governmental authorities, had not necessitated their migration.

The first village was piously named "Amana," from the Biblical term meaning "to believe." During the seven years that followed, more Inspirationalists came to the holy valley, and their towns, which radiated out from the first, took the names of West Amana, South Amana, East Amana, Middle Amana, and High Amana. Though they were all within several miles of one another, each was governed by a separately elected Council of Elders. The buildings and farmlands of each village were held in common, and all the work that was performed was done without wages for the common good. The sensual frivolities of the material world were frowned upon: the mode of dress was plain even to drabness; jewelry or any sort of personal adornment was forbidden; music, poetry, dancing, or any of the arts which did not relate directly to the Bible were not allowed. Even books were deemed evil influences, and only the Bible was to be found in an Amana home.

But life in the Amanas was far from unpleasant. Over a period of four generations the families lived in a sort of timeless, fairytale kingdom where personal conflicts and the disruption of change did not occur. There was little bitterness or selfishness, for their religion taught them that all men were alike in the eyes of the Lord — and to them religion was everything. There was no want — for food, clothing, and all necessities were furnished free to each society member. Neither was there the loneliness of the outside world, for the joy of daily prayer meetings and the comradeship of the community dining rooms provided the pleasure of close and friendly contact. Each Inspirationalist had a feeling of deep contentment, certain that he and his fellows had found the true and good life, that they were under the friendly direction of God and were finding favor in His eyes.

Of all the Midwestern utopian experiments, none came nearer to success than that of the Mormons, who were organized in 1830 by Joseph Smith, a serious young man of twenty-four. In that year Smith published a book that he claimed was the translation of mysterious golden plates he had found, under God's guidance, buried on a hill in upper New York. The plates told the story of an Israelite clan which had sailed to America in 600 B.C. Over the years this clan had split into two antagonistic groups: the cultured Nephi, who built the magnificent cities of Central and South America, and the savage Lamanites who devolved into the American Indian. In 421 A.D. the Indians destroyed the Nephi, but not before Mormon, the last survivor, hid the records of his race on the hill where Smith later found them.

Joseph Smith, firmly believing that the Book of Mormon showed God's desire that America should be the site of the new Zion, set out to form a church which would carry on the tradition of the Nephi. The Church of Jesus Christ of Latter-day Saints was accordingly begun at Fayette, New York, and though it had but a handful of members, missionaries were quickly sent out to bring the knowledge of God's revelation to the masses. These missionaries had a certain success wherever they went, but their greatest accomplishment — actually the turning point in the fortunes of the Mormons — was the conversion of a Campbellite congregation of a thousand members at Kirtland, Ohio.

Upon news of the events in Kirtland, Joseph Smith migrated there. Arriving in January 1831, he found himself on a wind-swept spur of the deeply eroded Appalachian plateau. In the far distance he could see the slate-gray waters of Lake Erie, bounded by the flat plain upon which the hamlet of Cleveland rested fifteen miles to the west. But Smith had little interest in the scenery. He believed he heard the voice of God during emotional revelations and was interested only in creating a new church based on these revelations. As word spread about this ardent young man who claimed such wonderful powers, thousands of frontiersmen and their families made their way to Kirtland, eager to join the dynamic movement.

On May 6, 1833, Smith told his people that God had directed

them to build a temple, even giving them the very dimensions He desired. Work was begun immediately, and as the walls rose, the joy of the congregation expanded until it seemed to know no bounds. The building of the church was a community project entered into with a spirit of hardy comradeship. Some men worked in the nearby quarries, happy to be laboriously fashioning the stones for God's palace. Others felled the trees from the surrounding forest and furnished teams to haul the fine-grained logs to the building site. There, carpenters, among them a stocky, muscular man by the name of Brigham Young, fashioned the lumber into pews, handsome pulpits, graceful Ionic pillars, and a hundred more needed items. The women, in the meantime, were busy spinning and weaving the cloth needed by the working men and, it is said, a few even donated their finest china to be broken and added to the mortar.

After three years of difficult labor, the temple was completed. As March 27, 1836 — the day of the dedication — approached, a tremor of excitement ran through the Mormon community, for it was believed that God would demonstrate His pleasure in some manner. When The Day arrived, such crowds were on hand that the church was filled to capacity and large numbers of disappointed persons were forced to wait outside. Joseph Smith spoke from the freshly painted pulpit, his voice trembling with emotion. And the congregation, all but overwhelmed with emotion, chanted, "Hosanna, Hosanna, Hosanna."

Then something strange and thrilling happened. There was a great rushing of wind through the surrounding trees and into the temple itself. Persons on the outside looked frantically about them, then saw what appeared to be a shimmering pillar of light glowing on the roof of the church. In the interior Smith cried out, "The heavens are opened to me and I behold the celestial Kingdom of God . . . I see the transcendent beauty of the gate through which the heirs of that Kingdom will enter, which is like unto circling flames of fire." Many others, too, said they saw Smith's wonderful vision. The expected miracle had occurred.

After the tremendous events of the dedication ceremony, the temple was used for the more routine meetings of the church. Yet, even so, the spirit of the Lord was always close, and more than once persons claimed to have seen Him seated before them on the altar, His omniscient eyes peering at them in columns of soul-searching fire, His visage glowing more brilliant than the sun, the hair of His head pure and as wondrously white as Christmas snow. Holiness and awe hung over the Mormon temple like an invisible cloud.

But the ways of the Lord are strange and not to be comprehended by mortals. On July 11, 1836, the Federal Government issued its famous Specie Circular which forbade the use of bank notes in payment for government land. The notes of all banks, but especially those in the Midwest which had little gold to back up their overabundant issues, rapidly lost value. Smith and his followers found that their creditors would accept only gold, not bank notes, for the debts contracted in the construction of the temple. Smith could not purchase enough gold to meet these debts and soon groups of angry creditors, including even many Mormons themselves, began harrassing Smith at Kirtland.

The deteriorating economic situation began to undermine the confidence of many of Smith's followers, who found themselves nursing doubts that God would be directing their affairs in such an unbusinesslike fashion. Bitterness broke out within the church to such a degree that not even the appeals of Brigham Young, one of Smith's staunchest advocates, could prevent many of the congregation from attending services carrying pistols and Bowie knives. Finally one cold winter night in 1837, Smith left Kirtland, fleeing for his life.

Yet the saga of Joseph Smith did not end here. With a persistence reminiscent of LaSalle or Tecumseh, he regrouped his loyal followers, of whom there were still thousands. And, after a brief and violent stay in Missouri, they began to build a new capital on the shores of the Mississippi River in an unsettled portion of Illinois.

The new town was named "Nauvoo," meaning "beautiful plantation" in Hebrew, and when the Mormons began arriving in the spring of 1839, they did indeed find it beautiful — the low land nestling close to the placid river, the skyline broken by high yet gently rounded bluffs. At the same time they found it swampy, filled with the malarial mosquito that caused the death of great numbers of Mormons, including Smith's father and younger brother. But the hard-working men and women, still unshaken in their belief in the personal guidance of God through His prophet, Joseph Smith, drained the swamp and built a thriving town. By 1841, Nauvoo boasted a population of 10,000 — with possibly 20,000 more Mormons living in the vicinity. From an uninhabited wilderness to the largest city in the state — it was a dramatic personal success for Smith.

The crowning jewel of Nauvoo was the magnificent temple which

Nauvoo, Illinois, 1846-47. The Mormon temple is on the hilltop. The two-story, square building at the river's edge is Nauvoo House, a guest home in Joseph Smith's day. His own home was one of those immediately left of Nauvoo House.

was built on the bluffs overlooking the city. Constructed at the phenomenal cost of some one million dollars, its impressive facade of three-story pilasters and its towering octagonal steeple surmounted by a gilded statue of the Mormon angel, Moroni, made it the finest building in the entire Midwest.

The concentration of population at Nauvoo and the tight political cohesiveness of the church organization enabled the Mormons to become an important force in Illinois elections. They actually came to hold the balance of power in the state, and both Democrat and Whig politicians found themselves currying favor with the Mormons at Nauvoo. Joseph Smith, quick to see the advantages to be gained from political success, even went so far as to announce himself candidate for the presidency of the United States in 1844.

But with all the apparent success, time was running out for the theocracy at Nauvoo. The people of Illinois, friendly at first to the Mormons, had gradually grown antagonistic. Some had been alienated by the haughty pride with which the Mormons referred to themselves as "Saints" while calling the non-Mormons "Gentiles." Others feared the rapidly growing political power of Joseph Smith that seemed to spell the end of religious freedom if it went unchecked. Still others were disturbed by rumors of a private Mormon army of many thousand young men called Danites.

But probably the greatest opposition to the Mormons came from the substantiated reports that Mormon leaders, including Smith himself, had proclaimed Biblical support for polygamy and were taking "spiritual wives" to be lived with for the day or the month as the occasion called for.

The opposition was brought to a head when two Mormon dissenters opened a newspaper in Nauvoo in which they printed a fierce attack against their former brethren. When the Nauvoo council ordered the press destroyed, the owners fled to nearby Carthage, the county seat, where they told the riled citizens how Smith was making a mockery of freedom of the press. The county authorities accordingly issued an order for Smith's arrest.

The anger of the Mormons in their formidable strongholds along the Mississippi at once threatened widespread violence if the warrant was served. The situation became so taut with danger that the governor himself hastened to Carthage and gave his solemn word that if Smith left Nauvoo and came to Carthage to stand trial he would not be molested by the hostile elements that had vowed his destruction. Smith consented to go to Carthage, though it was with forebodings of death that he, his brother, Hyrum, and two other Mormon leaders left the safety of Nauvoo.

When they arrived at Carthage, Governor Thomas Ford, seeing the ugly temper of the populace, placed the Mormons in a comfortable room above the jail and appointed the Carthage militia to guard them. Ford then set out for Nauvoo to investigate the charges. With Smith now far removed from the might of Mormon arms, virtually alone in a countryside burning with hatred, and with his protector, the governor, twenty miles away, the stage was now set for the final tragic events of Smith's turbulent career.

On the afternoon of June 27, 1844, the four Mormons heard an ominous rumble of approaching voices. Looking out the window, they saw a surly mob, their faces made ugly by the lamp-black they had smeared over them to prevent identification. The militia, Smith's only hope, gave way easily before the threatening crowd. In another moment the men were inside the jail. Then Smith and his companions could hear the heavy clatter of many boots stomping up the stairs which led to their room.

The Mormons sang a hymn, though the discordant harmonies of Death were ringing in their ears. Suddenly, a shot blasted through the door and Hyrum Smith, hit directly in the face, fell mortally wounded to the floor. Then a second Mormon was dropped by two bullets. Smith dashed for the window, intending to attempt a leap to freedom, but as he did gunfire roared, and riddled his body. He hung for a moment on the ledge, then slowly somersaulted onto the ground below. The mob had had its vengeance.

When the news of Smith's murder reached Nauvoo, cries for retaliation were heard but were quickly drowned by the decision of responsible men, led by Brigham Young, who saw that the hope of the Mormons lay, not in battling their much more numerous neighbors, but in establishing a realm of their own in the far western desert beyond the territory of what was then the United States. Once the decision was made, the mass of Mormons made haste to leave, and within a year and a half once-smiling Nauvoo lay all but deserted. A new city of Zion was taking form beside the Great Salt Lake.

The stories of the many attempts to create Shangri-Las in the Midwest give one occasion to ponder a most intriguing "might-have-been." What if the steamboat and the locomotive had not been invented just in time to insure the rapid flooding of the Midwest with rambunctious, individualistic immigrants? What if the Midwest had been populated at a more leisurely pace, giving each particular colony time to develop its own particular culture and mode of living?

This is how it might have been:

The Harmonist society, which passed into extinction with the death of its last member in 1906, might have evolved into a place of refuge for the old and discouraged from all over the country, becoming, perhaps, a vast old people's estate providing good care and pleasant companionship for the aged.

Robert Owen — unhampered by the encroachments of the materialism that caused the breakdown of New Harmony only a few years after it was founded — might have established a town which would have become, as originally intended, the inspiration for the founding of small, self-contained communities throughout the Midwest, communities that would form a sphere of common feeling reaching across county and state boundaries.

The colony at Amana, which managed to last almost eighty years before its communal economy was abandoned in 1932, would have continued its slow growth, and, if it was given enough time, might have become a theocratic federation encompassing the present state of Iowa.

The Mormon colonies at Kirtland and Nauvoo, which were broken by the hostility of the surrounding "Gentiles," might have become greatly-expanded, closely-allied districts controlling trade on Lake Erie and the Mississippi.

Then, instead of consisting merely of rotting buildings and fading memories, the colonies might exist today, making the Midwest a region rich in experiments to better mankind — experiments which, in the variations and improvements that the years would have brought, might have discovered the elusive touchstone that would help lead to human perfection.

It might have been. . . .

# CHAPTER TEN

# "Just a piece of driftwood"

*Introduction: the Illinois prairies*
*Abraham Lincoln as a Midwesterner: log*
*cabin birth, humility, self-education, a*
*fighter, hurt in romance*
*Love of politics*
*Republican Convention of 1860*

*There was nothing* there, yet the people were afraid. Their eyes scanned the horizon and the very boundlessness of the vista made them uneasy. There were no trees nor shrubs nor any evidence of human habitation; only the endless grass swaying beneath the vagrant breezes as if it were a thing with a mind. The grass was everywhere. It held the low, rounded hills in a furry embrace, it half smothered the struggling streams. There were no landmarks, nothing to tell a man where he was or where he might be going. There was only the billowing grass extending into the infinitely remote horizon.

During the endless centuries when the Indian held the land, this area belonged to the tribes of the Illini Confederation. But the red man was never at home here. The warriors and their families kept close to the rivers, hardly daring to leave their well-marked paths, fearful at the thought of becoming lost in the grasslands eight feet high. Yet, after the Illini had gone, the area kept its name: the Prairies of Illinois.

The early white men stood on the edge of the prairie and were as fearful as the Indian. Marquette and LaSalle seldom strayed from the waterways, and the little French trading villages clung to the banks of the rivers like children to their mothers' skirts. And even when the land-hungry American frontiersmen broke through the forests to the south, they paused before the awesome grasslands that rode the crest of every hill for three hundred treeless miles; preferring to live among the comforting trees, they built their capitol at Vandalia.

During the 1820's, however, the central prairies began slowly to fill with hardy men and women whose descendants still plow the rich, black earth. It was during this time that a little village was founded on the banks of the Sangamon not far from Springfield. It was called New Salem and its founders had great hopes that one day it would become a populous city. Yet the destiny of New Salem was to be otherwise, for within ten years it was a nearly deserted ghost town of decaying wooden buildings. But, though New Salem bloomed and died as quickly as a prairie dandelion, it achieved a renown that few cities, however large, can boast. From its muddy streets and ramshackle cabins its greatest son, Abraham Lincoln, began a career that would bring New Salem a reflected immortality.

Lincoln was not actually born amid the rolling prairies, but he lived there long and it is hard to imagine his growth in any other setting. The wide horizon broadened the feelings of many, and it would be surprising if Lincoln was not affected in a similar way. Prairie thoughts are expansive, different in so many ways from the localized emotions that are nourished in lands where forests and buildings hedge in the individual. A feature of Lincoln's greatness was that he could see all sides of a problem, could catch the basic issues in terms that brought the public to him. This lack of small-mindedness attuned him with the people as a whole; and it may very well have been the prairie vista that helped bring this about.

That Abraham Lincoln has universal appeal is undeniable. He was perhaps the only Christ-like figure America has ever produced, and it is little wonder that he has been transformed into a secular saint. From the sorrow and tragedy of his life, to all his humanness, there has emerged a universal sympathy. His life is an American legend and he himself has become the Savior of the Nation, the Great Emancipator of the Enslaved, the Fearless Defender of the Oppressed and Downtrodden.

In his every action there is something of the goodness and nobility that we all would like to find within ourselves.

Yet, oddly enough, the many traits of Lincoln, national hero that he may be, do not belong to the country as such, but strictly to the Midwest. Take, for example, Lincoln's much publicized log cabin birth. This was not so much a national ideal as it was Midwestern. An Eastern politician who wished to emphasize his actual place of birth would be happy if it were a middle-class, city dwelling; and a Southerner would prefer a magnolia-shaded plantation.

Lincoln appealed to people because in many ways his life was so common. As a young man, he spent most of his time plowing or working rugged boulders from the tough prairie soil, or splitting tree trunks into fence rails. Such farm life is a Midwestern ideal, far from the aristocratic life of the slave-labor South or the industrial and business life of the East. Where else but in the Midwest could a dirt farmer be carried to fame on the homey slogan "The Railsplitter"? It rang true in Illinois, but in Georgia or New York it would have had little attraction in this period of national history.

In humility, too, Lincoln is strictly Midwestern. One could scarcely imagine anyone except a person close to the common people making fun of his homely features. Certainly the city politicians of the East or the aristocrats of the South would never have told a story such as the one Lincoln told about being stopped by a stranger in Illinois who told him he had a jackknife that belonged to him. Lincoln, surprised, asked the man how that could be. The stranger, presenting the knife to Lincoln with a grand flourish, said that it had been given him by someone who insisted that he keep it — till he found a person uglier than himself.

The early Midwesterner was suspicious of the college educated gentleman — even as today there is a lingering distrust of the Ivy Leaguer type. The Midwestern ideal is the self-educated man whose learning consists largely of practical matters. The image of the young Lincoln lying on the firelit floor on his log cabin reading about his idol, George Washington, or studying grammar and surveying under a backwoods teacher in New Salem, or laboriously reading Blackstone's "Commentaries on the Laws of England" — these are events dear to the heart of Lincoln lovers. Lincoln was no learned philosopher but an ordinary, hard-working young man interested in politics, good grammar, and law. This appealed to the Midwesterner.

Lincoln was not merely a studious young fellow. Midwesterners insist that their heroes be two-fisted, able to match their might against any comer. The fight between Lincoln and the New Salem ruffian, Jack Armstrong, has become an integral part of the Lincoln story. Yet even more important to the development of the man were his two hazardous trips down the wild Mississippi to the "wicked" city of New Orleans. On one trip, when he was only nineteen, Lincoln's flatboat was boarded by a group of Negroes bent on killing Abe and his only companion and stealing their cargo. In a furious fight Lincoln drove off the Negroes but was left with a lifetime scar over his right eye — an ironic event for the man who was to release the Negro race from bondage.

It was at New Orleans that Lincoln got his first real exposure to the evils of slavery. He saw the auction blocks where human beings were treated like animals; saw the swarthy overseers roughly separate husband from wife, parents from children; heard the heartfelt sadness of the Negro songs and laments. It's reported that after his second trip to New Orleans he vowed if he ever got a chance to "hit" slavery he would. However, being a Midwesterner, his philosophy did not take him into the utopian regions of outright abolition of the institution; that was reserved for the more religious, more idealistic New Englanders. It was his desire — and this was made amply clear as his political career unfolded — to merely limit the expansion of slavery, not destroy it where it already existed.

This view of slavery reflected Midwestern opinion, which is invariably conservative. Although slavery was an admitted evil, the average Midwesterner had no burning desire to adopt the radical alternative of total emancipation.

Lincoln's romantic life reveals more of his Midwestern upbringing, for he had neither Southern grace nor Eastern sophistication. When in 1831 Lincoln arrived in the Illinois village of New Salem he fell under the spell of the lovely, blue-eyed Ann Rutledge, daughter of the tavern keeper. She was but eighteen and he was four years older; yet he, awkward, hesitant, and shy, was unable to turn her affection away from the handsome easterner, John McNamar. However, McNamar left for the East soon after he and Ann were engaged to be married, and for three years not more than a line or two was heard from him.

Lincoln must have watched Ann with a heart full of silent anguish, for, as Carl Sandburg puts it, "both were figures of fate — he caught with debts . . . she the victim of a betrothal that had become a mysterious scandal." But one day the waiting was over. On August 25, 1835, Ann, after an illness of six weeks, died — still faithful to her absent lover. Upon her death it is reported that Lincoln went temporarily out of his mind and was found wandering through the woods, half mumbling, half sobbing.

The affair with Ann Rutledge is the tenderest in Lincolniana. It brought him close to the people — in his day and now in ours — for it would seem all great men must have some personal tragedy in their lives, otherwise they remain as cold as marble statues: respected but devoid of appeal.

The tragedy of Ann Rutledge, while a deep and everlasting sorrow to Lincoln, was a blessing to the nation. Through Ann's death he was saved from possible mediocrity, since Lincoln needed a woman who would push him, who could channel his indolent, good-natured laziness into a surging tide of ambition. Gentle Ann Rutledge could not have done this; driving Mary Todd, whom he married in 1842, could and did. Though Mary Todd has been castigated and scorned by generation after generation of Lincoln's admirers, it is probable that without her Honest Abe would to this day be known only as a local politician of Springfield, Illinois.

After one has pointed out the Midwestern traits that made Abraham Lincoln a representative figure of the region, there remains the most important factor of all. It took more than a log cabin beginning, a youth of railsplitting and Mississippi adventure, a humility, a sense of humor about his homely features, a self-taught, practical education, a romantic tragedy, and a driving wife. All these qualities made him politically acceptable in the Midwest. But there still remains the man himself.

It is a common belief that Lincoln was reticent about entering politics; that he answered the call of his party and of the people with regret; that he would have liked to have been left alone to live his life away from the noise and turmoil of public life. This is quite contrary to the facts. Lincoln loved politics as he loved nothing else: one of the greatest disappointments of his entire life occurred when his Whig party broke up and he appeared to be left without any vehicle for remaining in politics. One has only to examine his career to see just how politically active he was.

When Abe was only twenty-one, his father abandoned his barren Gentryville farm and led his family out of Indiana onto the prairies of Illinois. The wide grasslands gave Abe a new, expansive feeling about his future, and in the same year, 1830, he made his first political speech. Only two years later, after he had left his father and migrated to New Salem, he ran for his first office — the Illinois legislature. Though he was defeated, he ambitiously ran again two years later. This time he was elected. Again, in 1836, he was returned to the legislature where, at the age of twenty-seven, he became Whig floor leader. At this time he was active in getting the capital moved from the sleepy, southern town of Vandalia to expanding Springfield on the prairies. When this was done, he moved from New Salem, which was dying, to Springfield.

During the "Log Cabin and Cider" campaign of William Henry Harrison, he took to the stump to aid the Whig candidate. In 1846 Lincoln achieved his, till then, greatest success by being elected to Congress on the Whig ticket. But the Congressional term was for only two years; and since the Whig party was breaking up, he believed his political career had by 1848 just about ended. As William

Barton states it: "One of the great disappointments of his life rose up and smote him when he went back to his dingy [Springfield law] office." At the age of thirty-nine Lincoln regarded himself as a has-been.

For six years Lincoln was content with the mundane life of a circuit lawyer, riding throughout the thirteen prairie counties of his district in a horse-drawn buggy. He probably tried to keep his mind on local doings, but the dramatic success of Stephen A. Douglas, his one-time co-legislator in Illinois and former rival for the hand of Mary Todd, must have left him distraught at his own lack of achievement. Yet in 1854 Douglas himself unwittingly brought Lincoln back into politics when he rammed the much discussed Kansas-Nebraska Act through Congress. By opening these territories to slavery, Douglas hoped to curry favor from the South in his bid for the Democratic presidential nomination.

Lincoln began speaking out against this unwarranted expansion of possible slave territory, and the favorable response made him enthusiastic over his chances of being elected to the Senate. With his wife's insistent urging, he redoubled his efforts. Politics again became a passion with him. Shortly after the Republican Party was organized, he joined it and quickly became one of its leaders in Illinois. His stature became such that the 1856 Republican Nominating Convention gave Lincoln 110 votes for the vice-presidency which, though not enough to put him on the ticket, increased his prestige and made him the logical Republican standard bearer to contest in Illinois the re-election of Douglas to the U.S. Senate.

During the summer and fall of 1858, Lincoln and Douglas met in a series of debates that took them to every section of the state. That the nationally illustrious Douglas beat Lincoln was no surprise — but that Abe came within five legislative votes of winning (Senators were at that time elected by the state legislature) was something that brought Lincoln's name to the tongues of thousands of Easterners who had never before heard of him.

Now Lincoln's star was rising fast. Knowing that the Republican Nominating Convention was to meet in 1860, Lincoln spent the preceding year delivering speeches that took him four thousand miles across the nation. At the same time he began writing letters to men of political importance recommending his merits and himself as at least second choice after their favorite-son candidate.

The Republican Convention was held in Chicago during the third week of May 1860. For the cheering and chanting, for the unbounded enthusiasm, for the sheer noise and hubbub, this convention was to be unlike any thus far experienced. Chicago was the site, chosen as a symbol of the growth and vigor of the expanding Midwest. The energetic city had built a huge structure known as the "Wigwam" especially for the convention.

It was in this building that the political future of Abraham Lincoln was to be decided. And while Lincoln waited nervously in Springfield, his capable lieutenants began the jockeying that would eventually send their leader to the White House.

But the convention was not a cut and dried affair for him. Lincoln was not the favorite; far from it. He was a dark-horse candidate scarcely mentioned in the same breath with William H. Seward, Salmon P. Chase, or John M. Bates. Seward was the heads on choice and his followers had come to town ready to win. Train after train arrived from his New York stronghold carrying rowdies and toughs, greasy politicos with ready bribe money, brass bands, pamphleteers, and, most awesome of all, Seward's unscrupulous manager, Thurlow Weed.

During the first two days, the convention was occupied with choosing the chairman and making the party platform. When the meeting of the second day was over, the Seward men gathered in their hotel planning for the victory they were so sure would be theirs when the balloting began on the morrow. But in other hotel rooms Lincoln's team began their secret attack.

David Davis, three hundred pounds of dynamic force, led the Lincoln men. Just as unscrupulous as Thurlow Weed, he was not so confident and thus was more dangerous. Davis moved with such rapidity that the Seward cause was undermined before Weed even suspected the battle had begun.

Davis began by printing a thousand counterfeit tickets and carefully distributing them to Lincoln rooters specially selected for their shouting ability. Next Davis had the seating chairman place Seward's New York delegation in an isolated portion of the Wigwam where they would not be able to disturb the Lincoln demonstrations. Finally Davis made his greatest play for votes. He brought the wavering Indiana delegation to the Lincoln side by promising their leader, Caleb B. Smith, the position of Secretary of the Interior in Lincoln's cabinet. To swing Pennsylvania he promised Simon Cameron the Treasury Department. When Lincoln, fearing that the enthusiasm of his followers would lead them too far, wired, "Make no contracts that will bind me," Davis drawled, "Lincoln ain't here," and the steamroller kept moving.

The next morning the Wigwam was stuffed with ten thousand shouting, perspiring, shoving people while outside twenty thousand more eagerly awaited news of the proceedings. When the first ballot showed that Seward had only 173½ votes to Lincoln's startling 102, the Lincoln galleries let forth with a well rehearsed roar that was deafening. "Lincoln, Lincoln, Lincoln" was the chanting and the managers for Seward grew uneasy as they saw many of the other delegations, overcome with the Lincoln enthusiasm, beginning to waver.

Then the second ballot was taken. Thurlow Weed was in a rage as the men from Cameron's group swung to Lincoln. Delegates pledged to Chase added their support to the Railsplitter. Lincoln jumped to 181 votes and the leather-lunged cheering section became even more boisterous. Amid an almost unbelievable clamor, the third ballot was taken.

The New England states, supposedly citadels of Seward strength, were the first called. But when Massachusetts suddenly switched four of her votes from Seward to Lincoln, the uncontrollable avalanche was on. There was nothing now that Weed and his cohorts could do. Rhode Island and New Jersey turned to Lincoln. Then Pennsylvania; then Maryland — Lincoln was not to be stopped. Yet when the third ballot was completed, it showed Lincoln lacking two votes for the nomination!

There was a profound silence as everyone in the packed hall grasped this fact. Then an Ohio delegate stood on his chair and through the hush loudly cried a change of four votes from Chase to Lincoln! According to reports on the spot, the crowd gasped as if it were one; then the wildest bedlam that frontier Chicago had ever heard broke out. A cannon on top of the Wigwam boomed the news and sheer pandemonium spread throughout the city — their man, the Illinois railsplitter, had won! It was a great day for the Midwest.

And what did Abraham Lincoln think when the news was flashed to him in Springfield? He found himself sobered, strangely sad, overcome with humility. Perhaps he stared at the telegram in disbelief.

A campaign rally in front of Lincoln's home in Springfield, Illinois, August 8, 1860. Lincoln is the tall figure in white at the right of the door. The home today is virtually unchanged.

He had fought hard for the nomination, but, now that he had it, there may have been a sensation of bewilderment; all this could not actually be happening to him. He had never been absolutely sure of himself. When he came to New Salem many years earlier, he had compared himself to a piece of driftwood, a purposeless, bobbing twig that was swept willy-nilly along life's river. And several years later, as he stood on the field at Gettysburg, he would again express his sense of uncertainty and insecurity when he said: "The world will little note nor long remember what we say here . . ."

But the call had come, and Lincoln was ready. The whirlwind caught him up, taking him from his beloved prairies to the White House; there to transform him into a national hero.

This was Lincoln, a common man with common faults and common failings, yet so very much above commonness! And this was Lincoln, the Midwesterner whose physical likeness was incorporated in the emerging figure of Uncle Sam, legendary symbol of the entire nation.

This was the man who shall live forever — the Man of the Prairies.

# CHAPTER ELEVEN

# Comet over the Mississippi

Introduction: The Comet of 1835 —
Mark Twain's portent
Florida, Missouri
Hannibal, Missouri
Life on the Mississippi
Adventures of Tom Sawyer
Adventures of Huckleberry Finn
Death, 1910

*This* was not the Dark Ages but the year 1835, and the bright object which hung silvery in the night was not an evil omen, but merely Halley's Comet. Yet each night, as the comet grew larger and brighter, Midwesterners from all walks of life watched the ghostly sign and wondered what it could portend.

Some men, old and tired, turned their thoughts to the past: William Clark, then sixty-five years of age, may well have dreamed of the grand days of his youth when with Meriwether Lewis he had gazed at the new lands and ocean which they found beyond the headwaters of the Missouri; or the doughty Chief Black Hawk, three years older than Clark, who yearned for the glorious days when the upper Mississippi River had belonged to him; or William Henry

Harrison, three years younger than Clark, who wistfully relived the days long past when he had been the youthful governor of the boundless Indiana Territory and had defeated the warriors of Tecumseh at Tippecanoe. To men such as these the comet must have appeared as a harbinger of the End. They were ready to go, for the world of their youth had already died.

But there were other men who were ready and eager to meet the challenges of changing times: Abraham Lincoln, a beardless youth of twenty-six, who had just been elected to the Illinois legislature; Ulysses Grant, barely in his teens, whose father would soon send him to West Point and thus start him on his spectacular military career; Joseph Smith, four years older than Lincoln, who had joyfully begun to gather his militant Mormon forces at Kirtland in preparation for the coming of the Lord. To men such as these the comet must have appeared as a harbinger of the Grand Beginning. They were young and the world was young with them.

Gradually, Halley's Comet turned about the sun and sped again into the black outer reaches of the solar system, not to return again for seventy-five years. As it dwindled into the merest speck and then into nothingness, it ceased to be a topic of conversation and within a short time had been all but forgotten by the millions who had once spoken of little else. Yet there were a few who did not forget the comet, and to those few it remained something that seemed to forecast events both wonderful and at the same time tragic.

One of these was a young mother whose second son was born on November 30, 1835, while the cold light of the comet cast speckled shadows through the cracks of a little frame cottage in Florida, Missouri. She christened her baby Samuel Langhorne Clemens, and from his earliest childhood repeated to him the story of the comet which had announced his birth.

Sam's mother, Jane, had lived something of a tragic life. A vivacious, impulsive redhead, she had been in love with a Kentucky doctor, but had married Clemens in a fit of spite. Perhaps because she did not love her husband, her emotions turned toward the superstitious. Her first son she named Orion after the stellar huntsman and, when the brilliant comet shone at the birth of Sam, she immediately believed it a sign of great importance. She instilled her starry fantasies in her son to such a degree that he later confessed to believe "I came in with the comet and I shall go out with the comet."

Sam's father, John, deprived of the love of his wife, nevertheless did the best he could to bring her happiness; but all his efforts seemed predestined to failure. His law practice in Tennessee had proved unprofitable, partly due to his cold personality; and a venture in land speculation had brought him close to bankruptcy. He moved to Missouri at the encouragement of his wife's brother-in-law, John Quarles; but, after attempting to manage a store in the tiny village of Florida, he gave it up as another bad venture and decided to try his luck in the nearby and bustling town of Hannibal on the Mississippi. Thus it was that young Sam found himself at the age of four in the town that would be his home for the next fourteen years and which he would make famous.

Hannibal during the 1840's was a boy's paradise. The river was a broad highway filled with lead barges from the mines of Galena, long rafts of timber from the forests of Wisconsin, flatboats filled with pioneer families crossing to the fertile fields of Missouri, and, most glorious of all, there were the flamboyant, bespangled steamboats that swept into the Hannibal levee with a flourish that in later years would never again be seen on the inland waterways. Boys would long watch for the approaching steamboats; and, when the upright silhouette finally appeared on the horizon, they would drop whatever they were doing and dash to the shore.

In a sense the river was Sam's mother. Her lapping water nurtured him with the milk of first awareness. From her beckoning capes came his first concept of distance; from her tangled islands he learned the joy of adventure; and from the men and women whom she transported to the town he was educated in the ways of the wide world.

In 1847, when Sam was twelve, his father died. Jane Clemens, left with almost nothing, was forced to take her son out of school — which scarcely displeased him — and apprentice him to the printer of a local newspaper. Two years later Sam's older brother, Orion, bought *The Hannibal Journal,* and Sam was dignified with the title of Assistant Editor. Orion even let him put a few of his own lines in the paper. The lad took to writing, and by the time he was sixteen had the satisfaction of seeing two anecdotes he had written appear in no less a magazine than *The Saturday Evening Post.*

But by the time he was eighteen, Sam, feeling the urge to see the world beyond the valley of the Mississippi, left Hannibal and, vagabonding through the East, worked as a typesetter in New York, Philadelphia, and Washington. Then a year later, he returned to the Mississippi to work in the print shop Orion had set up in Keokuk, Iowa. He remained with Orion for two years but, when fate blew a fifty dollar bill into his startled hands, he gave in to his wanderlust and set off for Cincinnati.

He got a job in his old typesetting trade, yet in two months the river called him again and he took passage on the steamboat *Paul Jones* for New Orleans. The trip down the Ohio and Mississippi was so fascinating that before he was half way down he knew the river was in his blood and he could not leave it. During the days and far into the evenings he talked with the rough, but gentle, pilot, Horace Bixby, and by the time they had arrived in New Orleans, Bixby had agreed to teach Sam, now twenty-two, the difficult profession of piloting. Then for the two happiest years in his life Sam plied the Mississippi as a pilot.

When the Civil War closed the Mississippi, Sam returned to Hannibal where he was induced to join the forces being prepared to help the secessionist governor, Clairborne Jackson, against the federal troops stationed in St. Louis. Yet Sam's heart was not with the Confederates, for his trips down the river had shown him that he was not a Southerner. Later, in *A Private History of a Campaign That Failed,* he described his farcical military experiences that ended when, at the approach of the Union Army, Sam and his group told the rest of the companies that "the war was a disappointment to us and we [are] going to disband." Then they hurriedly fled just before the men of Ulysses Grant came galloping into their camp. And here is an irony, for Grant nearly made a prisoner of war the very man who would later publish the General's *Memoirs* and thereby save him from near poverty!

After leaving the "disappointing" war, Sam found that Orion had just received an appointment from Lincoln's Attorney General, Edward Bates, to be secretary to the Governor of the Nevada Territory. Sam, quickly renouncing his former Confederate alliance, went with Orion to Nevada, later describing the rugged stage coach trip in his book *Roughing It.*

Once out West, Sam's writing career began to open. At Virginia City he was hired by *The Territorial Enterprise,* a newspaper that quickly recognized the high quality of the sketches the young man submitted. In the environment of untamed miners, hostile Indians, and outlaws of every description, Sam Clemens found himself at home; and these humorous sketches soon caught the fancy of everyone. Some of his work even began appearing in eastern newspapers.

Yet, though the Nevada desert was a long way from the flowering lands of the Mississippi, the whisper of the river still ran through his thoughts, and when he chose a pen name it was taken from the old term used by the steamboatmen: "mark twain" — two fathoms, safe water. From that time on Mark Twain he was.

The young writer was soon involved in the violent life of the Territory to such an extent that he was expelled for attempting to fight a duel with a rival newspaperman. From Nevada Mark Twain's trail led to San Francisco, to distant islands in the Pacific, and to a passage through the jungle paths of Panama. When in 1867 he landed in New York after five and a half years of the wildest sort of adventures, he was received with a great deal of attention, for his writing had by then become well known throughout the nation. But the young man, now thirty-one, was not ready to settle down and, contracting to write travel letters for a California newspaper, he boarded a steamer for Europe and the Holy Land. As a result of this trip, he wrote *Innocents Abroad,* a humorous portrayal of Europe as seen by a Western American.

While aboard ship, he saw a picture in a locket of a girl with a rare, delicate beauty. The locket belonged to a chance acquaintance, Charles Langdon, the girl's brother. Mark fell passionately in love with her — even though they had never met. When he returned from his trip, he gained an introduction to Olivia Langdon. He then ardently wooed and finally won her — although it was with some misgivings that the well-born Olivia married the boisterous Westerner.

After their marriage in 1870, Olivia set out to tone down her husband. They took a house in the conservative city of Hartford, Connecticut, and there Twain began to work on a new novel in collaboration with one of his neighbors, Charles Dudley Warner. Entitled *The Gilded Age*, it was so well received that it eventually gave its name to the entire period it was intended to describe. A satire on the low business and political morals that had overtaken the nation during the Reconstruction Era, it was at the same time profound and raised Twain to high rank among American authors.

Yet Mark Twain, lionized everywhere, wealthy from the sale of his many books and from his numerous lectures, was not entirely happy. His humor, while beguiling his readers, was actually a mask for his disdain of the world around him; and within his jests there was usually found the grit of bitterness. Typical of this bitterness are the Twain witticisms: "Few things are harder to put up with than the annoyance of a good example," and "Nothing so needs reforming as other people's habits."

He saw life in fatalistic terms. Man was a poor, helpless creature buffeted by chance, perhaps even controlled by the stars. He knew his life had been one of chance: the fifty-dollar bill that started him on his steamboating career, the escape from Grant that had let him begin his writing career, the portrait of the girl that had led him to his wife. And his mother had even seen his future foretold by the comet which had appeared at his birth.

And so the successful author, saddened by life's apparent futility, turned back to those sweet dreams of yesterday when he was young and when each golden day broke as if the happy times would never end. He imagined himself not approaching the decline of middle age, but as a young man piloting the steamboats up and down the Great River.

He saw again the majestic Mississippi tinted pale green with twilight's afterglow, or molten orange at sunrise, or stained with the silver and purple of a moonlit night. He heard again the clanging steamboat bells as the hours were tolled, heard the powerful mumbling of the boilers, heard the shouts of the man at the bow: "mark twain," safe water. And he felt again the throb of the rotating paddle wheels, felt the shiver of the boat as it spun through an eddy, felt the spray as the churning water broke over the railing. Those were the days when everything was an adventure.

He remembered his apprenticeship to Horace Bixby when the notebook he kept gradually began to bristle with the names of all the picturesque towns and villages along the river, all the dim capes and shadowy islands, all the mysterious sandbars that were never in the same place twice. Each river bend had to be noted and the capricious currents that swept around them recognized. He even had to memorize every one-limbed cottonwood or obscure wood-pile that might serve as a landmark.

And slowly he had grown to know the Mississippi even better than he knew his best friends. He had seen her when she was sullen, with the water low and moving slowly, exposing hidden sandbars, turning once safe channels into dangerous shoals, bringing to the surface derelict hulls that rose like black nightmares. He had seen her when she was wild as an enraged tigress, with the water rising and turbulent, sweeping the fragile steamboat along at breakneck speed, tearing its bottom on rocky snags or battering its sides with the gigantic logs that careened through the rushing water. And he had seen her when she was contented as a slumbering woman, with the water gently rustling against the sandy shore, calling him to swim in her quiet pools.

In 1875 Mark Twain wrote these reminiscences in a series of articles entitled *Old Times on the Mississippi.* They were published in *The Atlantic Monthly,* and eight years later, augmented by more memories, were brought out in book form as *Life on the Mississippi.* This book, more than any other, has immortalized the Mississippi as it was during its age of Midwestern greatness. It was fortunate that he wrote when he did, for the railroad was even then destroying the river as a route of commerce and would soon leave it almost as deserted as it had been during the days of the redman.

But Twain was still not happy after he had finished this book. He had opened the floodgates to the past and could not close them. He revisited his childhood hometown of Hannibal and let himself be carried backward on the current of time to the days when he was the leader of a gang of boys. And, as he dreamed, he began to recreate his past in the character of a fictional youth, Tom Sawyer.

How pleasant must have been the memories of the weary author as he began writing *The Adventures of Tom Sawyer*. He himself was the hero, but the other main characters were people from his past. His mother was restored as she had been thirty years earlier to become Aunt Polly. His sister, Pamela, became Cousin Mary. His younger brother, Henry — tragically killed many years before in a steamboat explosion — was returned to life as Tom's half-brother, Sid. And, of course, there was pretty Laura Hawkins, who once charmed Mark from her house across the street; she became Tom's sweetheart, Becky Thatcher.

But *Tom Sawyer* was more than a book of memories. It brought something new and important to literature. For the first time the plot of a major novel revolved around the lives of common American villagers — not sophisticated, Eastern aristocrats or romantic, hardly believable, generals and frontiersmen. A Midwestern dialect was spoken and episodes typical of interior Amerca were used. Mark Twain had, in effect, created a new national literature.

After Twain finished *Tom Sawyer*, he took an extensive European tour which resulted in the popular books *A Tramp Abroad* and *The Prince and the Pauper*.

Then in 1884 he entered the publishing business and soon made a fortune on General Grant's *Personal Memoirs*. Yet, even with these successes, Twain could not prevent his thoughts from returning to his boyhood days on the Mississippi. The same year that he entered the publishing field he completed the manuscript of what is regarded as his greatest book: *The Adventures of Huckleberry Finn*.

The main portion of *Huckleberry Finn* concerns the dual escape of Huck from his drunken "Pap" and of Jim, a Negro slave, from the mistress who he thinks is about to sell him. As Huck and Jim drift down the Mississippi on a flatboat, they meet two likeable scoundrels who call themselves the Duke of Bridgewater and "the pore disappeared Dauphin, Looy the Seventeen." The Duke and the King are bungling swindlers who lead Huck and Jim on a series of escapades that take them out of town after town barely one step ahead of the law. Yet these adventures are more than merely a series of incidents; they are, in reality, acute portrayals of small-town life as it was lived along the middle Mississippi prior to the Civil War.

Again, as in *Tom Sawyer*, the characters and settings have life, because Twain molded them on what he had actually known in Missouri. Huck was a boyhood chum, Tom Blankenship, whose father was the town drunkard. Jim was Uncle Dan'l, a middle-aged slave who belonged to Twain's Uncle John Quarles. And, for the purposes of the story, the entire farm at Florida, Missouri, was moved to Arkansas to be used as the setting for the recapture of Jim and the happy ending that followed.

*Huckleberry Finn* was a much loved story during the years following its publication and has since become regarded as an American masterpiece. It, even more than *Tom Sawyer*, broke the ground for the Twentieth Century writers. Ernest Hemingway has gone so far as to state that "all modern American literature comes from one book by Mark Twain called 'Huckleberry Finn.'"

The nine years between the publication of *Old Times on the Mississippi* and *Huckleberry Finn* brought Twain to the peak of his career. Thereafter the decline began. It all seemed to start with an invention in which he became interested — a machine that, by setting type many times faster than could be done by hand, promised to revolutionize the entire printing industry. Because Twain thought he could make millions in royalties, he backed the young inventor, James Paige, with sums which eventually ran up to a staggering $190,000! To invest this amount, Twain had far overextended himself and, when the machine could not be perfected, the entire investment was lost. This left the fifty-nine-year-old author bankrupt at an age when he should have been able to retire, and forced him to undertake an exhausting series of lectures which, though he eventually was able to repay every cent he had borrowed, was a severe hardship on the elderly man.

The most unfortunate thing about the Paige fiasco was that there was really no need for Twain to seek the gigantic profits that he hoped to make. He already had sufficient money from his books, his publishing house, and his lectures. But there was something that drove him; something that can only be explained by his sense of insecurity. Perhaps the comet under which he had been born symbolized this insecure feeling. Just as the comet moved beyond the control of men, so did his own affairs seem to move irresistibly beyond his control. Yet, in a futile attempt to escape from his own fatalism, Twain tried to make himself safe by making the kind of fabulous sum that the typesetter seemed to promise.

His later years were filled with an unhappiness that must have made the author long for the return of the comet and the peace of death. While lecturing overseas to repay his debts, his favorite daughter died in the United States, and a second daughter later became an epileptic. In 1897 his brother Orion went. Then his wife, the beloved Olivia, sank into permanent invalidism to finally pass away in 1904.

After his wife died, Mark Twain had nothing left for which to live — yet his own sturdy health would not let him die. For six long, sad years he waited, spending much of the time dictating his autobiography to Albert Bigelow Paine.

At last it was 1910, the year he had so long awaited. Faintly and indistinctly Halley's Comet appeared in the nighttime sky. Slowly, as it approached, it grew brighter and brighter. Then the necks of the humble and the mighty turned upward to look at the spectacle that was beginning to fill the sky — just as their fathers and grandfathers had seventy-five years earlier. Industrial tycoons, such as Elbert Gary and Henry Ford may have paused a moment from their empire building to wonder if the blazing comet might not portend something of their destinies.

But to Mark Twain there was little question what the comet signified. In January his heart began to give him trouble and by mid-April it was clear that the end was not far off. Finally on April 21, just as the comet was beginning to appear through the scarlet haze of sunset, the author began fading. "Good-bye, if we meet . . . ," he mumbled as if speaking to someone in the unseen distance — perhaps someone being born at that moment who would carry the fear of the comet to the year 1985. Then he sank into a coma, and a short time later he was dead.

# CHAPTER TWELVE

# Climax in Chicago

*Theodore Dreiser*
*Edgar Lee Masters*
*Carl Sandburg*
*Sherwood Anderson*
*Decline of Chicago in the 1920's*
*James T. Farrell*

*The years* did strange things to the swampy wastelands that extended for many miles around the sluggish Chicago River. Gone were the days when the wandering Indian tribes shunned the region for its bad smell and unhealthy atmosphere. Gone were the French portage paths and the little shack in which the ascetic Father Marquette spent a dreary winter. Gone was old Fort Dearborn whose tiny, helpless garrison had been massacred by Indians during the War of 1812. Gone even was the ramshackle Wigwam in which Lincoln received the Republican nomination for President during the uproarious convention of 1860. Chicago was no longer a struggling frontier village begging for loans from imperious Shawneetown. During the years after the Civil War it became a boomtown, whose fantastic growth was well known even in Europe, where Germany's Iron Chancellor, Otto Von Bismarck, confessed he wished to go to America if only to see Chicago.

Chicago's rise was not due to chance. Situated at the far end of Lake Michigan, it was the natural hub around which the railroads turned as they reached northward into the opening lands of Illinois, Wisconsin, Minnesota, and the Great Plains. Soon the ancient swamp was traversed by broad bands of steel rails and by connecting brick roadways, along which were clustered the homes and factories of the thousands flocking to the expanding city. Before the end of the nineteenth century the glitter of Chicago began to hang over the Midwest like a throbbing aurora — attracting all those who yearned to replace the uneventful life they were living with the vigor, the novelty, the chance for self-improvement and financial advancement that could only be found in such a dynamic city.

Chicago was something new on the American landscape — a city not psychologically subservient to England as were the cities of the Eastern coast, nor deeply involved with tortuous racial problems as the cities of the South, nor humble provincial outposts as other Midwestern cities. Chicago was the proud capital of the Midwest, a region beneficially isolated from foreign influences. It was strictly American, and this fact made it more appealing to those with literary bents than the other, shop-worn cities. The new Chicago called for men to tell its story — and they came.

One of the first writers to be attracted to Chicago was a frail young lad named Theodore Dreiser. As a boy he knew poverty, having been carried by his parents on their wanderings through half a dozen Indiana towns. Chicago had always been a symbol of Romance to him ever since the days when he had picked up coal along the railroad tracks at Terre Haute, watching as he worked the trains rumbling northward toward the city which was on everyone's lips. And so it was that when his mother died and the family broke up, Dreiser was quick to catch a train to Chicago, eager as a medieval knight to find his fortune in the world which lay just over the horizon.

The furiously growing city brought scenes to the young man

which would never leave him. He was fascinated by the ponderous homes of the wealthy and the pomp of their owners. But his job as a collection agent for an easy-payment furniture company also took him into the poorer sections of the city, there to walk with fear as well as wonderment through the dreary yet curiously interesting neighborhoods where the foreign-born lived. At times he would find himself near the vast railroad yards where the air was thick with smoke and the buildings grimy with soot from the vast herds of snorting engines. And he saw too, in vivid contrast, the clean, blue horizon of Lake Michigan, its water whitened by the sails of scores of luxury yachts. Occasionally, too, his path led him along the murky banks of the Chicago River, past Goose Island, where upturned boats became miserable shanties for squalor-ridden families.

As he made his rounds, seeing for the first time the raw, seamy side of big-city life as well as the dazzling world of wealth, he was possessed with a strong urge to write, for Chicago was acting on the country lad like a strong stimulant:

> After a time I ventured to commit some of these things to paper, scarcely knowing what they were . . . And I had a singing feeling, now that I had done this much, that some day I should really write and be very famous into the bargain.

This urge to write kept the young man frequenting newspaper offices, begging for work of any kind, looking all the while like a homeless cat — as Dreiser later described himself — meowing to be taken in. At last he had his chance. A small, struggling paper, *The Daily Globe,* took him on. He had at long last been provided with his grand entry into writing.

Dreiser's success at newspaper work eventually took him to other cities, but Chicago was still very much in his thoughts. There were stories in Chicago that cried to be told. He saw again the endless processions of country folk, people like himself, being drawn irresistibly toward the city like iron filings to a magnet. He remembered the faces and incidents of the countless persons he had seen and talked to during his days with the furniture store and *The Globe.* With his perceptive, sympathetic mind he could feel their fervent longings, their burning hopes, their unbounded pride when they made good or overwhelming despair when they failed. He dreamed of writing the great novel that should catch this mass of humanity at its crest — not a romantic story where love conquers all nor mere anecdotes describing local color in the Mark Twain tradition. He dreamed of a new kind of novel, about common men and women caught in the cold, impersonal life of the pushing, shoving, trampling city — a life where goodness was not always rewarded and badness not always punished. He dreamed, and then he began writing —

> When Caroline Meeber boarded the afternoon train for Chicago. . . . Her heart was troubled by a kind of terror. The fact that she was alone, away from home, rushing into a great sea of life and endeavour, began to tell.

Dreiser saw this eighteen-year-old girl as an innocent bird about to flit into the tangled, rank jungle; soon to be innocent no longer. Dreiser would lead his heroine, Sister Carrie, through the tortuous paths of big-city life, exposing her to the drudgery of work in a shoe factory, of bleak living in an unattractive tenement, of seduction by a traveling salesman. And as Dreiser wrote, he created the events not out of the fantasies of thought but out of real life, for *Sister Carrie* was to a large extent the retelling of the misadventures of one of his own sisters.

The book was published in 1900 but was quickly withdrawn from circulation when the publisher's wife voiced her violent disapproval of the unthinkable plot which found Carrie content to live with a man not her husband yet which resulted, not in her punishment, but in fame and fortune as a famous actress. Nonetheless the book brought Dreiser international respect and eventually was hailed as a milestone in the advance of American literature toward a realistic portrayal of contemporary life.

Though Dreiser was greatly disturbed by the repression of *Sister Carrie*, the theme of Chicago life still rang in his ears. A few years later he completed two more novels with settings largely in that city: *Jennie Gerhardt* and *The Genius*. Then, in 1913, he returned to Chicago to delve into the life of one of the city's great tycoons,

Charles T. Yerkes. After careful deliberation, he had decided upon Yerkes as one of the best representatives of that fast-moving Gay Nineties era when the powerful men of big business fought titanic battles for the loot of a nation while riding roughshod over the people.

Dreiser ferreted through the city, interviewing persons from all walks of life who had known Yerkes before his death in 1905, examining the newspaper files of that period, visiting the locations Yerkes had frequented. Then he wrote *The Titan,* a book which has become both a valuable historical study of an important man and a vivid description of a period in the growth of a mighty city.

Dreiser's pen caught the man and the city in sharp outline. There were the supercilious ladies of high society, quick to dispute the right of Yerkes and his wife to encroach upon their exalted status; the hard men of big business, fighting with all the weapons at their disposal, fair and foul, to prevent Yerkes from gaining a monopoly on the public transportation system; the bungling, bribe-taking politicians of Chicago and of Springfield, the state capital, all eagerly grasping the money Yerkes offered them for his invaluable transportation franchises; the crafty, yet somehow likeable, ward bosses who fought or helped Yerkes as his money or their inclinations directed them. And there was Yerkes himself (or Frank Cowperwood, as Dreiser names his hero) — an engaging, domineering titan, whose quick mind instantly made him master of any situation, whose self-centered morals were described by his motto "I satisfy myself," yet whose inner personality was that of an unsure introvert, and whose groping for certainty in a world of ceaseless change led him to spend a fortune on works of art and beautiful women.

But Dreiser was not the only writer who found inspiration in Chicago. When he returned to the city in 1913, he was the guest of Edgar Lee Masters, a lawyer enjoying a profitable practice in partnership with the famous Clarence Darrow. Masters had written a friendly letter to Dreiser, whom he had not then met, when he had read *Sister Carrie.* The correspondence had continued over the years and it was Masters who had helped convince Dreiser to come to Chicago prior to writing *The Titan.* Though Masters had writ-

ten only a few inconsequential collections of poems and plays,
Dreiser found his friendship stimulating and it was partly through
Dreiser's encouragement that Masters decided to write a series of
poems about life in a small Midwestern town.

Just as *Sister Carrie* had shown a new, realistic side of city life,
so did the verses collected as the *Spoon River Anthology* show a
country town as it actually was, not as something quaintly romantic in the usual tradition. By living in Chicago, Masters had gained
the perspective necessary to see the remarkable pettiness of the
small towns where everyone knew all the dirt about his neighbor
and where personal feuds often brought forth a deep vendetta that
broke the village into irreconcilable factions.

Masters knew well the area from which he drew the material for
his free verse poems. He took for his example Lewistown, Illinois,
the place where he had grown up and from which he had fled in
disgust in 1892. He remembered his boyhood there: evenings brim-
ming with accomplishment when his high school teacher talked
with him about Emerson, Dickens, and Thackeray — and the sadness that overtook him when the same teacher, discouraged with
the lack of response at the high school, left for another town. He
remembered the bitter political fights of his father against the entrenched politicians who controlled Lewistown. He remembered
the contempt with which the townsfolk, and even his father, held
his love for learning and his desire to write. He remembered lonely
days spent wandering over the country hills or watching the water
of the Spoon River cascade over the mill dam at nearby Bernadotte.
These bitter memories served as the basis for Masters' biting picture of what he regarded as a typical small town.

The *Anthology* consisted of 244 epitaphs written by the inhabitants of the Spoon River graveyard — each relating to the aspirations,
triumphs, or disappointments of the particular person concerned.
There was, for example, Benjamin Pantier complaining against the
narrowness of his wife:

> In the morning of life I knew aspiration and saw glory.
> Then she, who survives me, snared my soul
> With a snare which bled me to death,
> Till I, once strong of will, lay broken, indifferent . . . .

Or there is Pantier's wife who saw him as the country bore he
may have been:

> But suppose you are really a lady, and have delicate
>     tastes,
> And loathe the smell of whiskey and onions . . .
> And the only man with whom the law and morality
> Permit you to have the marital relation
> Is the very man that fills you with disgust . . . .

As Masters wrote he felt haunted by the souls of the dead he
was describing "who were watching me and protesting, and yet inspiring me to go on." And well might Masters feel the eyes of the
dead, for most of his characters were taken from actual persons he
had known. There was Kinsey Keene, a character possibly based
upon his own father, who fought the domineering Thomas Rhodes,
president of the bank. Rhodes scoffed at Keene with sentiments
Masters must have heard many times:

> Very well, you liberals,
> And navigators into realms intellectual . . .
> You found with all your boasted wisdom
> How hard at the last it is
> To keep the soul from splitting into cellular atoms.

There was Masters' school teacher who cried out:

> Where is my boy, my boy—
> In what far part of the world?
> The boy I loved best of all in the school?—
> I the teacher, the old maid, the virgin heart . . .

Masters epitaphs himself as Webster Ford who, disillusioned with
the work-a-day life he is leading, longs to follow Apollo, the god
of poetry:

> 'Tis vain, O youth, to fly the call of Apollo.
> Fling yourselves in the fire, die with a song of spring,
> If die you must in the spring. For none shall look
> On the face of Apollo and live, and choose you must

'Twixt death in the flame and death after years of sorrow,
Rooted fast in the earth . . .

In *Spoon River Anthology* the man and the theme had found each other. But, oddly enough, though the *Anthology* was a great success from the moment the first verses were published in 1914 and though the future seemed to promise great things for the author, none of the numerous works he wrote in the following years approached the *Anthology* either in originality or sparkle. The pen had caught fire only once, yet by this one work Masters shattered the idealized image of the country town and set the style for scores of writers who were to follow him.

Almost at the same time that Masters was exposing the unhappy life in the country towns, another Chicagoan was describing the seamy side of life in the big cities. This man was Carl Sandburg, a close acquaintance of Masters, though eleven years his junior. While Masters had seen the city as being on a cultural plateau far above that of the country towns, Sandburg discerned that the cities had their own particular brand of tragedy.

The course that Sandburg's poetry would take was largely determined by his childhood experiences. His father, a poor, illiterate working man who had immigrated from Sweden, spent long hours as a blacksmith at the railroad yards in Galesburg, Illinois, yet he could never do much better than provide his family with the bare necessities. Carl was born at home in 1878 on a cornhusk mattress and did not know the luxury of a feather bed until after he was ten. His youth was spent among children of the laboring class, and in the strife that periodically filled Galesburg, Sandburg inevitably found his sympathies on the side of his friends against the railroad.

He began working full time when he left school after the eighth grade, holding a number of menial jobs, the most permanent of which was as a bootblack. But the slow, ritualistic life at Galesburg did not appeal to him and at the age of sixteen he embarked upon a three-year period of vagabondage; ending up, as did most questioning Midwestern youth, at the city of Chicago.

Chicago was majestic, yet somber to the drowsy-eyed country youth. He slept on used linen in a cheap hotel on South State Street. During the day he walked many miles along the city streets, drinking in the roar of the city, so different from quieter, duller Galesburg. He would watch fascinated as the trolley cars of Chicago's transportation tycoon, Charles Yerkes, rumbled over the elevated loop of shaking steel girders that circled the city's business section. He would walk through the bustling department stores, marveling at the wealth of merchandise so elaborately displayed. He would drop in at a saloon where a free lunch was included with a glass of beer, there to meet workmen of every class, and streetwalkers with painted faces. Then he would peer in at the Board of Trade where grain speculators waved their fingers like conjuring magicians, winning and losing fortunes in the twinkling of an eye.

Sandburg spent only three days in Chicago this first time, but he was struck with an image that never left him — an image of a mighty giant with a myriad of faces and a voice that shouted not merely "I will," as the local cartoonists claimed, but "I won't," "I can't," "I wouldn't," "I couldn't."

In 1907 Sandburg returned to Chicago, having spent four years at a Galesburg college in the interim. He obtained a job on a small, liberal magazine and focused his interest on that portion of the city which contained the poor, the struggling, and the hopeless. In March 1914 his first book was published, a collection of strong, free-swinging verses aimed to shake the reader like the punch of a champion boxer. And shake they did. Even his friend, Edgar Lee Masters, was startled by such a brutal portrayal of city life.

Some of the verses from the book, entitled *Chicago Poems*, gained a sharp intensity by contrasting city bleakness with the loveliness of nature:

> Passing through huddled and ugly walls
> By doorways where women
> Looked from their hunger-deep eyes . . .
> I came sudden, at the city's edge,
> On a blue burst of lake,
> Long lake waves breaking under the sun
> On a spray-flung curve of shore . . .

But it was the people, not nature, that appealed to the young poet. Most of his poems told of the poor, smothered in the roar of the city, the dust of dismay choking their throats; of middle-aged parents, burdened with sick children who would never know the smell of new-mown hay; of the rich, well-fed and smug, living behind sturdy palisades of steel spikes that shut off all thoughts of the rabble. The poems told of the misty girls in a thousand Mid-western towns watching the railroad trains speeding toward Chicago while they dreamed of Romance and Big Things — little knowing the bitter sadness that was waiting for them at the end of the line; the sound of fish criers on Maxwell Street, shouting their wares with voices as forlorn as a north wind blowing over December corn stubble. Other verses pictured the thousands of bewildered immigrants — men like Sandburg's own father — who were writhing beneath the heel of the strange, uncaring city: an Italian shovel man, once a romantic hero to a Tuscany maid, now splattered with dry clay; a proud Bohemian sweeping the bloody floors of the stockyards. Or there were the Negroes smiling the slumber dreams of old jungles, with features softer than a fluff of cotton yet harder than dark earth.

And behind the struggle, the dismay, the tragedy, was Sandburg's Chicago, an inspiring city nonetheless:

> Fierce as a dog with tongue lapping for action, cunning
>     as a savage pitted against the wilderness,
>         Bareheaded,
>         Shoveling,
>         Wrecking,
>         Planning,
>         Building, breaking, rebuilding
> Under the smoke, dust all over his mouth, laughing with
>     white teeth,
> Under the  terrible burden of destiny laughing as a
>     young man laughs,
> Laughing even as a ignorant fighter laughs who has
>     never lost a battle,
> Bragging and laughing that under his wrist is the pulse,
>     and under his ribs the heart of the people . . .

While Sandburg and Masters were experimenting with new forms of poetry, another writer was probing far deeper than them into the submerged emotions that rule men's lives. This was Sherwood Anderson who, after renouncing his business career in 1912, had come to the city which was generally regarded as most sympathetic to writers: Chicago. Once there he spent day after day in the peopled-solitude of the Grand Central Station, observing the crowds that swept past him and writing down his thoughts on many reams of paper. Anderson was an emotional man who felt compelled to expose the hidden drives of others. His analytical mind was always questioning, questioning — never content with the usual answers.

In Chicago Sherwood Anderson sought and found a group of people with similar bents living on Fifty-Seventh Street near Stoney Island Avenue. He would spend long evenings with them talking of the new type of literature they were going to write or criticizing the cool, emotionless New England writers who had dominated American literature for almost a hundred years:

> No doubt Emerson had been a great writer. But while he could sing "Give All to Love," we were sure he could not express love in the way we of the Middle West were coming to feel desirable.

Anderson's first novel, *Windy McPherson's Son,* was in effect an autobiography. Theodore Dreiser had met Anderson while working on *The Titan* and had enthusiastically recommended this work to a New York firm that subsequently published it. The novel concerned a man from a small Midwestern town who rose to leadership in the small arms industry, but, at the moment of success, abandoned his career for a vagabond pilgrimage around the country searching for meaning in life.

Other stories and novels followed, but the book that eventually became Anderson's greatest, *Winesburg, Ohio,* was begun late in 1915. This book was in actuality a series of penetrating sketches of Midwestern life as seen through episodes in the lives of twenty-two persons living in a little Ohio town. For models of his characters Anderson took persons he had known in Chicago or at Clyde, Ohio, his hometown. Though Winesburg was a small town, Anderson was not so much concerned with its size as with the human emotions that seldom, if ever, had been expressed before in American fiction. He had criticized earlier writers, such as Nathaniel Hawthorne, William Dean Howells, and Mark Twain, for leaving sex out of their writings and thereby losing the tang of realism. This omission Anderson set out to rectify, but not in a blatant, sensational way. Instead, his sketches were done with great delicacy — yet with an edge even more keen for that very reason.

There was, for example, Elizabeth Willard, wife of the hotel owner, who before her marriage had a shaky reputation in Winesburg. Confused and uncertain with men, she could not understand those strong urges that welled up within her, yet were not shared by her male consorts:

> It was always the same, beginning with kisses and ending, after strange wild emotions, with peace and then sobbing repentance. When she sobbed she put her hand upon the face of the man and had always the same thought . . . She wondered why he did not sob also.

Or there was the Reverend Curtis Hartman, who from his room in the church tower watched the pretty school teacher, Kate Swift, reading in her bed; watched her night after night while he tormented himself with lascivious thoughts and heartfelt recriminations:

> He was horror stricken at the thought of a woman smoking and trembled also to think that his eyes, just raised from the pages of the book of God, had looked upon the bare shoulders and white throat of a woman.

And Kate Swift herself, lonely and alone, felt a love for her pupil, George Willard, which she fought to repress:

> A passionate desire to have him understand the import of life, to learn to interpret it truly and honestly, swept over her. Leaning forward, her lips brushed his cheek. At the same moment he for the first time became aware of the marked beauty of her features . . . "What's the use? It will be ten years before you begin to understand what I mean when I talk to you," she cried passionately.

Were the people of Winesburg typically Midwestern — women without sex education, bewildered at their desires; men ashamed of their emotions yet longing for a peek at the forbidden; teachers isolated from the community, finding their only means of sexual expression with pupils who were too young to appreciate them? Perhaps the answer to the question was in the violent reaction to the book. Anderson found his mail filled with indignant letters accusing him of immorality. Library committees even burned *Winesburg*. And though the vilification made Anderson ill for months, he had indeed discovered a taproot that few people cared to admit existed in themselves — and he had thereby opened a new door in American literature.

During the early nineteenth century Chicago seemed on the point of becoming the literary capital of the United States. H. L. Mencken, self-styled spokesman for the nation, even stated that for a score of years almost every literary movement of importance had its beginning in Chicago. Yet with all the pomp and bluster of the Windy City, the 1920's saw it lose much of its vigor and settle down into the resignation and stagnation reflected in its new name, the Second City — no longer a serious challenger to New York, no longer Sandburg's lusty fighter who had never lost a battle.

Masters left the city in 1919. Anderson made his final break in 1922. Dreiser no longer wrote novels about Chicago. Sandburg alone remained, but his far-reaching eyes were looking beyond the towers of Michigan Avenue — and his poetry was taking on a national hue.

This desertion by the intellectuals foretold the decline of Chicago in other respects. During the Prohibition Era the frightful excesses of Al Capone and his dark-visaged gangsters gave Chicago a new reputation that would hardly have attracted even old Bismarck, if he had been still living. Then the Depression hit, and with the catastrophic demise of Chicago's greatest tycoon, Samuel Insull, the once swaggering city was struck so hard a blow it seemed as though it would never recover.

The decline of Chicago is probably best seen in a trilogy of novels written during the twenties and early thirties by one of her native sons, James T. Farrell. This trilogy, grouped under the title *Studs Lonigan,* describes the life of a young Irish tough from his graduation from grammar school in 1916, through his wild, pugnacious life during the high-living twenties, to his sad end in the early thirties. It portrays Studs as a ruffian anxious to be recognized by fellow gang members, yet at the same time frightened by the violence and dissipation engulfing him.

The world of Studs Lonigan is in many ways a microcosm of Chicago itself. Picture Studs at the age of twenty-one, a strutting young man, head held high, a young fighter:

> Studs emerged from the building and walked along, taking loose, easy strides, strides that he considered self-confident... He looked at his clenched fist ... Now he was a man ... And there were many years ahead of him, drinking, jazzing, poker-games, plenty of things.

These were the days of the youthful gangs that held many parts of Chicago in a grip of fear; gangs that were based partly on race hatred and partly on the sheer love of violence:

> Studs, Red, Tommy, Weary, Kenny, and Benny Taite led the gang ... For two hours, they prowled Wabash Avenue and State Street, between Garfield Boulevard and Fifty-ninth Street, searching for niggers. They sang, shouted, yelled defiance at the houses, and threw bricks into the windows of houses where they thought niggers lived ...

But as Studs grew older he began wondering not only just what he was accomplishing, but what his future would be in the world of violence he had helped create:

> He felt himself trapped like a rat in a cage. All this life around him, the sky, everything, were bars, and here he was... in this cage.

Chicago too was trapped in a cage of its own making. The very rapidity of its expansion had created the ruthless businessmen that Dreiser had described and the festering neighborhoods pictured by Sandburg and Farrell. The people had no deep-seated loyalties, no convictions based on the firm rock of generations of tradition. The buoyant spirit that had changed Chicago from a wild onion swamp to a major metropolis in fifty years had not had time to develop enough momentum to let the city meet and conquer adversity when the halcyon days came to a close. The young blustering Midwestern giant, once so certain of a glorious destiny, suddenly lost its drive; and soon gangs like that of Studs could challenge the rights of law-abiding citizens.

Thus, by the late 1920's the climax was over. The Midwestern capital had become merely another provincial city; and while the years after World War II would see it continue along the road of progress, it would never again be the fighter who had never lost a battle. From the Second City it would soon become the Third City, as Los Angeles overtook it, and would be content to read books published in New York and see TV programs and movies made in Hollywood — while looking back to its days of glory like Studs Lonigan who:

> tapped with his foot, dreamily thinking of himself as just going along the same as he had in the old days, strong and tough and with nothing serious to cramp his style and his fun . . . His lips twisted in a sneer at himself, and he thought that he was just a goddam washed-up has-been.

# ʊhe broken diagonal

*This* was not really the most likely place for a giant corporation to arise, this pleasant little town of about 20,000 persons. The rustic homes and commercial buildings were clustered around a New England style village green and were surrounded on two sides by a dense forest, on one by a small river, the Cuyahoga, which meandered crazily through its marshy channel, and fronted by the choppy waters of Lake Erie. The site had been chosen for a town by one Moses Cleaveland only a year after "Mad" Anthony Wayne had ended the Indian menace at Fallen Timbers; but being far from the route of immigration along the Ohio River, it had long languished. The town was inhabited mainly by New Englanders who had settled in a 115-mile strip along Lake Erie that had once been part of Connecticut called the Western Reserve. With their firm attachment to business conducted on a family basis and their disdain for novelty or any break with tradition, it would seem unusual that out of this struggling town of Cleveland would emerge an industrial colossus who would not only gain a nation-wide monopoly but would found the largest corporation then known to mankind.

Picture a scrawny, quiet, sanctimonious young man who had to leave high school after the third year in order to help his family make a living. In 1855, at the age of sixteen, he is working as a clerk for fifty cents a day, barely enough to pay for the food he must eat. Yet the name of this unlikely tycoon is John D. Rockefeller — and when you have said that, the outcome of the story becomes clear.

The rise of Rockefeller and the gigantic company he created is more than a tale of a single man; it is also the story of the coming of age of the Midwest. Rockefeller, brilliant as he was, entered the Midwestern scene at the precise moment when events entirely beyond his control had prepared the way. He was a creation as well as a creator of the tremendous economic growth that began during the closing days of the Civil War — a growth that threatened the smug money-lenders and tyrannical commercial barons of the East Coast with a new and earnest industrial rival.

One event that laid the ground work for the Rockefeller saga was the great population influx into the Midwest. The flatboats that floated down the treacherous Ohio and the Conestogas that rocked over the rutted National Road brought, year after year, an ever-increasing tide of farmers into the region. Agricultural towns and villages blossomed at every landing and crossroads to provide these farmers with markets for their produce. It was not long until factories and larger cities rose on the major transportation routes, to provide the tools and materials sought by the town merchants and farmers. Thus it was that when the time came for the enterprising Rockefeller to make his move, there was already a large regional market and supply of city workmen.

Just as important was the new network of railroads that began binding the region together. The New York Central, the Pennsylvania, the Erie, and other lines linked the Midwest with Eastern markets, insuring a faster and less expensive flow of raw materials to cities that were distant from the source of supply.

The young Rockefeller began his career in 1859 when, with the aid of a thousand dollar loan from his father, he went into business on his own. Though only nineteen, he quickly proved his canny business sense. Within a year his produce and grain commission house could boast gross sales of almost half a million dollars.

But it was not in farm products that Rockefeller was to make his fortune. The young man turned to an enterprise which was so recently developed that the field was wide open for small businessmen such as himself. News of a remarkable discovery was sweeping through Cleveland. In Titusville, Pennsylvania, just across the Ohio line, a rich field of oil had been discovered. The black liquid was so bountiful that there were not enough containers ready, and it oozed sluggishly into the creeks and was swept in multicolored ripples down the streams. Cleveland, on direct rail line from the fields, was a logical place to refine the thick material into the kerosene that would provide America with a light better than sputtering candles or costly whale oil. Soon refineries were built in Cleveland and, as the malodorous fumes began spreading over the little town, John D. Rockefeller sniffed the polluted air and with an unfailing instinct that never left him, smelled the sweet scent of money.

He began dabbling in oil in 1863. He built his first refinery on the land around a quiet little creek, called Kingsbury Run, which flowed into the Cuyahoga a short distance south of the main part of Cleveland. By 1865 he was doing well over a million dollars worth of business yearly and had the largest of the thirty Cleveland refineries. Quite a success for a twenty-five-year-old.

Rockefeller was of a new breed of Midwesterners: one who looked at the awesome financial power of the East fearlessly and saw in it something to challenge. Money and power he wanted, but he sought more — envisaging a gigantic, monolithic monopoly controlling the entire nation's oil production. From his office overlooking the Cuyahoga this thin, spider-like man spun great webs of power that eventually enabled him to dominate 90 per cent of American oil. Every home, store, or office, be it in the frontier Dak-

otas or on the island of Manhattan, would pay Rockefeller's price
or would simply do without oil.

And so Rockefeller built more refineries on the Kingsbury Run.
Then he began absorbing his Cleveland rivals — by fair purchase
or by crippling price war, depending upon the power of his opponent. The railroads, too, felt the irresistible pressures of Rockefeller and his associates. Eastern millionaires, including William
Vanderbilt himself, soon learned that even they could not do business with Rockefeller without rebating a significant portion of their
freight rates.

Rockefeller was a strange man to be trespassing in the realm of
the Eastern titans. Modest and soft-spoken, disdaining tobacco and
liquor, content, even when he was piling his fortune, to live in an
unpretentious house on Euclid Avenue, he was a far cry indeed
from the bellowing, hard-living, flamboyant Eastern robber barons
and "captains of industry" of his day. Rockefeller's mind did not
run along the then normal channels, he did not care to be a dashing stream roaring through the countryside; he wanted to be none
other than the mighty Mississippi itself, placid, all encompassing,
calling his own tune and rhythm.

Oil, oil, oil — it was all Rockefeller could think or speak of. Even
at night he would suddenly awake with new plans for his rising
empire. He read few books, and though he would sometimes indulge himself by racing his horses down Euclid Avenue, it was in
oil that he found his chief pleasure.

In January 1870 Rockefeller organized his refining companies under the name of Standard Oil. His momentum rose faster. With
breathtaking speed he eliminated competition in Cleveland; moved
on to Pittsburgh; Philadelphia; finally, New York. Within eight
years Standard had all but eliminated competition in the entire
United States. The money that then began flowing into Standard's
coffers was beyond belief. The Midwestern company did not bow
to Eastern bankers and plutocrats, as had been the custom; instead
it made its own bankers, and plutocrats. And when the big boys
that Standard made moved into the New York stock market, few
combinations could withstand them.

Rockefeller was not the only Midwesterner to burst into the staid commercial realm of the Easterners. The masters of the country's largest corporations, namely the railroads, found that other Midwesterners were challenging them. One such challenger was George M. Pullman who had come to Chicago in 1855, a wide-eyed youth of twenty-four. His profession as a cabinet-maker proved invaluable, for the vibrating atmosphere of Chicago, rapidly becoming the railroad center of the nation, helped inspire him with the idea of building a sleeping car which would completely revolutionize the entire system of overnight travel.

Pullman began working on his new sleeping car in 1864. It was to be a luxurious affair, far superior to the unimaginative cars then in use. There was to be plush carpeting, an amplitude of mirrors, hand carving on the woodwork, the very best upholstery, and an interior design that would appeal to the most discerning. But most important of all Pullman hit upon the idea of hinging the upper berth to the wall where it could be stored out of sight during the day. The hinge was patented, and soon all the old cars with the cumbersome permanent bunks had become obsolete.

At first it was tough going, for Pullman insisted upon forcing the railroads to pay him a rental for his sleeping cars instead of allowing them to purchase them outright. He would also permit only his own specially trained employees to operate the Pullman cars. These facts meant that the railroads had to pay the Chicago manufacturer a large and continuous percentage of their overnight-trade profit. It was a bitter pill to swallow, but Pullman held the patent and had organized his business with such efficiency as to achieve a virtual monopoly. The nationwide publicity that ensued when Mrs. Abraham Lincoln insisted that a Pullman car be attached to the funeral train carrying her martyred husband back to Springfield made the Chicago firm famous. From that time on there was no stopping George Pullman.

But Pullman had more in mind than merely manufacturing one of the best traveling cars ever invented. He saw himself as a beneficent father to the thousands of men who labored in his factory. He wanted to guide them, poor creatures that he believed they were, along paths he deemed worthy. And so in 1880 he chose a deserted site by Lake Calumet twelve miles south of Chicago and built there what he imagined would be a workers' paradise — a self-contained town, landscaped with shady trees, graced with ample parks, and boasting paved streets, a theater, a library, and a school where education was free through the eighth grade. Liquor was banned and sports encouraged. After the workers and their families moved into the neat, row houses provided by Pullman, an eighty-piece military band was formed. It became the pride of the town of 12,600 when it won first place in statewide competition.

Unfortunately Pullman, man-god that he was, had not built the town (which he named after himself) merely out of altruism. The money that he collected from his high rents enabled him to make a good return on his investment. In addition, by having most of his labor force directly under his thumb, he could control not only their absenteeism, but the attempts at unionization that might tend to raise his wage scale. He had spies everywhere who were quick to report the names of trouble-makers to the all-powerful employer. Local politics were, of course, controlled by Pullman; and any worker who ran for office against his wishes was promptly fired. Thus, although the town of Pullman gained fame throughout industrial circles, the workers found much to be desired.

Trouble began to brew when the nation was hit by a severe depression in 1893. The railroads slowed down their orders and Pullman correspondingly began to lay off his workers. The men who were out of work quickly found themselves destitute, for although Pullman kept charging them rents that were 25 per cent above that of the surrounding towns, they were afraid to move since the plant usually rehired those men who lived in Pullman. In some instances children had to lie in bed most of the winter because they had no shoes to go to school. Seldom were there hot meals for there was no coal. The town had no provision for relief not only because Pullman frowned upon the socialism that it implied, but because, since everyone in the town was beholden to a single employer, there were none who could afford to help his co-worker. Seldom, if ever, has any large group of Americans been so completely under the despotic rule of one man.

Yet in the spring of the following year a faint glimmer of hope appeared. Down in Terre Haute, Indiana, a man of awesome activity had organized a union of railroad employees. This man, Eugene V. Debs, was an idealist whose love and sympathy for his fellow men was exceeded only by his genius at organizing amorphous masses of persons into a powerful, well-disciplined force. Debs was not a rabble-rouser, for his temperament tended strongly toward the peaceful solution to problems. Yet the early days of America's new industrialism indicated that the working man could not hope to win any significant gains from his much more powerful employer unless he was prepared to back up his demands with the power of a crippling strike. The earlier unions, such as the American Federation of Labor and the Railroad Brotherhoods, had been organized strictly for the skilled worker, ignoring the much more numerous men who worked at the more routine jobs. Debs saw that what was needed was a strong union composed of the entire working class; and so in 1893 he began recruiting for his new American Railway Union. He had such amazing success that by the following year the ARU could boast 150,000 active members. Centered mainly in the Midwest, though having strong units on both coasts, the ARU could control much of the national rail commerce and had suddenly become an uncomfortable factor the Eastern railroad men had to take into account.

The national headquarters of the ARU was in Chicago. During the spring of 1894 the desperate workers at Pullman flocked to Debs, begging him to marshall the force of his huge union for their aid. Although Debs cautioned the men against a strike, they quit work on May 11. George Pullman angrily refused to negotiate with delegations from the ARU and prepared to starve his workers into submission.

On June 12 the national convention of the ARU met at Chicago. Amid a tremendous ground swell of emotion it voted to retaliate against Pullman by calling all its members out in a nationwide boycott of all Pullman cars: the trains would go through but not before the ARU members had detached the sleepers.

Now the once local strike took on a new and far more serious aspect, for the entire railroad community, the mightiest aggregation of wealth in the country, was beset. Since the railroad owners

KING DEBS.

A cartoonist's view of Eugene V. Debs during the Pullman strike
of 1894 taken from *Harper's*.

refused to operate their trains without the Pullman cars, the ARU
in effect had declared war upon them as well. The general managers
of the twenty-four lines running out of Chicago met to decide what
action to take against Debs. Debs, who had hitherto been a little
known Midwestern labor leader, now gained national prominence.
He was no mean opponent, for his union controlled the actions of
nearly 70 per cent of the men working for the lines radiating
out of Chicago. Wisely cautioning his men against acts of violence,
he nonetheless was able to stop virtually all rail transportation not
only in the Midwest but throughout much of the nation. In depots
across the country the freight piled up like mountains. Midwestern labor had entered upon the national economic scene in a powerful, forceful way.

But though most of their trains were stalled in what many newspapers called the Debs Rebellion, the General Managers Association had powerful weapons on its side. The United States Marshal
at Chicago was anti-Debs, and he quickly authorized the formation of a force of 3,600 special deputies who were to serve as strike-
breakers under the pay and supervision of the railroad managers.
When the ARU members met the deputies with forceful resistance, the Managers demanded that President Cleveland send federal troops to protect their property. Within a week General Nel-
son A. Miles had established his headquarters in the Pullman Building. The 2,000 regulars, encamped along the Chicago lakefront, protected the movement of freight from the city, but not without bloodshed. The ugly climax came when twenty persons were killed by
federal gunfire. The situation was almost as grave in Michigan,
Iowa and California.

It was not the use of federal deputies or army troops, however,
that finally broke the strike. The General Managers Association,
attacking the ARU on all fronts, prevailed upon the Attorney General
to issue an injunction prohibiting the strike leaders from encourag-
ing the boycott of Pullman cars. When Debs, who had no real
choice, ignored the writ, he was arrested along with seven hundred
other ARU leaders and sent to jail. With the leadership gone the
strike collapsed and by August 2 George Pullman was again op-
erating his non-union factory.

Again, as with Rockefeller and Standard Oil, the emerging Midwest had entered America's new industrial and urban scene with phenomenal impact. No longer was the region a rustic, agricultural farmland figuring little in the important affairs of Eastern businessmen. Pullman dominated overnight rail travel. Debs showed the power of labor, when organized, in the first nationwide strike in the history of the United States.

At about the same time that Pullman and Debs were creating their national furors, a new endeavor was beginning in distant Minnesota, a region barely out of the frontier stage — an endeavor which would be an essential factor in drawing the Midwest into a mighty industrial unit as important as many a European country.

Minnesota in 1893 was a far different place from what Hiawatha and his braves had known. Vanished were the playful spirits who filled every glade with their laughter and trickery — gone, because the traders of the American Fur Company had induced the redmen to kill most of the fur-bearing animals within whose breasts lived the spirits. Vanished too were the swaying, humming pine forests, the secluded haunt of many a Chippewa clan — for the fast-moving lumber companies had swept over the area like a wrathful scourge. And without the tree cover, erosion had turned the water of the streams and lakes into repositories of reddish silt. As the weary, beaten Indians huddled in their miserable reservations, they must have mused sadly upon the white man's wasteful, gluttonous ways; and they must have looked at each other in mournful comprehension at what they regarded as the death of their Minnesota, "land of the sky-tinted waters."

Yet oddly enough, the Indians could not have been more wrong, for the region was about to enter a stage of fantastic growth. The harbinger of the new era was George Stuntz who had become the first permanent settler in the area one day to be named after the early French explorer, Sieur du Luth. It was in 1852 that Stuntz constructed a tiny trading post on a long finger of land that jutted into Lake Superior, later to form Duluth's marvelous harbor. From this Minnesota Point he wandered far into the wild northern hinterland, marveling at the deep red soil that he found in a hilly region to be known later as the Vermilion Range. Stuntz was sure it was an exceedingly rich lode of iron ore, and in 1884 interested a millionaire, Charlemagne Tower, to open a mine there. Soon, scores of long ore boats were docking at the growing town of Duluth, carrying valuable cargoes back to the mills that were rapidly going up in Cleveland.

The Vermilion strike was valuable, but the best was yet to come. From their homestead at Oneota, high on the bluffs overlooking Duluth, the seven Merritt brothers watched the activity in the harbor with envy. Because their father had been a timber scout, they knew the country like the palms of their hands. They had seen a place visited by few white men, called by the Indians the "Mesabi," or "Height of Land." So certain were the Merritts that the Mesabi was even richer than the Vermilion Range, that they hired an experi-

Hull-Rust open pit mine of the Mesabi Range, Minnesota.

enced mining engineer to make a report. When their beliefs were confirmed, they enthusiastically began digging at a location prophetically called Mountain Iron. The ore all along the Mesabi was so close to the surface that the brothers had only to scoop it out and send it by sagging wagon to the waiting ships at Duluth. The Mesabi ore proved to be of such high quality that in 1892, only two years after the excavating was begun, the Merritts built a railroad — the Duluth, Missabe & Northern — to haul the ever increasing traffic.

During these first frantic years it seemed as if the seven brothers were on their way to becoming not only millionaires, but the powerful owners of one of the most valuable ore deposits on the face of the globe. But just when wealth and power seemed within their grasp, they were hit by the Depression of 1893. The sudden expenditures for rail and digging equipment that had seemed so wise at the time had left them momentarily without funds. In desperation they turned to the one man who seemed not bothered by the depression, crafty John D. Rockefeller. The good John D., ever quick to sense an opportunity, was happy to aid the Merritts — but his benevolence had so many strings that before the unsuspecting brothers could sense their peril, their entire holdings had been digested into Standard Oil.

Now things really began to happen. Rockefeller leased the land to Andrew Carnegie, whose steel operations at Pittsburgh had already started the nation well on the road to industrialization. Gradually, as Carnegie began to depend more and more on the Mesabi, the little pits of the Merritts became so wide and deep that railroad spurs were constructed along the sides, and freight trains puffed down to the ever sinking bottom where an army of steam shovels clawed away at the bright ore. The Mesabi became known far and wide among iron men — and they spoke of it with awe, for there had never been anything like it. More and more yawning excavations began turning the range into a Midwestern Grand Canyon. Towns sprung up — Coleraine, Hibbing, Mountain Iron, Virginia, Eveleth — that were continually "digging out" from the powdery ore that clung to the sides of their buildings like red stain, that rose like rust-colored smoke from beneath the tires of wagons or from the padding shoes of the workmen, that gathered, blood-scarlet, on the banks of all the streams.

The roar of activity along the Mesabi Range meant more than merely material for the blast furnaces of Pittsburgh. It also meant new plants would be built closer to the supply — plants which would bring new industry to the Midwest.

The most startling development occurred on the dunes along the Indiana shore of Lake Michigan. During the late 1890's many Midwestern steel companies had combined in order to compete better with Carnegie's giant corporation. In 1901 Elbert Gary, president of the new company, Federal Steel, united with J. P. Morgan, wizard banker of Wall Street, to buy out Carnegie. The resulting colossus was formed into the first billion dollar company in the nation — the United States Steel Corporation. Gary and Morgan were quick to see that their new company should take advantage of the dune land around Lake Michigan, for it was here that the ore boats from the Mesabi most easily met the coal trains from southern Illinois. The Inland Steel Corporation had just erected a large mill in the expanding town of East Chicago, but U.S. Steel chose a deserted location ten miles east where the land was cheap.

Work was begun in 1905. It was a mammoth undertaking, since not only did the mills have to be built, but an entire city — homes, streets, stores, municipal buildings. The dunes had to be leveled; the lakefront had to be elevated by pumping sand directly from the lake bottom; the Grand Calumet River had to be moved one hundred feet from its original bed; and a harbor had to be created by extending a long breakwater far into the lake. When the job was completed, the U.S. Steel works at Gary, as the town was named, was the largest steel plant in the entire world.

Thus it was at Gary and neighboring East Chicago that the saga of steel reached a climax. These cities, creations of the twentieth century, glow at night with pulsating flames from the immense furnaces. A ruddy nimbus hangs over the entire area, silhouetting the towers and chimneys of the mills and casting a strange aura over the still wild dunes and swamps that surround them. When the wind is from the lake, industrial smoke drifts over the cities, heavy with the sharp odor of flaming iron. The feeling is inescapable: here is Power being created, relentlessly forged into the tough metal that forms the sinews of the nation.

If one must choose a date when the Midwest came of age, it would be 1905 with the building of Gary, Indiana.

Two years before Gary's founding something just as momentous happened across the Michigan peninsula at Detroit. A gaunt farm boy with a flair for tinkering with the new-fangled gasoline engines talked twelve men into investing $28,000 of their hard-earned dollars into the manufacture of his sputtering flivver. The Ford Motor Company, as it was called, was a tiny enterprise able to produce but ten cars daily, even with Henry Ford himself working beside his dozen mechanics. Yet, even so, Ford had come a long way from the day seven years earlier when he had assembled his first automobile from a motley assortment of bicycle wheels, plumbing pipe, and other makeshift parts.

Slowly the output of the Ford plant increased. In five years it was producing five times as many cars as in 1903. Then production rose to one hundred cars a day. But Ford, a man with grease still on his hands, was not content. Master mechanic that he was, he cared little for making money. The manufacture of automobiles was everything to him, and virtually every penny he earned was plowed back into larger plant facilities. He could ignore competition, for he was a genius with machines and could produce a car much more cheaply than anyone — even the General Motors Corporation, formed in 1908, did not worry him. Ford production rose with such rapidity that by 1914 two hundred and fifty thousand Model T Fords were on the road, accounting for 45 per cent of all cars made that year.

Efficiency and practicality were everything to Henry Ford. His thoughts were Midwestern, unfettered by the traditions of the Easterners. He viewed the world in a Midwestern way, with a willingness to try out new ideas. And so he began expanding on a scale hardly imaginable to Easterners, using machines as far as possible in place of temperamental, slow-moving human power. And, as the gleaming black Model T's began pouring from the assembly line in great numbers, Ford gradually hit upon a new idea which would revolutionize industry the world over. Since specialization was the key to mass production, he reasoned, why not install men on a *moving* assembly line where they would perform one job at the pace prescribed by the machine itself — the pace of the embryonic automobile being about two feet a minute? When Ford established his moving assembly line, he had at last accomplished his unconscious ideal: he had turned men into machines.

In the early 1920's Ford crowned his success by erecting a huge plant to house his assembly and sub-assembly factories. It was constructed beside the River Rouge — a small stream just south of Detroit, once the solitary haunt of Frenchmen who gave it its name, "Red River," and later a favorite hunting and fishing area for American farm families who settled there when Detroit was still a quiet river town. Ford as a youth had enjoyed wandering among the cattails and sweet flags which grew along the Rouge; and it must have been with mixed emotions that he saw his monstrous plant turn the lower portion of the river into the largest integrated factory in the world.

One could see a glimpse of the future at the River Rouge plant — an intriguing, fascinating — and disquieting glimpse. The two-square-mile area was a kingdom unto itself where the Machine was the ruler. Everything was done here, from the forging of iron ore into steel to the painting of the bright new cars which rolled off the assembly line every sixty seconds. Machines did most of the work, men performing only the labor that was uneconomical for machines. More than a dozen sub-assembly plants fabricated the particular parts necessary for the finished car — representing the highest degree of specialization ever achieved on such a scale. In the main assembly plant endless belts and continuous overhead hooks moved slowly but relentlessly, bringing the various parts of the car together at the precise moment they were needed. The plant was on the very brink of Tomorrow where the Machine had become not only an indispensable ally but a subtle ruler of mankind.

Yet with all his worship of the Machine, Henry Ford was strangely quixotic in loving too the very past that he was helping destroy. In 1928 he built a huge museum where the nostalgic items of yesterday could be preserved — old handicraft china, silverware, and pottery, primitive farm equipment, outdated automobiles. In the ad-

The River Rouge plant of the Ford Motor Company. The River Rouge is in the foreground, and the Detroit River and the Canadian shore are in the distance.

joining two hundred acres he collected almost a hundred original buildings in which events of importance in the early business or inventive life of the country occurred — the shop of the Wright brothers, the laboratory of Thomas Edison, the birthplace of Luther Burbank. The Henry Ford Museum and Greenfield Village soon were attracting tourists from all over the nation, curious to see the homes and artifacts so significant to their material culture.

The construction of Greenfield Village marks an important divide in Midwestern history. It was as if Henry Ford, last and greatest of the Midwestern pioneers, unconsciously provided a monument to the liquidation of his region as a separate, viable entity in the nation. By the end of the 1920's much of the individuality had gone from the region — the "diagonal progress," which had jumped like a spark between the Midwest and the East and which had enabled the nation to go forward with great rapidity, had largely ended. The challenge of the opening farm, fur, and lumber frontiers had long passed — thus diminishing the self-reliance and tough individuality of the Midwesterner, qualities that had given new strength to the nation as a whole. Between the election of Lincoln in 1860 and that of Herbert Hoover in 1928 the Midwest had provided the nation with nine out of fifteen presidents — but there was only one, Truman, after Hoover. By the 1920's the renaissance of literature in Chicago had faded and never again was that unofficial capital of the Midwest to regain its position in American letters.

As for Midwestern industry, control gradually passed into Eastern hands. Rockefeller left Cleveland for New York in 1878. The Midwest continued to be vital to the railroads, especially with Chicago as the rail center — but the transportation monopoly held by the railroads was rapidly displaced by automobiles, busses, trucks, and airplanes; and by the end of World War II the Pullman plant was forced to discontinue the production of the famous sleeper. The monsters of steel and transportation, United States Steel and General Motors, were increasingly absorbed into the Eastern-based Morgan and Du Pont interests. And when the Ford Company went public after the war, one of the last of the major and exclusively Midwestern concerns lost its strictly regional character. It was the same with the labor unions, most of which are now parts of national organizations centered in New York.

What has happened to the Midwest? Why has this region which gave so much to the nation become so unsure of itself? Why does it have so little of the Southern pride in its past; so little of the Eastern pride in its present; so little of the Western pride in its future? Surely the Midwest can be proud of its beauty: the hazy canyon of the Mississippi, the sparkling blue of the Great Lakes, the rounded hills of eastern Ohio, southern Indiana, and central Wisconsin. Surely the Midwest has a stirring history: the daring Frenchmen, heroes like Anthony Wayne and George Rogers Clark, the sturdy pioneers who rafted the Ohio or rocked over the National Road. Surely there is a Midwestern literature demanding respect: the idyllic tale of Hiawatha, Mark Twain's Mississippi stories, the new American realism that Dreiser and the Chicago school fostered. And no one can deny that the Midwest has played an important part in the economic development of the nation — important not only for its natural resources, but for the leadership and new ideas that came from such men as Rockefeller, Gary, and Ford.

Is it too much to hope that in this day of centralization in government, industry, labor, and literature there will be a realization of the harm done the country by not giving the separate regions more autonomy, more chance for individuality, more opportunity to create and contribute its own particular mode of living to the nation? Perhaps if there is such a realization, the history of the Midwest will not end with the building of Greenfield Village but will continue with new heroes rising, new challenges being met, and continued "progress along the diagonal" of regional interchange. Let us hope so.

# VAGABOND
*Section*

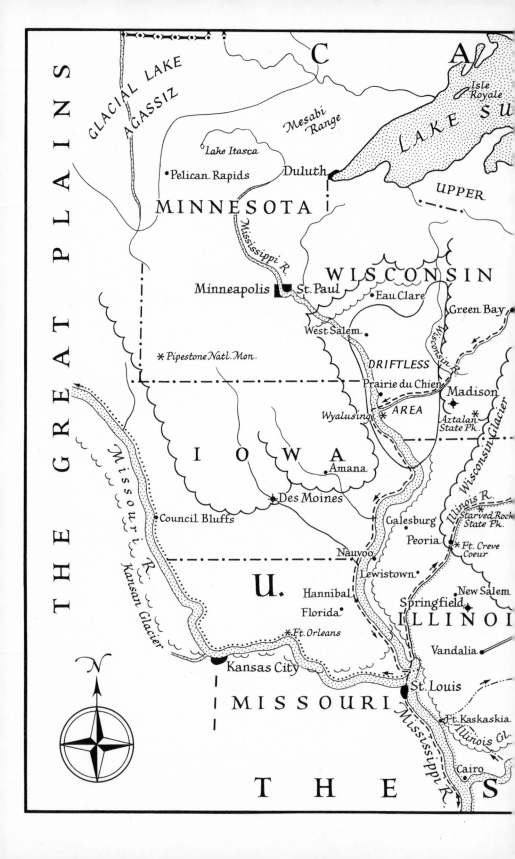

ROUTES
- — — — Joliet and Marquette 1673
- · · · · · La Salle 1680-82
- — · — · La Salle 1680-82
- — ·· — G.R.Clark 1778-79
- + + + + Wayne 1793-94
- · · · · · Lewis and Clark 1804-06
- Harrison 1811
- State Capitals
- Wisconsin Glacier
- Portion of Illinois Glacier not overlaid by Wisconsin Glacier
- Portion of earliest glaciers not overlaid by Wisconsin or Illinois glaciers

N  A  D  A
PERIOR
MICHIGAN
Sault Ste. Marie
St. Ignace
Mackinac I.
Ft. Michilimackinac
LAKE HURON
Marquette Burial
LAKE MICHIGAN
Milwaukee
MICHIGAN
Lansing
Detroit
LAKE ERIE
A  T  H  E
Chicago
St. Joseph
Kirtland
Fallen Timbers
Toledo
South Bass Is.
Cleveland
South Bend
Maumee R.
Ft. Meigs
Hudson
Gary
Warsaw
Ft. Wayne
Clyde
Zoar
Schoenbrunn
Pittsburgh
E  A  S  T
Battle of Tippecanoe
Ft. Ouiatenon
Greenville
OHIO
Wheeling
Washington R.
S  INDIANA
National Road
Columbus
Old Piqua
Muskingum R.
S  A.
Indianapolis
Terre Haute
Cincinnati
Ft. Ancient
Serpent Mound
Wabash R.
Madison
Ohio R.
Vincennes
Gentryville
Louisville
New Harmony
Shawneetown
Miles
50    0    50    100    150    200
O  U  T  H

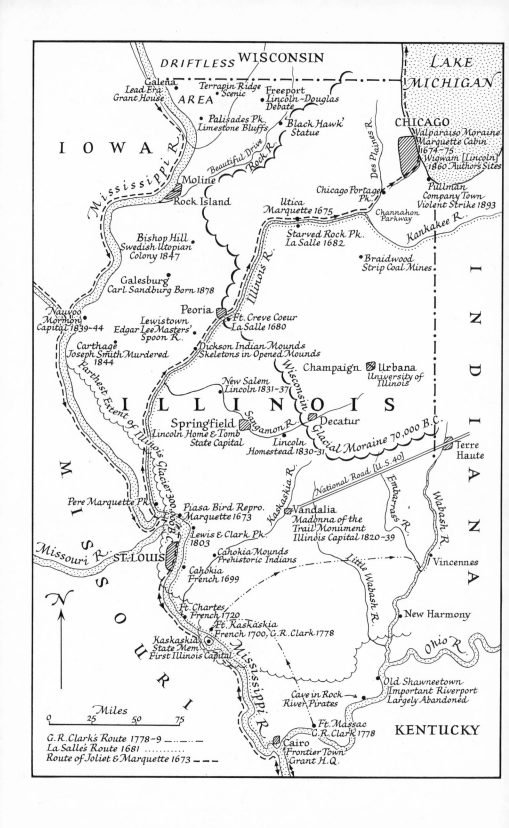

# Illinois

ALTON
BISHOP HILL
BRAIDWOOD
CAHOKIA MOUNDS STATE
  PARK
CARTHAGE
CAVE-IN-ROCK STATE PARK
CHANNAHON STATE PARK
CHICAGO
DECATUR
DICKSON MOUNDS STATE
  PARK
FORT CHARTRES STATE
  PARK
FORT CREVE COEUR STATE
  PARK
FORT MASSAC STATE PARK
GALENA

GALESBURG
KASASKIA STATE PARK
LEWIS AND CLARK STATE
  MEMORIAL
LEWISTOWN
LOWDEN MEMORIAL STATE
  PARK
NAUVOO
NEW SALEM STATE PARK
NORTH UTICA
PERE MARQUETTE STATE
  PARK
ROCK ISLAND
SHAWNEETOWN
SPRINGFIELD
STARVED ROCK STATE PARK
TERRAPIN RIDGE
VANDALIA

**ALTON** As Marquette descended the Mississippi in 1673, he saw a grotesque bird-god painted on the eastern bluffs. Modern artists have created a reproduction, called the Piasa Bird, which may be seen a few miles north of Alton on the Great River Road. The painting shows a bearded serpent with long fangs, high antlers on his head, wide wings, and a tail which almost entirely encircles its body. It is certainly hideous enough to be the one that the Illini tribes worshipped.

The Great River Road is a beautiful drive in itself, sweeping quite close to the Mississippi banks. It is ultimately to be joined with other segments now being completed to form a magnificent paved highway from the river's source to its mouth.

179

**BISHOP HILL**    Bishop Hill, a quiet little village, contains a large park in its center which was once the meeting place for a group of Swedish utopian colonists (*Chapter 9*). Just north, at the corner of Front and Bishop Hill Streets, is the steepleless, barn-like building where church services were once held. Although it is currently in use as a museum, its displays are limited.

West 1 block on Front Street is the gulley in which the Swedes spent the first terrible winter in hand-dug caves that gave them the most meager protection from the lashing prairie wind. The gulley soon became a place of death as cholera took its terrible toll. (In one week alone 114 died out of the original 800 settlers.) The gulley, which should be preserved as a monument to pioneer fortitude, has now, unfortunately, been abandoned to weeds and trash.

Two other locations of interest are the field on the other side of Front Street from the gulley, which is the site of the "Big Brick," the principal residence, and the cemetery on a low ridge on the eastern edge of town, which contains the grave of the Swedish leader, Erik Janson, who was murdered by a malcontent follower in 1850.

**BRAIDWOOD**    Braidwood, a small town 60 miles south of Chicago, is in the midst of a large open-pit coal mining area. For a most unusual drive, take one of the county roads that branches off from U.S. 66 southwest of town. Barren rock mounds reach, row upon row, almost as far as the eye can see. Mining is still done, and it is more than likely you will come across some of the huge machinery resting on a flat vein of coal a hundred or more feet below the ground. Once it was part of a vast, murky swamp that existed here (*Chapter 2*) amid the lush fern forest. Mazon Creek, crossing Alternate 66 a few miles southwest of Braidwood, is famous among geologists for the fine impressions of ferns found in the coal along its sides.

**CAHOKIA**    The village of Cahokia is 5 miles south of East St. Louis, Illinois, and should not be confused with Cahokia Mounds State Park, which is 9 miles to the northeast. (Both were named after the Cahokian tribe of the Illini Confederacy.) The village, founded in 1699 as a mission among the Indians, was one of the most important French towns along the Mississippi — and is today the oldest permanent settlement in the Mississippi valley. When the fur trade developed, the population of Cahokia eventually rose to over 3,000 — many times larger than the current 800. The single story log courthouse, built in 1735, still stands, and the interior contains a museum of French relics. The historical value of the site has now been somewhat marred by the railroad embankment which hides the river that meant even more to the Cahokians than the courthouse.

**CAHOKIA MOUNDS STATE PARK**   The famed Cahokia Mounds (*Chapter 3*) are located on U.S. 40 and 66, 9 miles northeast of East St. Louis, Illinois. Within a radius of a mile and a half there are 80 mounds — all part of the complex that was once a populous Indian town. Monks Mound, named after a colony of Trappist monks who lived on it from 1809 to 1813, is a huge, partially forested, manmade mountain covering an area three times more extensive than that of the Great Pyramid of Egypt — certainly a most impressive monument to the skill and energy of the Moundbuilders. The view from the top is inspiring, with the gray limestone walls of the Mississippi bluffs in the distance, the flat, alluvial plains below, and the echoing chants of long dead Indians all around.

**CAIRO**   Cairo is a "frontier town" (*Chapter 1*) reminiscent of the South in many ways. As one stands in the small triangle of land between the bridge that takes federal highways over the Ohio on one side and the Mississippi on the other, he can smell the dampness and feel the hotness that billows up from the muddy river valley that extends all the way to the Gulf of Mexico. A drive through the city, crouching behind its high levee, reveals a number of large, southern-style homes with spacious verandas. Cairo was recognized as a border town during the Civil War, for it was here that Ulysses Grant mobilized an army of Midwesterners for the invasion of the South in 1861. The Grant headquarters may be seen at 609 Ohio Street.

**CARTHAGE**   The jail where Joseph Smith met his end (*Chapter 9*) has been purchased by the Utah Mormons and is located at the corner of Walnut and N. Fayette Streets. With its pleasant tan limestone walls, it has more the appearance of a charming home than a place of death. One can visit the second story room where Smith and his three companions were housed and see the door that still has the hole made by the bullet which felled Hyrum Smith. The building is a reminder of the religious persecution that sometimes erupted on the frontier but which is today a thing of the past.

**CAVE-IN-ROCK STATE PARK**   Few of the locations in the Midwest have the bizarre fascination of Cave-in-Rock. One has an eerie feeling from the time he reaches the point where Illinois 1 ends abruptly at the Ohio River (where a picturesque little ferryboat carries cars and passengers to Kentucky) to the moment he stands in front of the black, gaping mouth of the cave. Although there are camping and picnicking facilities, the park, remote from the normal tourist treks, is usually deathly still. As one walks into the cave, he will hear the ghostly sound of breathing, but it will only be the soft cooing of pigeons which nest along the walls. When he nears the end of the cave, which is almost 200 feet long, he will see a sliver of light appearing from an opening in the roof that was once used by the outlaws (*Chapter* 8) for emergency escapes. At this point the view toward the entrance is most impressive — the cave mouth forming a natural frame around a gnarled, yet gracefully grotesque sycamore, the Ohio River shimmering behind it, and the pencilled line of trees on the Kentucky shore in the dim distance.

**CHANNAHON STATE PARK**  Channahon State Park is built around a mossy canal lock and ancient lock-tender's house on the old Illinois-Michigan canal, built in 1848. This canal, by making navigable the Illinois River and connecting it with the Chicago River and Lake Michigan, caused the population spurt which soon made Chicago the state's largest city.

Highly recommended is a 10-mile drive along the old tow path, which begins immediately across the DuPage River from the park. It is a narrow, gravel road (running one way only) built on the path once used by horses and mules to pull the freight-laden canal boats. The canal is on the right and to the left is at first the DuPage River, which shortly merges with the DesPlaines, and a little distance on is joined by the Kankakee to become the wide Illinois River. Although scenic turnouts make any season an enjoyment, the best time to take the drive is in the spring when the path is strewn with myriad wild flowers and the canal and rivers are not obscured by tree foliage.

**CHICAGO**  Most of Chicago's historical and scenic sites can be visited by making a north-south tour as will be outlined shortly. There are, however, two locations connected with the French era that cannot be included on the tour. They are:

1. *The Chicago Portage National Historic Site.* This small park, on Illinois 42A, 2 miles south of U.S. 66, is built at the point where Marquette, and the hundreds of French traders who followed him over the years, carried their canoes between the DesPlaines and the Chicago Rivers. During the spring rains the entire area became so swampy that canoes could actually be paddled over it. The tiny park is a restful, secluded place — strangely aloof from the whir of traffic that sounds from all sides.

2. *Marquette's Cabin Site.* A plaque on the Damen Avenue bridge commemorates the frail priest who spent four desolate months in this once uninhabited marshland beside the Chicago River during the winter of 1674-75 (*Chapter* 4). All around him were the spicy wild onions which caused the Indians to call the area "Chicago," or the "bad smell." Nowadays the cabin site is in the midst of warehouses.

It is strongly recommended that the tour which follows be taken on Saturday or, even better, on Sunday in order to avoid the congestion along the city streets. The tour should begin (or end if one is proceeding from south to north) at CARL SANDBURG'S HOME: 4646 N. Hermitage. (Take Lake Shore Drive — U. S. 14, 41, Business 12 — to the Lawrence Avenue turnoff, which is 4800 north. Go 12 blocks west to Hermitage, then 1½ blocks south.) Sandburg lived here most of the years he worked for the Chicago *Daily News*. The house is privately owned, and is in a modest but well-maintained neighborhood.

CHICAGO HISTORICAL SOCIETY: Clark Street and North Avenue. (Return to Lake Shore Drive. Go south to North Avenue, which is 1600 north. Then go west 4 blocks to Clark. The building is on the northeast corner.) The Society museum contains a blockhouse constructed of logs from the second Fort Dearborn, built 1816, shortly after the Chicago massacre described later. There are also extensive displays concerning such periods as the French, the War of 1812, and the great Chicago fire.

FRANK COWPERWOOD'S HOME: Michigan Avenue near Goethe Street. (Take North Avenue 4 blocks east to Michigan Avenue, then go 4 blocks south to Goethe.) This portion of Michigan Avenue was once the location of the most opulent homes in the city. Theodore Dreiser's hero of *The Titan (Chapter 12)*, Frank Cowperwood, lived along here. There are still a few of the original mansions tucked in among the luxury skyscraper apartments.

THE OLD CHICAGO WATER TOWER: Corner of Chicago and Michigan Avenues. (Continue south on Michigan Avenue to Chicago Avenue, which is 800 north.) The Water Tower was one of the few buildings to survive the disastrous fire of 1871, and has since become a symbol of the city's indomitable will to conquer obstacles.

SHERWOOD ANDERSON'S ROOMING HOUSE: 738 Wabash Avenue. (Take Chicago Avenue 2 blocks west to Wabash, then go half block south.) The building in which Anderson wrote *Winesburg, Ohio (Chapter 12)* has been destroyed, but a Victorian house that is probably similar is across the street. This area is still in the heart of Chicago's Bohemian quarter.

THE SUN TIMES-DAILY NEWS BUILDING: Corner Wabash Avenue and the Chicago River. (Continue south on Wabash for 8 blocks.) Carl Sandburg worked for the *Daily News* between 1919 and 1923. Although the old News Building that Sandburg knew at 30 N. Wells is no longer in existence, tours of the present, ultra-modern plant still give one the feeling of being part of the hustle that helped inspire the poet. There are no Sunday tours, however, and Saturday tours should be arranged in advance.

The view of Chicago from the Sun Times-Daily News riverside promenade is rewarding. Immediately to the west are the spectacular circular Marina Tower skyscrapers. To the east is the white-faced Wrigley Building, illuminated at night by hundreds of floodlights. Across the river, on the southwest corner of Michigan Avenue, is the location of old Fort Dearborn — the lonely outpost which suffered a massacre during the War of 1812. Boats at the foot of the Michigan Avenue bridge take tourists on regular trips up the river for a short distance, then out on Lake Michigan.

THE TREMONT HOUSE: The southeast corner of Lake and Dearborn Streets. (Take Wabash Avenue over the bridge 2 blocks to Lake Street, then go 2 blocks west to Dearborn.) The Tremont House (now demolished) was once Chicago's foremost hotel. Many of the delegates to the convention which nominated Lincoln in 1860 (*Chapter 10*) stayed here — as did Lincoln himself whenever he came to the city. Stephen A. Douglas, Lincoln's arch adversary, met him here and made a speech from the Tremont balcony.

Across from the Tremont House was the stage coach terminal, built in 1840. The coach line ran down Dearborn Street, bringing visitors and immigrants from the east to the town which then was strung out along the Chicago River.

EDGAR LEE MASTERS' LAW OFFICE: Corner of Clark and Randolph Streets. (Take Lake Street 1 block west to Clark, then go 1 block south to Randolph.) Masters shared his office with Clarence Darrow, famous criminal lawyer, in a building on the site of the present Greyhound Bus Terminal. Here, in the partial seclusion of his back office, Masters wrote many of the verses of the *Spoon River Anthology* (*Chapter 12*). The Sherman House, one of the city's best known hotels, is across Clark Street. Across Randolph is Chicago's new Civic Center, a complex of gardens and gigantic buildings that are justly the pride of the city.

THE WIGWAM: Southeast corner of Wacker Drive and Lake Street. (Return to Lake Street. Go west 4 blocks to Wacker.) On this site (now an office building) in 1860, the Republican convention nominated Abraham Lincoln for the presidency (*Chapter 10*). Before the huge Wigwam was erected, just prior to the convention, the location was occupied by the Sauganash Hotel, where the first Chicago town meeting was held in 1833.

FRANK COWPERWOOD'S OFFICE: Corner of Madison and La Salle Streets. (Take Wacker Drive 2 blocks south to Washington. Go 3 blocks east to LaSalle, then 1 block south to Madison.) Here, in the shadows of the LaSalle Street financial canyon, the hero of Dreiser's *The Titan* (*Chapter 12*) began the machinations which would eventually lead him to a monopoly of Chicago's transportation lines. Cowperwood's (*i.e.* Charles Yerkes') Elevated Lines still encircle the Loop — though they are now owned by the city.

THE BOARD OF TRADE BUILDING: 141 W. Jackson Blvd. (Continue on LaSalle Street 3 blocks south where it ends at the towering Board of Trade Building.) Be sure to visit both the Grain Exchange, which is the world's largest (open weekdays 9:00 A.M. to 1:15 P.M.), and the observation deck at the top of the 44-story building (open Monday through Saturday 9:00 A.M to 6:00 P.M.).

HURSTWOOD'S LOUNGE: The north side of Adams Street between Clark and Dearborn. (Take Jackson 2 blocks east to Dearborn, then go 1 block north to Adams.) Hurstwood, tragic lover in Dreiser's *Sister Carrie* (*Chapter 12*), depended on businessmen from the LaSalle Street district for many of his customers. Carrie Meeber worked for a while in a sweat shop at the corner of Adams and Wells (Fifth Avenue in Dreiser's day), which is 2 blocks west.

SITE OF THE PULLMAN BUILDING: Corner Adams and Michigan. (Three blocks east from the Hurstwood site.) The old Pullman Building has recently given way to the sleek, modern Borg-Warner Building. The commander of the federal troops sent to break the strike at the Pullman plant 12 miles south made his headquarters here in George Pullman's Chicago office (*Chapter 13*). The troops camped due west in Grant Park.

GRANT PARK is probably the main tourist attraction in the entire city. In it are: the Art Institute, the nation's second largest art museum (open 7 days a week); the Band Shell, where open air concerts are given Wednesday, Friday, Saturday, and Sunday evenings during the summer; the Chicago Natural History Museum, famous for its collections of jewels, Egyptian artifacts, reproductions of mammals and birds, etc.; Buckingham Fountain, 280 feet in diameter, illuminated by constantly changing colored lights on summer evenings; John G. Shedd Aquarium, with a complete display of fish from the entire world swimming in large tanks; and the Adler Planetarium, giving regular displays of the heavens, past, present and future, on its indoor dome. One of the most scenic views of Chicago is from the end of the long causeway connecting the Planetarium island with Lake Shore Drive.

SITE OF THE PULLMAN MANSION: 1729 Prairie. (Take Michigan Avenue 12 blocks south from the Pullman Building site to 16th Street. Then turn 2 blocks east to Prairie Avenue.) Prairie was once one of the ultra-fashionable thoroughfares, described so well by Dreiser in *The Titan*. George Pullman, along with most other Chicago notables, maintained a large home here. The Pullman home is no longer in existence, but a fine mansion at 1801 Prairie is probably of a similar style.

A marker at the corner of 16th and Prairie denotes the site of the Fort Dearborn massacre. Here in 1812 Potawatomi and other Indians massacred half the garrison at Fort Dearborn during an attempt to flee through the area which was then rolling dunes — ideal for ambush.

STEPHEN A. DOUGLAS TOMB: 35th Street and Lake Park Avenue. (Go 1 block east to Calumet Avenue. Take Calumet 3 blocks south to Silverton, then go 1 block southeast to South Park Way — U. S. Business 20 and 12, Alternate 30. South Park Way runs south to 35th Street. At 35th turn east 6 blocks to Lake Park Avenue.) Douglas, one of the most powerful and influential men ever elected to the United States Senate, had an estate here overlooking the lake, which then covered the Illinois Central tracks and Lake Shore Drive beyond. The park, later in the center of Negro slums, is now part of an area being renovated. Scores of gleaming, skyscraper apartments surrounded by grassy knolls now give one a most pleasant glimpse of the City of the Future.

EDGAR LEE MASTERS' HOME: 4853 S. Kenwood. (Take Lake Park Avenue south to 47th Street. Go 1 block west to Kenwood and a half-block south to the house.) Masters lived here during much of his Chicago career (*Chapter 12*). The area is currently part of the Kenwood-Hyde Park experiment in interracial living which, guided partly by families from the nearby University of Chicago, seems to be largely succeeding.

SHERWOOD ANDERSON'S TEMPORARY RESIDENCE: 57th Street and Stony Island Avenue. (Return to Lake Park Avenue. Go south to 57th Street, then a half-block east to Stony Island.) The unique little string of one-story buildings between the Illinois Central railroad embankment and Stony Island Avenue still houses groups of Bohemian writers and artists, just as in the days when Sherwood Anderson made his first contact with Chicago writing here (*Chapter 12*). Directly across Stony Island Avenue is Jackson Park, the artificially created site of the Columbian Exposition of 1893. The only building remaining from this World's Fair (which put Chicago on the cultural map for the first time) is the Museum of Science and Industry. The huge building houses displays that have made it one of Chicago's most visited museums (open 7 days a week).

THE STUDS LONIGAN NEIGHBORHOOD: Indiana Avenue and 58th Street. (Take Stony Island Avenue south to 60th Street. Then go 21 blocks west to Indiana Avenue, and north 2 blocks to 58th. For 11 blocks, 60th Street parallels the grassy Midway of the University of Chicago — the university buildings are concentrated on the north side of the Midway. At the corner of Woodlawn and 57th Street is the architecturally renowned Robie House, now part of the University, built by Frank Lloyd Wright. It is a precursor of virtually all modern architecture.)

The fistic success of James T. Farrell's hero, Studs Lonigan (*Chapter 12*), was crowned when he beat Weary Reilley, his deadliest rival, in a rugged fight at 58th and Indiana. Studs' girl, Lucy Scanlan, lived in the row of buildings immediately north of that corner. Studs himself lived in a house opposite the Carter School, which is on the corner of Michigan and 58th, a block west of Indiana. The poolhall where Studs spent so many of his days was on 58th under the Elevated tracks a block and a half east of Indiana Avenue. A block and a half further east is Washington Park, the site of a football game between Studs' and another gang — surely one of the most ferocious athletic events ever described in American literature.

THE FORMER TOWN OF PULLMAN: 111th Street and St. Lawrence Avenue. (Return to Stony Island Avenue. Go south to Doty Avenue, then continue south. At 111th turn west 4 blocks to St. Lawrence.) The Florence Hotel is at the corner of 111th and St. Lawrence. Here George Pullman once entertained visiting dignitaries. Opposite is the deserted factory where the Pullman Palace Cars were made, site of the violent strike of 1894 (*Chapter 13*). At 112th and Champlain Avenue (1 block east and 1 block south) is the old market place, surrounded with an arched arcade and containing in the center a square still used by shops. A block west is the gloomy, stone church, the only one Pullman allowed in his town. Row houses — all of similar styles — line street after street. They are currently inhabited by workers from surrounding plants. The area is now incorporated in the City of Chicago.

**DECATUR**   In the spring of 1830 Abraham Lincoln, then a young man of twenty-one, and his family arrived in frontier Decatur on their way from Indiana to their new homestead on the Sangamon River (*Chapter 10*). They camped near the log cabin courthouse before moving on — a plaque in the Courthouse Square indicates the campsite. Later that summer Lincoln made his first political speech at Decatur. Years after, when he became a lawyer, his circuit often led him back to the old courthouse — which is now on display in Fairview Park.

The Lincolns left Decatur to settle on their homestead 10 miles west — the site of the Lincoln Trail Homestead State Park. Here Abe and his parents spent the exceedingly harsh winter of 1830-31 when huge snow drifts cut them off from civilization and left them with barely enough parched corn to keep them alive. One winter like that was enough for Abe's father; the next year he moved farther south. Abe, however, determined to strike out for himself, took a canoe down the Sangamon to Springfield where a new life opened up. The parting with his father left a bitterness between the two that never healed.

**DICKSON MOUNDS STATE MEMORIAL**   There is something ghostly, yet at the same time compelling, about Dickson Mounds Memorial. The mound itself is crescent shaped, extending about 500 feet from tip to tip. But it is the museum that has been constructed over an excavated area 30 by 60 feet that holds the interest — for here are the grinning skeletons of over 200 Mississippian Indians lying in exactly the same position, and in the same packed earth, as when they were laid to rest hundreds of years ago. One cannot help but feel that he is very, very close to the elusive past as he gazes into the burial pit. On the surrounding walls are cases displaying Moundbuilder artifacts.

**DIXON**   The town of Dixon was begun as a ferry point across the Rock River. When Chief Black Hawk and his warriors returned to their old hunting grounds, which were in this vicinity, the countryside rose in panic. The call went out for help and among the thousands of frontiersmen and army regulars who answered the call were two strange companions: Abraham Lincoln, a young captain of a small militia force from down-state New Salem, and Jefferson Davis, handsome lieutenant in the regular army, later to be President of the Confederate States. Both men were at the Dixon blockhouse while news was being awaited concerning the activities of Black Hawk, but it is probable neither knew of the other. Black Hawk did not appear at Dixon, but artfully skirted it while making his way up the Rock River to supposed safety with the Winnebagoes. (See ROCK ISLAND for a résumé of Black Hawk.)

A momument now stands on the site of the Dixon blockhouse. At the junction of routes 2 and 30 is the old Nachusa House built in 1837, only five years after the Black Hawk scare. It still provides comfortable lodging and good meals.

**FORT CHARTRES STATE PARK**   Although Fort Chartres now stands in a lonely, little frequented corner of the state, it was once one of the most important centers of French Midwestern power. First built in 1720 as a wooden stockade, it was reconstructed of sturdy limestone taken from the nearby bluffs in 1753. The fort was built to control passage along the Mississippi, yet this very proximity to the river brought a constant harassment of floods and finally forced the British to abandon it shortly after they had taken it from the French. Continued floods washed away most of the fort, but the impressive gateway has been rebuilt, as has the long barracks (in which there is a good museum). However, the original Powder House claims the main attention, for it, along with the courthouse at Cahokia, is one of the small number of authentic buildings of the French era remaining in the Midwest.

**FORT CREVE COEUR STATE PARK** Fort Creve Coeur was to have been LaSalle's central stronghold in the Mississippi valley (*Chapter 4*) — yet now only a plaque high on the bluffs overlooking the Illinois River (in the modern town of Creve Coeur) marks the fort site. The large Illini village, which formerly was in the valley below, is now the active city of Peoria. But the vista is still sweeping and even the smokestacks, railroad yards, and warehouses below do not materially detract from the wide view that must have thrilled the French explorers.

**FORT MASSAC STATE PARK** Fort Massac was built in 1757 by the French who wished to take advantage of the strategic location which commanded a 30-mile vista along the Ohio River. The extensive public park built around the site of the fort is dedicated to George Rogers Clark who, when he and his army disembarked near here in June 1778 (*Chapter 5*), brought the first American flag into Illinois. Public camping and picnicking are allowed, and there are facilities for boating and fishing.

**FREEPORT** Freeport is the site of the most important of the Lincoln-Douglas debates. In a cove of trees (now a parking lot at North State Avenue and East Douglas Street) on August 27, 1858, Lincoln forced Stephen A. Douglas to admit that local laws could prevent slavery from expanding into the territories. This "Freeport Doctrine," by causing the Southerners to split the Democratic party two years later (thereby giving the election to Lincoln), became an important factor leading to the Civil War.

**GALENA** This hillside town, almost lost in the Driftless Area hills (*Chapter 2*), is one of Illinois' most picturesque, as well as historic locations. The discovery of lead close to the gravel-free surface of the ground brought large numbers of settlers into the mining town which took the name "Galena" after the ore that abounded. In 1855 the De-Soto House was built, at that time one of the finest hotels in the state. Lincoln once addressed an audience from its balcony. The hotel is still in good repair and stands at Main and Green in the heart of town. A visitor can sleep in the very room Lincoln once used.

Galena's main fame, however, is connected with one of her adopted sons, Ulysses S. Grant. Grant arrived in town in 1860, a broken man who had been forced to resign from the army due to bad drinking habits. He lived in a small, hillside house at 121 High Street and would descend the almost endless steps each day to work in his father's leather goods store at 120 Main. The house still stands, although it is privately owned. There is a plaque on Main Street to denote the store site.

When Grant returned to Galena in 1865, a military hero, the proud town presented him with a handsome mansion on the eastern bluffs. This house, in which he lived until he was elected to the Presidency in 1869, has been carefully restored to the condition in which Grant left it, and is open to the public.

**GALESBURG**    The frame home in which Carl Sandburg was born is at 331 E. Third Street (*Chapter 12*). The three-room cottage has been restored to its original condition and contains a small display of articles connected with Sandburg's career. Third Street ends a block west at the yards of the Burlington Railroad, the company for which Sandburg's father worked as a blacksmith.

Knox College, which both Sandburg and Edgar Lee Masters attended (although Masters was ten years earlier), is on South Street only a few blocks from the New England style village green. Old Main — a red brick building with two low towers — is a famous Knox College landmark, for it was the site of an important Lincoln-Douglas debate in 1858.

**KASKASKIA STATE PARK**    Kaskaskia was founded by Jesuit missionaries in 1700. Later French farmers discovered that the bottomland was excellent for the growing of food and soon Kaskaskia began furnishing supplies to the traders at Cahokia and the soldiers at Fort Chartres. Following the French and Indian War, the British took over, building Fort Gage on the bluffs across the Kaskaskia River from the town — which remained largely French.

The vista that greeted George Rogers Clark and his tiny army as they advanced on Kaskaskia in 1778 (*Chapter 5*) was far different from today. The narrow Kaskaskia River, which then ran close to the bluff base, has now been flooded by the Mississippi (which formerly looped far out to the west). This flooding wiped the town of Kaskaskia completely away. However, the bell that rang throughout the village the night Clark took it from the British is now called the "Liberty Bell of the West" and has been preserved in the Kaskaskia State Memorial, a handsome brick building on a nearby Mississippi island which is accessible by ferry from Fort Gage, Illinois, or by road from St. Marys, Missouri.

Kaskaskia State Park includes the area around the British fort, with a roadway running along the old earthen ramparts. The view of the Mississippi valley and the meandering river is wide and appealing.

**LEWIS AND CLARK STATE MEMORIAL**    Immediately prior to their leap into the wilderness in 1804, Meriwether Lewis and William

Clark trained their men at a camp on the Illinois side of the Mississippi opposite the mouth of the Missouri. The approximate site of this camp has been set aside as a state memorial, and though it is largely undeveloped, still gives the visitor an insight into the location and the feelings of the explorers as they must have stared day after day up the Missouri, wondering what adventures they would find on their long trek to the distant Pacific Ocean.

**LEWISTOWN**   The Lewistown of today has not changed a great deal from the 1880's when Edgar Lee Masters was growing up in it (*Chapter 12*). The Masters home stands 1 block north of the courthouse square on the northwest corner of Adams and Milton. The house, with its quaintly impressive Victorian tower, represents a period when Edgar's father was the four-term Democratic mayor of Lewistown.

In the center of Lewistown is the typically Midwestern Renaissance courthouse. It is surrounded on three sides by commercial buildings. Masters' father had a law office on the second story of The Beadles Block. Often young Masters would sit in his father's window watching the dull, yet absorbing panorama in the square below.

Oak Hill Cemetery, certainly a stop for anyone who has read the epitaphs in *Spoon River Anthology*, is on a gently wooded hill north of the main part of town. Although none of the markers carry names in the *Anthology*, there is a haunting presence about the graveyard that recalls passages from Masters' poems.

The mansion of Lewis Ross, founder of Lewistown, is at 409 E. Milton Avenue. In its deserted, decaying condition it seems to echo Masters' verses on Washington McNeely, who, bowed by tragedy, sat forlorn under his cedar tree, a poor millionaire.

Spoon River itself is 5 miles southwest of Lewistown. U.S. 24 crosses it at Duncans Mills on a site once occupied by a covered bridge. A country road leads west from Lewistown to a small congregation of summer cottages on the Spoon River. This is Bernadotte, described in the *Anthology* and a favorite place for Masters in his youthful wanderings. The river churns over a low breakwater at the place where a four-and-a-half-story grist mill stood in Masters' day. Bernadotte is a peaceful place, ideal for fishing, picnicking, or just musing.

**LOWDEN MEMORIAL STATE PARK**   Lowden Memorial State Park is built around a huge statue of an Indian, done by the famous American sculptor, Lorado Taft. Commonly called "Black Hawk," the statue was intended to symbolize the close association of the beautiful Rock River valley with the Indian tribes who made it their home for so many years. There is no more pleasant Midwestern drive than the 40 miles between Dixon and Rockford where Illinois 2 hugs the river bank and scores of grassy turnouts attract picnickers.

**NAUVOO**   Present day Nauvoo is a village of about 1,500 persons, built on the bluffs overlooking the Mississippi. The site of the once magnificent Mormon temple (*Chapter 9*) is indicated by a stone plaque on 11th Street a half-block north of Illinois 96. The temple was burned by an arsonist two years after Brigham Young led the Mormons from the town.

The main portion of old Nauvoo was on the alluvial flatlands between the base of the bluff and the river. Little remains of the 8,000 homes which formerly housed the thriving Mormon population, but the outlines of the streets give some indication of the extent of the vacated city. Of main interest are three buildings at the river's edge: the log homestead occupied by Joseph Smith (but built by an earlier occupant in 1823), the Mansion House where Smith lived from August 1843 until his murder in June 1844, and the Nauvoo House, a guest home which Smith had built as a result of divine revelation.

After the main body of Mormons left the town, Emma Smith, Joseph's first wife, used the Nauvoo House as a residence until her death in 1879. The plaque in front of the building serves to emphasize the fact that a small proportion of Mormons remained at Nauvoo with Emma Smith, where they recognized her eleven-year-old son, not Brigham Young, as the true successor of Joseph Smith. These persons, refusing to endorse polygamy, split from the Salt Lake branch and, even though the Utah Mormons renounced plural wives in 1890, still maintain their separate division: the Reorganized Church of Latter-day Saints. The Reorganized Church controls the shrines at Kirtland, Ohio, and Nauvoo — including the grave of Joseph Smith itself, which occupies a small plot of ground between the Nauvoo homestead and the Mississippi.

The bitterness which exists between the two branches of the Mormon Church is typified by the disrepair into which the home of Brigham Young has been allowed to fall. Now used as a private residence on Sixth Street, little attempt has been made to preserve it as a shrine of any sort.

**NEW SALEM STATE PARK**   When the twenty-two-year-old Abe Lincoln was hired by a Springfield merchant to float his flatboat down the Sangamon to the Mississippi, the boat became temporarily stuck on a milldam at the settlement of New Salem. Liking the village, Lincoln returned there to live for the next six years before moving to

Springfield. Although New Salem, located off the main transportation routes, was abandoned by the 1840's, the state has reconstructed the little village which has become so dear to the memory of Lincoln.

New Salem State Park is now one of the major tourist attractions in the Midwest. Here the visitor can see the mill and dam upon which Lincoln's flatboat became stuck; the Rutledge Tavern where Lincoln boarded for a while, there to fall in love with Ann Rutledge; the Berry-Lincoln store where Abe found that he was not cut out to be a store-keeper; and a total of 22 more cabins and shops of the 1830's. The New Salem Lodge offers overnight accommodations, and guides conduct regular tours of the village. There are also camping sites and pic-nicking facilities in the park.

The grave of Ann Rutledge is 2 miles north of New Salem at Peters-burg. Her death in 1835 left Lincoln disconsolate and utterly deject-ed. Edgar Lee Masters composed the poem which is on the headstone.

**NORTH UTICA**   North Utica is the supposed site of the village where Marquette (*Chapter 4*) spoke to a large assembly of Illini dur-ing his brief missionary work among them in the spring of 1675. Al-though there are no plaques here, a visit will help visualize the set-ting where the dying priest made his appeal to the tribe that itself had but a little time left.

**PERE MARQUETTE STATE PARK**   Pere Marquette State Park, lo-cated at the junction of the Mississippi and Illinois Rivers, commands the scenic bluffs that Marquette and Joliet saw as they turned up the Illinois in 1673 (*Chapter 4*). The park is exceedingly well-developed, containing an excellent lodge, good cabins, well-marked nature trails (complete with trained guides), and opportunities for horseback rid-ing, boating, and camping.

**ROCK ISLAND**   The Rock River, with Rock Island at its mouth, is the setting for one of the most interesting of Midwestern Indian wars. This area was once the homeland of the Sauk-Fox tribe, a fierce group of people who loved their beautiful homeland with a deep intensity. As early as 1808 they became concerned with the encroachment of the white men and began harrassing Fort Madison, a small outpost of the St. Louis garrison. During the War of 1812 the Sauk-Fox, led by their indomitable chief, Black Hawk, took sides with the British and effectively blockaded the Mississippi against the Americans. How-ever with the withdrawal of the British at the conclusion of the war, the Indians fell increasingly under white pressure, particularly when a strong fort was built at the mouth of the Rock River.

In 1832 Black Hawk and a portion of his tribe, having been forced to the western bank of the Mississippi, returned to the valley of the Rock to harvest their corn. The white community, fearing an Indian attack, rose en masse. The ensuing fight was called the Black Hawk War, although it was little more than the pursuit of less than 500 warriors and their families by white armies of several thousands. Black Hawk fled up the Rock River into Wisconsin, where he and his hopeless tribe met utter defeat as they tried to recross the Mississippi into Iowa.

The treaty which followed was far more important than the actual war. This treaty opened up much of Iowa to white settlement and, by ridding northern Illinois and southern Wisconsin of any likelihood of' Indian attack, brought great floods of settlers into those areas.

The area in and around Rock Island and the other members of the Tri-cities, Moline and Davenport, Iowa, abounds in Black Hawk sites. Black Hawk State Park is found on the south side of Rock Island. Here was the rocky roost from which Black Hawk's lookouts sighted any American boats attempting to ascend the Mississippi during the War of 1812. Each Labor Day weekend the Sauks and Foxes return from their trans-Mississippi reservation (see TAMA, Iowa) to hold impressive ceremonial dances in a scenic bowl that holds 5,000 spectators.

Campbell's Island, 7 miles up the Mississippi from Moline, was the site of an Indian ambush of a small American force attempting to supply the garrison at Prairie du Chien on July 19, 1814. The marker commemorating the American defeat is about 100 yards north of a restaurant and boat dock. A camping area is nearby.

Credit Island, near Davenport, Iowa, was the location of another Black Hawk victory; this one over an American force under tough Zachary Taylor (later President of the United States) that had been sent out from St. Louis to punish the Indians for the Campbell's Island affair.

On the island of Rock Island (as distinguished from the riverside city) a blockhouse has been constructed on the site of Fort Armstrong, built in 1816 to control the Sauk-Fox. Farther down the island are other interesting sights: the home of George Davenport, one of the region's first permanent settlers, who gave his name to the Iowa city across the river; the pylons of the first bridge over the Mississippi, constructed in 1856, defended by Abraham Lincoln in a law suit brought by irate steamboat owners; and the famous Rock Island Arsenal, built in 1862, serving as one of the largest prisons for captured Confederate soldiers during the Civil War, and still active in the development and manufacture of ordnance equipment.

**SHAWNEETOWN**    Once one of the most opulent towns in the Midwest (*Chapter* 8), Shawneetown began a gradual decline when railroads displaced riverboats as the chief carriers of commerce. Periodic floods of the Ohio River aided the demise until finally in 1937 almost the entire town was moved to higher ground 3 miles inland.

Old Shawneetown (to distinguish it from the newer settlement) now is virtually deserted, with the decaying buildings as sad reminders of greater days 125 years ago. Strangely out of place is the 3-story First National Bank still in business at the corner of Washington and Main Streets. With its massive Grecian pillars and 17 spacious sandstone steps, it seems to remain as proud and defiant as in the days when it refused to loan money to the hamlet of Chicago.

**SPRINGFIELD** Of all locations in the nation, Springfield is most closely associated with Lincoln memories, for it was here that he lived for 23 years. Of main interest is the Lincoln home, the only one he ever owned, which is at Eighth and Jackson. Lincoln purchased the home in 1844; here his four sons were born, and here he accepted the presidential nomination in 1860. The interior, open to the public, is virtually unchanged from Lincoln's occupancy.

Next of interest is the Sangamon County Court House, the state capitol during Lincoln's time. It was in this Greek Revival building, located at Sixth and Adams Streets, that Lincoln served as legislator between 1837 and 1842. His headquarters during the campaign of 1860 were in a room in the capitol. And here his body rested in state on May 4, 1865.

The site of Lincoln's first law office is at 109 North Fifth Street. The office he occupied from 1841 to 1844 may be seen on the third floor at 203 South Sixth — across from the old capitol.

Lincoln's body is in a massive tomb crowned by a 100-foot obelisk at Oakridge Cemetery on Monument Avenue two miles north of the capitol. Mary Lincoln and three of their four sons are buried in crypts along the wall.

**STARVED ROCK STATE PARK** Of all the historic locations in the Midwest, there is none better developed nor more frequented than that centering around LaSalle's old fort on Starved Rock (*Chapter* 4). The top of the isolated butte upon which LaSalle built his fort is gained by an easy hike, and the view of the Illinois River, spotted with green islands and frosted with white foam from the nearby dam, is most pleasing. Here LaSalle's faithful lieutenant, Henri Tonty, waited in vain for his commander to appear down the river, while in the meantime the huge Indian village, the nucleus of LaSalle's Midwestern empire, began breaking up.

The state has erected a large lodge with cabins surrounding it, and there are opportunities for boating, horseback riding, and hiking.

**TERRAPIN RIDGE**    Terrapin Ridge offers an excellent vista of the Driftless Area (*Chapter 2*) that extends from Wisconsin into the extreme northwestern portion of Illinois. The scenery from the turnout on U.S. 20 2 miles east of Elizabeth is one of many miles of rugged, unglaciated hills — so very different from the glacier-smoothed farmlands immediately east. The hills are composed of Ordovician limestone: shells of animals which swam here 400 million years ago.

Sixteen miles northeast is the Apple River Canyon State Park, a secluded place just right for picnics, hiking, or fishing. The Apple River, wending through the Ordovician hills, is millions of years older than the Mississippi, 25 miles west, which is a comparative baby, born from the glacial meltwater only 20,000 years ago.

**VANDALIA**    Vandalia, the terminus of the National Road (*Chapter 8*), contains a Madonna of the Trail monument in the courthouse square. The town was the state capital from 1820 until 1839 when Abraham Lincoln, legislator from New Salem, was instrumental in having the capital moved to Springfield. The old capitol building has been preserved as a state memorial.

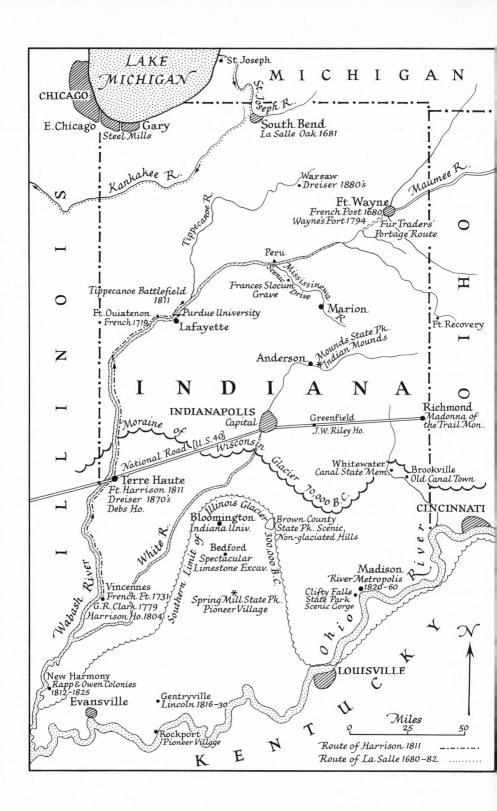

LAKE MICHIGAN

CHICAGO

E. Chicago
Steel Mills

Gary

St. Joseph

M I C H I G A N

South Bend
La Salle Oak 1681

Kankakee R.

I L L I N O I S

St. Joseph R.

Maumee R.

Warsaw
Dreiser 1880's

Tippecanoe R.

Ft. Wayne
French Post 1680
Wayne's Fort 1794

Fur Traders'
Portage Route

Peru

Frances Slocum
Grave

Scenic Drive

Mississinewa R.

O H I O

Tippecanoe Battlefield
1811

Ft. Ouiatenon
French 1719

Purdue University
Lafayette

Marion

Ft. Recovery

Anderson

Mounds State Pk.
Indian Mounds

I N D I A N A

INDIANAPOLIS
Capital

Greenfield
J. W. Riley Ho.

Richmond
Madonna of
the Trail Mon.

Moraine

of

Wisconsin

National Road [U.S. 40]

Glacier 70,000 B.C.

Whitewater
Canal State Mem.

Brookville
Old Canal Town

Terre Haute
Ft. Harrison 1811
Dreiser 1870's
Debs Ho.

White R.

Illinois Glacier

Bloomington
Indiana Univ.

Brown County
State Pk. Scenic,
Non-glaciated Hills

300,000 B.C.

CINCINNATI

Bedford
Spectacular
Limestone Excav.

Southern Limit of

Madison
River Metropolis
1820–60

Ohio River

Vincennes
French Ft. 1731
G. R. Clark 1779
Harrison Ho. 1804

Spring Mill State Pk.
Pioneer Village

Clifty Falls
State Park
Scenic Gorge

Wabash River

New Harmony
Rapp & Owen Colonies
1812–1825

Gentryville
Lincoln 1816–30

LOUISVILLE

K E N T U C K Y

N

Evansville

Rockport
Pioneer Village

K E N T U C K Y

Miles
0   25   50

Route of Harrison 1811  — · — · —
Route of La Salle 1680–82  · · · · · · · ·

# Indiana

**BEDFORD**  Nowhere does one gain a more vivid view of the vast limestone deposits left by the ancient oceans that once covered the Midwest (*Chapter 2*) than in the deep quarries easily visible from Indiana 37 and 58 just north of town. It staggers the mind to imagine the endless eons that must have passed by while the accumulation of tiny shells from the sea animals grew to become the quarry beds. Some of the nation's finest building stone, including much of that used to construct the Empire State Building, have come from Bedford. Tours of the quarry and stone-cutting mill are available through the Indiana Limestone Institute.

**BROOKVILLE**  Brookville is perhaps the most interesting town on

199

the old Whitewater Canal (see also the WHITEWATER CANAL STATE MEMORIAL). It was formerly the central town on the canal, being located on the turning basin. This basin, now dry and overgrown with weeds, can be seen from U.S. 52 on the south side of town. Across from the basin, once filled with heavily loaded canal boats and lined with wharves, is the Oregon Hotel, formerly a favorite place for the rowdy canal men who filled its rooms during the active days of the 1840's and 50's. At the corner of Fourth and Main (U.S. 52) is the Old Yellow Tavern, built as early as 1810, and used today as a residence. William Henry Harrison was entertained here in 1835, just before he made his first (and unsuccessful) bid for the Presidency.

**BROWN COUNTY STATE PARK**   Brown County State Park, one of Indiana's most popular scenic attractions, is located in the midst of lovely hills carved by torrents flowing from the melting glaciers which once surrounded it on three sides. The park has provided rustic cabins, a good dining room, fine hiking facilities, a swimming pool, horseback riding, and 27 miles of pleasant roadways. An art colony is centered in the nearby village of Nashville to take advantage of the sculptured countryside, and many of its paintings are for sale in the two local galleries. A summer theater is also active in Nashville, operated by Indiana University.

**CLIFTY FALLS STATE PARK**   Clifty Falls State Park, 4 miles west of Madison, is located at what geologists believe was the headwaters of the Ohio River in the pre-glacial days when it flowed east, not west (*Chapter 2*). The Ohio at this point now churns through a deep canyon where a large power plant takes advantage of the rapids. A clifftop inn is open the year around, and there are park facilities for horseback riding and hiking.

**EAST CHICAGO**   East Chicago boasts the huge plants of Youngstown Sheet and Tube and of Inland Steel, which actually produce more steel than neighboring Gary. Although the city is less accessible to the tourist than Gary, it should certainly be a point of call for anyone interested in Midwestern industry. Walter M. Jeorse Park on the lakefront opposite the Inland Steel plant offers a superb vantage point, and its extensive, colorfully landscaped grounds are ideal for all sorts of recreation. Go there in the evening to gain a spectacular close-up of the flames, the ever-changing colors, and the enthralling roar that combine to create a picture of modern steel.

**FORT OUIATENON**   Fort Ouiatenon was built in 1719 by François

Morgane de Vincennes, who was later to construct another fort bearing his name farther down the Wabash. Vincennes chose to throw up his guardian blockhouse at this particular point since the Fox War (*Chapter 4*) had closed the northern fur routes, and the Wabash had to be protected from war parties proceeding southward from the tip of Lake Michigan. The old fort has been reconstructed and now stands again in its original position about 5 miles below LaFayette on Indiana 526. Its country setting gives it an old time charm and authenticity not found in city monuments. The Wabash is close by, redolent with memories of singing French fur men and chanting Indians.

**FORT WAYNE** Fort Wayne, now one of Indiana's most important cities, was begun by "Mad" Anthony Wayne just after the Battle of Fallen Timbers (*Chapter 6*) to command the much-frequented portage route between the Great Lakes (via the Maumee River) and the Mississippi (via the Wabash). It consisted of a large stockade at the corner of Clay and Berry Streets and stood on a small rise above the point where the St. Marys and the St. Joseph Rivers merge to form the Maumee — a view unfortunately now blocked by a railroad embankment.

The area at the source of the Maumee had long been vital in the Indian economy. Quite early (possibly in 1680) the French had a trading post on the St. Marys where the Sherman Avenue bridge now stands. The British built a post on the St. Joseph after they had driven the French out; a fort garrisoned just in time to be massacred in 1766. The men of General Josiah Harmar met an equally disagreeable fate on the very same ground in 1790. This site may be found on St. Joseph Boulevard at Delaware, now shaded by deceptively peaceful, though somehow extremely appropriate, weeping willows.

**FRANCES SLOCUM TRAIL** One of the prettiest, off-the-beaten-path drives is along the Mississinewa River for 23 miles between Marion and Peru. The country road follows the placid, eddy-filled river through a land formerly dotted with the wigwams of the Miami Indian tribe. It was in a small Miami village that a most unusual drama was enacted during the last century.

In 1773 a four-year-old girl, Frances Slocum, was stolen by Indians from her parents in Pennsylvania. This girl grew up among the Indians and at the Battle of Fallen Timbers (*Chapter 6*) she was so taken by a wounded, handsome brave that she nursed him back to life and later married him. After she had lived with the Indians for 64 years, her brothers and a sister learned through a trader where she was living. Yet when they came to take her home, she refused to give up the only life she had known, dying ten years later among the Indians, "a stranger to her brethren," as the plaque on her grave quotes from Psalms. This grave, located on the site of Frances Slocum's cabin, is about a mile south of the hamlet of Peoria.

The Mississinewa roadway has been named the Frances Slocum Trail, yet there were other events of interest occurring along its byways. Tecumseh, the mighty Shawnee chief, once appealed to the Miami around a roaring council fire meeting held about 3 miles upstream from present Peru. William Henry Harrison (*Chapter 7*) in Vincennes, upon learning of the discontent of the Miami, sent an army against them in December 1812. The Battle of the Mississinewa was fought 2 miles north of present-day Marion, and, although the Miami were victorious, the loss of Indian life was so great that they never again were a powerful factor in frontier life.

**GARY**    The industrial complex formed by Gary and East Chicago is probably the most extensive in the world. The steel mills in these two Indiana cities roar day and night, producing 30,000,000 tons of steel a year — 4,000,000 tons more than their nearest American competitor, the Pittsburgh region, and more than most European countries.

Gary is unusual among industrial cities, for not a building in it is more than 60 years old (*Chapter 13*). The United States Steel plant dominates the city, with Gary's main street, Broadway, ending blankly at the wire gates of the mills. At night there is an incessant illumination from the blazing furnaces (which can be seen by motorists on the Indiana Toll Road for 25 miles), and the hum of the sintering plant grates uncomfortably against the ears of those not accustomed to it. Although the mills themselves are not ordinarily open to the public, tourists may pass through the gates and drive east along a roadway which parallels the Grand Calumet River. The short drive is fascinating, for one will pass a monstrous jumble of blast furnaces, rolling mills, and coking plants, view (though from a distance) the narrow harbor where the long ore boats unload, and hear the roar, see the flames and taste the heavy odors of steel in the making.

**GENTRYVILLE**    When Tom Lincoln led his family across the Ohio River from Kentucky in 1816, young Abe was only seven years old. The family built a small cabin near the present village of Gentryville, the site of which is indicated by the excavated hearthstones. Near the homesite is the grave of Lincoln's mother, Nancy Hanks, who died in 1818. The grave is in a quiet cove of trees, mostly hickories, which form an arching woodland cathedral.

Contrasting with the simple grave is the almost overly impressive Nancy Hanks Memorial building nearby. On the exterior walls are five live-size sculptured panels depicting scenes from Lincoln's life. One of the buildings is a chapel seating 250 people.

Adjacent to the Nancy Hanks Memorial is Lincoln State Park, which is centered historically on a reconstruction of the Little Pigeon Baptist Church, the place where the Lincoln family worshipped. Abe's only sister, Sarah, is buried in the churchyard. A large artificial lake has been created around the church and has been well stocked with fish. Boating, swimming, and hiking facilities are available.

**GREENFIELD**   Greenfield is the hometown of James Whitcomb Riley, an author whose verses, while not generally considered to be of first rank, are so descriptive of the Hoosier Midwest that he must be included in any résumé of Indiana. Riley was born in a two-story, clapboard home along the old National Road around 1852 (he was very secretive about his birth date). At the age of 30 he made his literary bow with a collection of poems entitled *The Old Swimmin' Hole*. Over the years he wrote other poems that have become a permanent part of Americana, including "When the Frost is on the Punkin," "Little Orphant Annie," "The Raggedy Man," and many others.

The home in which Riley was born, and to which he returned almost every summer as a grown man, is at 246 W. Main Street. It has been refurnished in period pieces and is open to the public. The high school Riley attended is at State and Main. Brandywine Creek, the location of "The Old Swimmin' Hole," meanders past Greenfield on the east. There is a large park around the river and a more splendid swimming pool than the poet ever dreamed of.

**MADISON**   Madison is a border town (*Chapter 1*) where the influence of the South is everywhere in evidence. During the 1840's and 50's great numbers of Southerners migrated here, fanning out over the countryside and producing the easy-going, rustic individual known as the Hoosier. During the days when the Ohio River was *the* grand highway of commerce, Madison grew to be Indiana's largest town (*Chapter 8*). Then Greek Revival mansions sprung up along the riverfront, the handsomest being that of James F. Lanier, which has now become a museum. The Lanier mansion, with its spacious grounds, its four huge Corinthian pillars, and its magnificent spiral staircase, recalls bygone days of leisure and luxury. Many other southern-style homes grace the streets of modern Madison.

**MOUNDS STATE PARK**   Mounds State Park, 4 miles east of Anderson, consists of nine earthworks, some oval, some guitar shaped. The main mound — proclaimed by many as Indiana's finest — is an embankment about 10-feet high and some 384-feet in diameter. It encircles a depression, 18-feet deep, in the center of which is a small raised area that was probably used by the Hopewellian builders for religious ceremonies. Paths lead from this mound to the White River, a remarkably beautiful stream, where there are fishing possibilities for those interested. The park also contains picnic sites and refreshment stands.

**NEW HARMONY**    New Harmony, a village of less than 1,500 persons, is tucked away in a little frequented corner of southwestern Indiana. Many of the buildings used by George Rapp and his Harmonist followers (*Chapter 9*) are in good repair and still used as residences. Rapp's home (at what is now Main and Church — U.S. 460) burned after his departure, but Alexander Owen built in 1844 a pleasing Greek Revival mansion which stands today on the same location. In the yard is a stone with the imprints of two feet, which Rapp claimed were made by the Angel Gabriel when he came to deliver a message. Many scientists, however, believe the imprints were made by a prehistoric Indian when the rock was still soft.

Immediately west of the house is the large, stone building constructed by the Rappites as a combination granary and fort. Still to be seen are the long slits through which muskets could be fired against any enemy. The best time to visit the fort is in June when it is ornamented by a cloud of Golden Rain trees imported from the Orient. After the Rappites left, the fort was used for many years as the headquarters for the United States Geological Survey.

Across Main Street from the site of the Rapp home is Community House Number Two, a long, three-story, brick building in which the single men were housed. During Owenite days it was the residence of the scientists and is now a museum. Community House Number Three, Owen's headquarters, is 1½ blocks east on Church Street.

The Rappite church stood at the southeast corner of Church and West Streets, on the present site of the public school. The Rose Door, formerly part of the church, is currently used as the west entrance to the school, a constant reminder to the children of their heritage. In 1874 aged Rappite survivors returned to New Harmony to supervise the demolition of the abandoned church. The bricks were used to build a low wall around the cemetery which was (and still is) on the Wabash River bank due west of the fort. This must have been one of the saddest moments for the Rappites, for now not only was their church gone, but the cemetery, formerly deemed only a temporary resting place of no consequence for their comades who would momentarily ascend bodily to heaven, had now become something quite permanent.

Another monument to the misled idealism of the Rappites was the intricate garden known as the Labyrinth, which they laid out 4 blocks south of the fort. This maze of paths bounded by shrubs and small trees was intended to demonstrate the difficult path to heaven, represented by a small, stone hut in the center. However, the End of the World did not come, and the Labyrinth gradually became a meaningless jumble of overgrown plants. It has now been reconstructed using low-growing privet bushes.

**SOUTH BEND**　The south bend of the St. Joseph River was an important location in the French fur empire long before the American city was founded there. The 10-mile portage between the St. Joseph (which led to the Great Lakes) and the Kankakee (which led to the Mississippi) was used by LaSalle many times, and it was over this portage that he passed on the monumental voyage which resulted in the discovery of the mouth of the Mississippi (*Chapter 4*).

A large oak tree which stood at the South Bend terminus of the portage was often used by Indians and Frenchmen for councils and treaty-making. In 1681 LaSalle met representatives of the Illini and Miami tribes here and negotiated a friendship pact between them in order to resist the aggressions of the far-ranging Iroquois. The old tree, known as Council Oak, still stands, supported by wires and posts, in Highland Cemetery on the northern end of Portage Avenue. It is a thrill to stand beneath the very living boughs that once shadowed the tragic LaSalle.

**SPRING MILL STATE PARK**　Spring Mill State Park ranks with New Salem, Illinois. as one of the best Midwestern reconstructions of pioneer living. The little village was begun in 1815, and, though it was later abandoned because it was too far from the developing trade routes, for a while it actively supported a gristmill, sawmill, post office, distillery, and tavern — which have been painstakingly rebuilt. The gristmill, turned today as yesterday by water channeled to it through a quarter-mile, elevated aqueduct, is in daily operation; and the ground corn meal is sold to visitors.

Spring Mill is in the midst of a region abounding in limestone caves. Experienced guides take visitors through some of them in boats, though Donaldson Cave may be partially explored without a guide on foot. The park has rental boats, horseback riding, fishing, hiking, picnicking, and swimming. The Spring Mill Inn is open for food and lodging all year around.

**TERRE HAUTE**　Terre Haute received its name from the French who found this "high land" protruding from the flat valley which extended for many miles southward. William Henry Harrison chose this "terre haute" as the place for a supply base, which he named Fort Harrison, while on his way to attack the Indians along the Tippecanoe River (*Chapter 7*).

Theodore Dreiser (*Chapter 12*) was born in a single-story shanty at 115 Walnut near the corner of First Street. The dilapidated house has been torn down to make way for a modern supermarket, but there are shanties across the street that are similar to the old Dreiser home.

When Dreiser returned to his hometown in 1913, a successful author, he stayed at the Terre Haute House on Seventh Street and Wabash Avenue — still one of the city's finest hotels. In *Hoosier Holiday* he remembered how his brother, Rome, used to stand in the doorway in his best suit of clothes, sucking a toothpick to make everyone believe he had just eaten there. Dreiser's mother worked in the hotel during the bleak days when his father was unemployed. Here, too, brother Paul was later feted in honor of his hit song "On the Banks of the Wabash" — for which Theodore composed the words.

The home of Eugene Debs (*Chapter 13*) is privately owned at 451 North Eighth Street. With its modest size it does not look like the residence of a man who once challenged the mightiest millionaires of the nation. Debs built the house himself in 1889, planning his bedroom in the back to overlook the railroad yards. The Hoosier poet James Whitcomb Riley (see Greenfield) visited Debs so often that another bedroom was called the Riley Room. The two friends would often be found at the bar of the St. Nicholas Hotel one block east drinking with the railroad workers.

During the First World War, Debs spoke out so strongly for peace, even after the United States had entered the conflict, that he was sentenced to a long term in prison. After the war he was pardoned, and a large group of friends gathered at the railroad depot several blocks east of his home to welcome him back. When Debs died in 1926, his funeral was held on his front porch to permit the thousands of saddened admirers to be present.

**TIPPECANOE BATTLEFIELD STATE MEMORIAL**    Standing on the hillock upon which Harrison and his men encamped on November 6, 1811, it is easy to see the events as they occurred (*Chapter 7*). The Americans were bedded down in a hollow triangle, with the horses and supply wagons in the center. On two sides were low downward sloping bluffs formed by Burnet's Creek to the northeast and the Wabash flatlands to the south. Just east of the base of the wedge-shaped piece of land was a dense thicket, and it was through this underbrush that the savages crept toward the camp from Prophetstown which was 4 miles up the valley.

About 4:00 A.M. a sentry awoke the camp as he fired at the Indians who were climbing up the bluff formed by Burnet's Creek. Markers on the battlefield indicate how deeply they penetrated the American lines to scalp Captain Baen and two others. A second attack came from the underbrush on the side facing the Wabash. Major Daveiss led a counterattack at which time he was killed — another marker indicates the location where he died. Then a third attack came from the rear. A tall monument is located at the place from which Harrison directed the charge which broke the Indian lines.

Picnic tables now dot the lowland along pretty Burnet's Creek. The atmosphere of the park is quiet and peaceful, in distinct contrast to the autumn days of 1811.

**VINCENNES** François Morgane de Vincennes built the fort named after himself in 1732, when the Fox Indians, by closing the Wisconsin River to the fur trade, forced the opening of a new route up the Wabash (*Chapter 4*). Soon a considerable company of *coureurs de bois* gathered around the fort in a ramshackle village. The Old Cathedral, the main building in the French settlement, stood on the location now occupied by the St. Francis Xavier Church, which itself is quite old (built in 1826). The tower bell is the same (though it has been recast) that hung in the first French church. It was in the Old Cathedral that George Rogers Clark received the formal surrender of the British in 1779 (*Chapter 5*).

The George Rogers Clark Memorial, an impressive Doric style building costing $2,500,000, stands between the Old Cathedral and the Wabash. Built on the site of Fort Sackville, it is one of the largest historical monuments in the Midwest. The entrance is by way of nineteen steps which represent the states of the Union when Indiana became a state in 1816. In the interior is a handsome bronze statue of Clark, and on the walls are seven large murals depicting events connected with the winning of the old Northwest. The spacious grounds border the Wabash River at a point where Abraham Lincoln and his parents crossed into Illinois in 1830 (*Chapter 10*) — a statue just over the bridge being dedicated to this event.

For those who wish to follow the route of Clark and his men as they marched on Vincennes, there is a marked county road which leads south from Vincennes past plaques indicating the then swampy camping sites at Upper Mamell, Sugar Camp, and Warrior's Island. The road ends abruptly at the Wabash, where a quaint, paddlewheel ferry takes cars and passengers across to St. Francisville, Illinois, approximately along the passage used by Clark.

William Henry Harrison's mansion, Grouseland, has been restored and stands a mile upstream from the Clark Memorial. When one visits the fine old house, he should be sure to note the beautiful, semi-circular Council Room where the governor signed so many Indian land treaties. Indications of the frontier state in which the governor found himself are the lookout in the attic, the heavy wooden bars over the basement windows, the gunpowder room, and a hole in a living-room shutter blasted by an Indian sharpshooter trying to kill Harrison. There is even a persistent rumor of a secret escape tunnel to the Wabash, although it has never been found.

In front of Grouseland, in what was once the grove where Harrison held a turbulent meeting with the Shawnee chief, Tecumseh (*Chapter 7*), is the small, two-story building that was the first Capitol of the Indiana Territory. From this unimposing structure the laws that governed what would be the future states of Indiana, Michigan, Illinois, Wisconsin, Minnesota, Iowa, and Missouri were made.

**WARSAW**    Theodore Dreiser devoted six chapters in *Hoosier Holiday* to recollections of his childhood in Warsaw, and the tourist who wishes to fix in his mind the image of a typical Midwestern town could do no better than to read these chapters, then spend several hours browsing through the streets of this proud county seat of 7,000 persons.

Visit first the courthouse square where the county building, so archaically Renaissance, yet at the same time so very Midwestern, dominates the town. When Dreiser lived in Warsaw during the 1880's, the southeast side of the square contained a poolroom that was "the very center and axis of all youthful joy and life in my day." The site is now occupied by a staid bank!

Dreiser attended seventh and eighth grades at the West Ward school. The old building has been replaced by a sleek, modern one and renamed Madison school, but it occupies the same site on Union Street at the end of West Main. Dreiser played in the mysterious swamp which still calls to adventuresome youths from its bed behind the school.

The first Dreiser home bordered the school at 121 North Union Street. In its back yard was an ash tree which he sometimes climbed; there, aloof from the world, to cling to its rocking branches as if he were a part of heaven. The Dreiser family later moved to what was then the 600 block on West Center Street (now the 400 block), first on the north side, then on the south side of the street. The later house, which is no longer standing, always appealed to the author as his true home. He loved to listen to the chimes of the clock in the courthouse tower, remembering as an adult how it carelessly ticked off the hours of his childhood.

Center Lake, too, was important in Dreiser's memories of his hometown. In the summer the lake, only a quarter-mile north of the court-house square, was much frequented for swimming. And in the winter on glorious moonlit nights he and his friends would skate on the ice that was "as thick as a beam and as smooth as glass."

There is something universal in the fond recollections of one's childhood hometown, and in his descriptions of Warsaw Dreiser has caught that something and made it accessible to all his readers.

**WHITEWATER CANAL STATE MEMORIAL** The influx of pioneers into the interior of the Midwest (*Chapter 8*) brought the problem of how to get their farm produce to the distant markets. One of the most successful solutions, until the advent of the railroads in the 1860's, was the canal. The Whitewater Canal State Memorial at the village of Metamora commemorates the important canal traffic by setting aside a picturesque lock that formerly lowered the boats as they made their long grip down the Whitewater Valley to Cincinnati.

U.S. 52 parallels the Whitewater Canal during most of its course to the Ohio River. The drive southward is pleasant, with the moss-covered canal, the rushing river, and the quaint little towns that were once active ports (see BROOKVILLE) lending interest to the highway. A marker on Boundary Hill, a few miles south of Metamora, indicates the Fort Greenville line (*Chapter 6*) which ran from the Ohio River to Fort Recovery and which still forms the western boundary of Dearborn County.

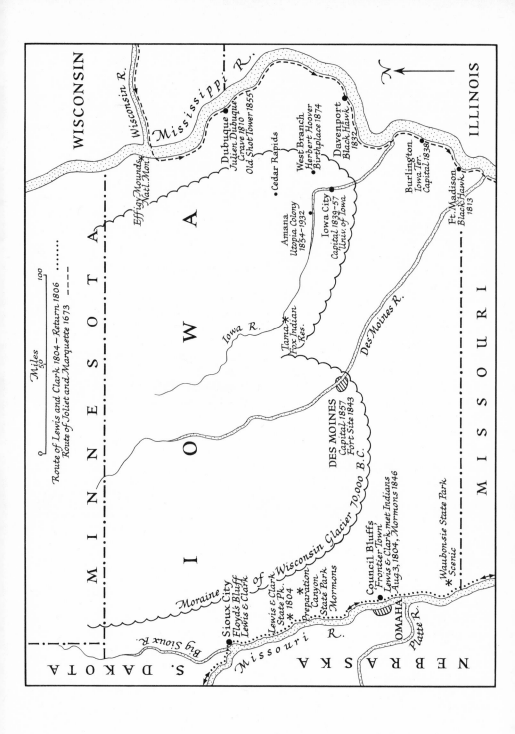

WISCONSIN

ILLINOIS

*Wisconsin R.*

*Mississippi R.*

*Miles*
0    50    100

Route of Lewis and Clark 1804−Return 1806 ········
Route of Joliet and Marquette 1673 − − − −

Effigy Mounds
Natl. Mon.

Dubuque
Julien Dubuque
Grave 1810
Old Shot Tower 1855

• Cedar Rapids

West Branch
Herbert Hoover
Birthplace 1874

Davenport
Black Hawk
1832

Burlington
Iowa Ter.
Capital 1838

Amana
Utopia Colony
1854−1932

Iowa City
Capital 1839−57
Univ. of Iowa

Ft. Madison
Black Hawk
1813

I O W A

*Iowa R.*

Tama*
Fox Indian
Res.

*Des Moines R.*

MINNESOTA

DES MOINES
Capital 1857
Fort Site 1843

Moraine of Wisconsin Glacier 70,000 B.C.

Sioux City
Floyd's Bluff
Lewis & Clark

Lewis & Clark
State Pk.
* 1804

Preparation
Canyon
State Park
Mormons
*

Council Bluffs
Frontier Town
Lewis & Clark met Indians
Aug. 3, 1804, Mormons 1846

*Waubonsie State Park
Scenic

*Big Sioux R.*

S. DAKOTA

*Missouri R.*

OMAHA

*Platte R.*

NEBRASKA

MISSOURI

# Iowa

**AMANA**   A tourist entering the valley of the Iowa River along U.S. 6 will at first find it hard to believe that the Amana towns were once aloof from commercial enterprises, for he will be virtually deluged by signs advertising the merits of Amana hams, woolens, furniture, and the products of the Amana Refrigeration plant, which is located at Middle Amana. These items made with Old World skill are of high quality, and tours may be arranged through most of the various factories.

Although this Americanization of the Amanas seems to have proceeded quite far, the six little villages still retain much of the flavor of the days when they were German religious outposts far from the civilized world (*Chapter* 9). The homes are of brick or locally-quar-

211

ried stone and are free from adornment — for the Inspirationalists disdained ostentation. There are no curbs on the streets, no alleys, few sidewalks, and no porches on the houses. The raising of flowers was considered a needless frivolity and vegetable gardens still predominate (although a large flowering lily pond was allowed to grow between Amana and Middle Amana — a pond that is still a beautiful sight during the mid-summer blooming time). Fruit trees, more utilitarian than shade trees, were mainly planted, and even today it is difficult to find relief from the scorching Iowa summer sun while in the Amanas.

A highlight of any visit is dinner at one of the old community dining rooms, which in Amana proper have been converted into fine restaurants. The Ox Yoke Inn is one of the best.

Opposite the Ox Yoke Inn is the main office of the Amana Company, now and in Inspirationalist days one of the central places of business for the villagers — most of whom are direct descendants of the Inspirationalists. Diagonally across the street from the Inn is the home of Christian Metz, leader of the Amana colonists until his death in 1867.

**BURLINGTON**   The first American flag to fly in Iowa was raised by the twenty-six-year-old explorer, Zebulon Pike, on August 23, 1805, from what is now Crapo Park on Burlington's southern outskirts. Young Pike was leading a government expedition to explore the then unknown upper Mississippi — an exploration that was designed to open the north as Lewis and Clark had recently opened the west.

Burlington, oddly enough, was once the capital of Wisconsin. This was in 1837 when the legislature convened here while the new capital at Madison was being prepared. The very next year the Territory of Iowa was sliced off from Wisconsin, and Burlington, as the largest and most distinguished town in the area, was chosen for the capital. However, the immigrant flood moved so fast to the westward that in 1839 a new capital was established at Iowa City.

Burlington has, unfortunately, done little to publicize its unique history. The Wisconsin assembly met in a house on the banks of the Mississippi, currently Front Street, between Columbia and Washington, but there is no marker there. The Iowa assembly met on Third Street between Columbia and Washington, but again there is no marker.

**COUNCIL BLUFFS**   Council Bluffs, overlooking the Missouri, is a "frontier town" (*Chapter 1*) in more than one respect. Motorists crossing into Nebraska and continuing west will soon find themselves out of the rolling hills of the glaciated Midwest and into the level lands of the Great Plains. The Platte River, which flows into the Missouri just south of the town, long marked a division that made the bluffs a place for councils between the Indian tribes of the plains and those of the hills. Lewis and Clark merely conformed to the Indian custom when they met with representatives of the Plains tribes here in 1804. The exact site of their meeting is not known for certain, but a monument has been erected on a bluff-top a few miles north of town on Rainbow Drive. The view from the monument, always panoramic, is particularly interesting in mid-March when millions of ducks and geese funnel up the valley from their wintering grounds on the Gulf Coast.

A marker at the corner of State and Broadway (U.S. 6, 75, and Alternate 30) indicates the location of a blockhouse built here in 1837 to protect the Potawatomi Indians, a Midwestern Algonquin tribe forced to leave their native land around Lake Michigan, from the hostile tribes of the Great Plains. This is another indication of the transitional character of the area.

The Mormons, too, found western Iowa to be on the edge of a vast wilderness not at all comparable with their former Midwestern homes in Ohio and Illinois. In 1846 Brigham Young, leading the Mormons from their abandoned capital at Nauvoo to the Great Salt Lake, established one of his camps in Bayliss Park at First Avenue and Pearl Street. Here the harrassed people gathered supplies and courage in preparation for their difficult push across the parched, Sioux-infested Great Plains.

For many years American political leaders considered the Missouri River to be the western limit of white expansion. The Union Pacific, first (and at that time thought by many to be the only) of the great trans-continental railroads, was begun here — as this was the logical point at which to start the long leap across the infertile, drearily-flat plains. A tall replica of the famed golden spike which linked the Union Pacific with the Pacific line will be found on the railroad grounds at 21st Street and Ninth Avenue.

**DAVENPORT**  Davenport is the largest of the Tri-Cities, which include Rock Island and Moline on the Illinois side of the Mississippi. The beautiful Davenport waterfront, a credit to the city, has been named LeClaire Park after one of the city's founders, Antoine Le-Claire, a French halfbreed who was the interpreter when the Black Hawk treaty was signed here in 1832 (see ROCK ISLAND for a résumé of the Black Hawk story). LeClaire's home, which can be seen on the grounds of the public museum at 704 Brady Street, became the first railroad station west of the Mississippi when the Rock Island line bridged the river in 1856 — a memorable event.

The home of the city's other founder, George Davenport, still stands on Rock Island. Davenport, an English trader, was murdered in his home by bandits in 1845.

Credit Island, 3 miles south of the city, is the site of a victory by Black Hawk and 1,000 of his braves aided by a detachment of British soldiers over an American army sent out to punish him during the War of 1812. The island has been turned into a recreation area with a well kept-up golf course, tennis courts, picnic grounds, fishing, and a scenic riverside drive of over two miles.

**DES MOINES**   Des Moines, receiving its name from the French adaptation of the Indian word for "mounds" (referring to the Moundbuilder hills once abounding in the area), illustrates the almost unbelievable rapidity with which Iowa was populated. When the Sauk-Fox Indians relinquished claim to much of Iowa at a treaty signed in 1832 in Davenport, eager settlers began fanning out over the extremely fertile new land. So rapidly did the white tide move that in 1843 a fort was built at the junction of the Des Moines and Raccoon Rivers, then far west of the frontier, whose purpose was not to protect the oncoming settlers, but to protect the Indians from the lawless white vanguards. Three short years later the fort was abandoned, for by then the population of the village growing up around it had swollen to sufficient size to maintain civil law. In 1857 the booming town became the state capital.

The speed with which Des Moines changed from frontier village to state capital was such that natives have attached little significance to the sites of its early history. The location of the army fort is now indicated only by an inconspicuous marker across from the baseball stadium; and the site of the first capitol building is obliterated by the huge shaft of the Soldiers and Sailors Monument on the grounds of the present capitol.

The view of the city from the 85-acre park upon which the present capitol (built 1871-84) stands is rewarding: the Des Moines River running leaden-colored below, the sparkling spires of the business section beyond, and the haze-enshrouded outline of the valley wall in the distance. The State Historical Museum adjacent to the capitol contains a fine collection of exhibits showing Iowa's development.

**DUBUQUE**   The early history of Dubuque concerns itself mainly with the mining of lead, which, because this region is part of the Driftless Area (*Chapter 2*), was found close to the surface of the ground — not overlaid with glacial gravel deposits. The city's first settler was Julien Du Buque, a French-Canadian who began mining in 1788 with the permission of the Spanish authorities who then ruled the trans-Mississippi region. Du Buque had great influence over the generally unfriendly Fox Indians, even inducing some of them to work in his mines. Du Buque died in 1810, and was buried on the bluffside near his homestead cabin. The gravesite is now marked by a somewhat inaccessible limestone tower on the city's southern outskirts, a half-mile beyond the end of Rowan Street.

Lead mining continued to be the town's major industry. In 1855 a tall tower was constructed at the river end of Fourth Street where lead shot was formed by dropping the molten metal into vats of water at the bottom. The waterfront around the tower then developed into one of the most active portions of the city, especially when huge rafts of northern timber began to arrive down the Mississippi. The Shot Tower was then used by a lumber mill as a lookout to sight the approaching rafts. Portions of the old stone levee, once aswarm with rafts, steamboats, canoes, and boats of every type and description, still remain — complete with the iron loops once used as anchorage.

Excellent views of the river and the city are gained from Eagle Point Park on the north or from the top of the Fenelon Place incline railway connecting Fourth Street with the blufftop. The railway itself is a monument to the past, having been built in 1882 to relieve buggy-horses from the staggering uphill climb.

**EFFIGY MOUNDS NATIONAL MONUMENT** Although much of the Effigy Mounds National Monument is still undeveloped, this very primitiveness lends an interest not found in the more frequented parks. The mounds, built nearly 1,000 years ago by Indians culturally related to the Hopewellians of Ohio (*Chapter 2*), are in forms interpreted as foxes, eagles, panthers, dogs and many other animals. Of main interest is the Great Bear Mound, 137 feet long. It can be reached only by a footpath that takes the hiker up the tree-covered bluffs of the Mississippi for about a mile. The mouth of the Wisconsin River, forever associated with Joliet and Marquette, is only a few miles downstream. The lookout over the marvelous canyon from Fire Point is spectacular.

**FORT MADISON** Fort Madison was built in 1808 by a detachment from the St. Louis garrison. Although its purpose was to quiet the Indians along the upper Mississippi, the troopers found themselves harassed to such a point by Chief Black Hawk during the War of 1812 that they were forced to abandon the fort, burning it as they left. For many years thereafter the upper Mississippi remained in Black Hawk's hands (see ROCK ISLAND, Illinois) and the blackened chimney of the ruined fort became a monument to the high tide of Indian power. This famous Lone Chimney, as it became known, has been reconstructed and now stands on its original location between the Mississippi and U.S. 61 on the east side of the modern town of Fort Madison.

**IOWA CITY** Iowa City, originally laid out amid the boundless prairie wilds, became the territorial capital of Iowa in 1839. At this time a farmer was paid to run a furrow from Dubuque, a major port of embarkation, across the treeless grasslands to the capital — for there were no other directional indications! A fine capitol building was built in the Greek Revival style that was then sweeping the nation. After the capital was moved to Des Moines in 1857, the graceful building became, and still is, the administration center for the University of Iowa.

Five years after the seat of government was established at Iowa City, the first governor, Robert Lucas, built an impressive brick residence on the southeastern outskirts of town. Plum Grove, as the home is called, is an interesting museum filled with period pieces and exhibits illustrating Iowa's history.

**LEWIS AND CLARK STATE PARK** Lewis and Clark State Park is centered around a loop of the Missouri where the explorers camped during the summer of 1804. The river has since formed a new channel, leaving a landlocked lake with a sand beach around which have been constructed a bathhouse and picnic facilities.

**PREPARATION CANYON STATE PARK** Preparation Canyon was named by a group of Mormons who encamped here, preparatory to making the long trek across the Great Plains to Salt Lake. They were leaving behind almost everything they held dear, and one can well imagine the apprehension, mingled of course with religious joy, with which they viewed their coming journey.

Good views of the rolling countryside, which the Mormons would one day contrast with the sharp desert scenery around their new western home, are to be gained from the surrounding ridges.

**SIOUX CITY** The site of Sioux City, located at the point where the Missouri makes a long, arching turn toward the west, was the burial place for Sargent Charles Floyd who died here, probably of appendicitis, on August 20, 1804 — the only member of the Lewis and Clark expedition to lose his life on the journey. Floyd's grave, originally denoted by a huge cedar post which stood for many years as a landmark to traders and a totem of superstitious awe and fear to the Indians, is currently indicated by a 100-foot pylon on Floyd's Bluff 3 miles south of town. There is an excellent view of the Missouri from the heights.

**TAMA** The Fox Indians, long one of the fiercest of Midwestern tribes, and their equally fierce blood relatives, the Sauk, now live on a semi-reservation a mile north of the village of Tama. The two tribes joined after the Fox were almost wiped out during the vicious war with the French and their Indian allies between 1712 and 1732 (*Chapter 4*). There are over 1,000 Indians here. making their living partly from the bead-work they sell from roadside stands. In mid-August they hold a four-day pow-wow at which time the public can witness some of the ancient ceremonial dances by descendants of the mighty Black Hawk. On the Labor Day weekend representatives of the Sauk-Fox tribe return to Black Hawk State Park (see ROCK ISLAND, Illinois) where they hold more ceremonies in what was once their cherished homeland.

**WAUBONSIE STATE PARK** As the humbled Potawatomi Indians, once conquerors of the garrison at Chicago, were pushed westward, they found momentary sanctuary in the area now bounded by the park named after their chief, Waubonsie. Although it is a beautiful place where wild hills tumble down forested slopes to meet the flat bottomland along the Missouri, the helpless tribesmen must have often yearned for the limitless waters of Lake Michigan and the flashing, fish-filled streams of Wisconsin.

A multitude of trails now take the tourist through land still partial wilderness. There are also camping and picnicking grounds.

**WEST BRANCH** West Branch, a hamlet of 800 persons, contains the tiny two-room house in which former President Herbert Hoover was born in 1874. The Rugged Individualism, so much a part of Hoover's beliefs, was essential on the near-frontier where he grew up. There were no government agencies to aid him or his parents, who had traveled from Ohio to West Branch in a covered wagon. When Hoover was only six, his father died, and four years later his mother went. The road from the little farm to the White House was to be long and hard, and the visitor to the Hoover Birthplace will gain a deeper appreciation for the man who was the last of the pioneer presidents (1929-33).

The environs of the birthplace house have been made into a fine park. Near the house, which has been refurnished with period pieces, is a bronze statue presented to Hoover by the Belgians after his superb relief work during the First World War. A short distance beyond is the modern Library and Museum, which houses exhibits and valuable papers relating to Hoover's many-sided activities.

Beyond the park are other locations of interest: the old swimming hole in Wapsinonoc Creek where Hoover swam as a boy by the Burlington railroad bridge; Cooke's Hill, just south of the creek, used by Hoover for sledding; and the Quaker meetinghouse, attended by Hoover's parents, at the corner of Water and Second Streets.

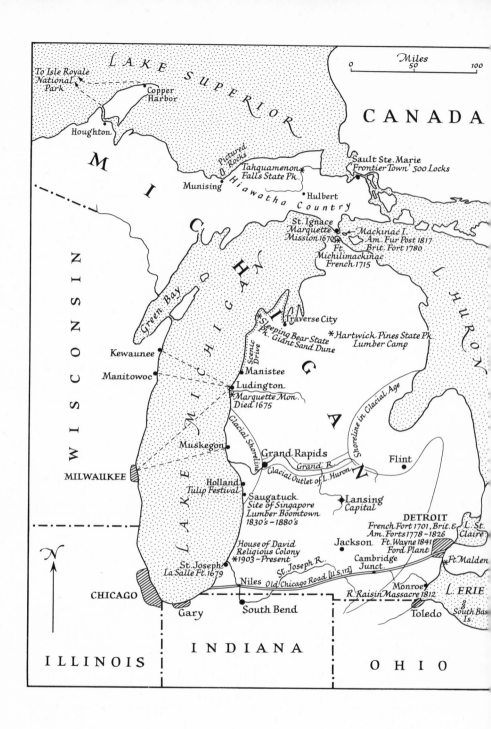

# Michigan

**CAMBRIDGE JUNCTION**   In 1832, Sylvester Walker built a tavern at a point, then deep in the wilderness, where the Sauk Trail, which had for centuries led Indian warriors around the tip of Lake Michigan to the Detroit Straits, split with the La Plaisance Trail, which ran to an old French settlement on the Raisin River (see MONROE). The next year Walker reaped the benefits of his planning, for the Chicago Road (destined to become a great immigrant route to the rich farmlands opening up in northern Illinois, Wisconsin, and Iowa) was constructed directly past his establishment. The Walker tavern still stands beside U.S. 112, which follows the old Road from Detroit to New Buffalo, where the pioneers then drove their conestoga wagons along the beach to Chicago. The interior of the tavern-inn has displays of old guns, wolf traps, pottery, blacksmith tools, furniture, and other relics of the pioneer era.

The hamlet of Cambridge Junction was begun a short time later by English immigrants, who wistfully named their tiny settlement after the famous university town in England. The Episcopal Church, built in 1858 and locally famous for its stained glass windows, is a quarter-mile south of the Walker tavern. Many were the squabbles the Englishmen had with their inveterate antagonists, the Irish, who settled only a few miles to the east (see the IRISH HILLS).

**DETROIT**    Detroit, founded in 1701 by Antoine de la Mothe Cadillac, received its name from its location on the strait which connects Lake Huron with Lake Erie — Ville d'Etroit, or "City of the Strait," the French called it. The site of the French riverside fort is now occupied by the impressive Civic Center, where a series of seven sculptured pylons record Detroit's history. Indians once built a council chamber a block southeast (now the site of the Old Mariner's Church) where the French made treaties and exchanged gifts with them. When the Fox Indians arrived in 1712 expecting the gifts Cadillac had promised them, they were massacred on the location of Detroit's tallest skyscraper, the Penobscot Building at Fort (U.S. 25) and Griswold Streets — a plaque on the Fort Street side recalls the bloody and important event.

After the British drove the French army from the Midwest, they replaced the old French fort with a new, much stronger one on the long ridge that overlooked the river — a location now occupied by the Federal Building on Fort Street, a block southwest of the Penobscot Building. It was from this fort, called Lernoult by the British, that "Hair Buyer" Hamilton set out to drive George Rogers Clark from Vincennes (*Chapter 5*).

The Americans occupied Detroit in 1794, after the victories of "Mad" Anthony Wayne in the valley of the Maumee 60 miles to the south (*Chapter 6*). At the outset of the War of 1812, General Hull ignobly surrendered Fort Shelby, as it had been renamed, to the British and Indians; and it was from here that General Proctor and Tecumseh boarded the ships that would take them to beseige William Henry Harrison at Fort Meigs (*Chapter 7*). A plaque at the entrance to the Federal Building displays a drawing of the fort. Other mementoes of the War of 1812 are on the grounds of the Old City Hall, kitty-corner from the Penobscot Building, where there are two historic cannons: the longer one used to bombard General Hull, the other used by Commodore Perry to help win the Battle of Lake Erie.

During the war scare of the 1840's, when Americans and British were disputing the occupation of Oregon, a massive American fortification, named in honor of Anthony Wayne, was built several miles south of central Detroit on what is now W. Jefferson Avenue 2 blocks east of Livernois Avenue. The 17-foot thick walls were honeycombed with tunnels in which were cannon embrasures and rifle ports. Fort Wayne, now open to the public, clearly demonstrates the frontier aspect of Detroit (*Chapter 1*).

As the years passed, industry came to Detroit. Because it was in the region of inexpensive timber and, at the same time, at the head of a crowded overland route to Chicago, great numbers of carriages and wagons were manufactured here. And when the automobile began to displace the horse-drawn vehicles, Detroit was the logical place to find men skilled at body-making. Henry Ford, a native son, was one of the first of the auto manufacturers — soon to be followed by many others.

Many of the gigantic factories which now make the Detroit area the automotive center of the world are open to the public. General Motors makes provision for visitors at its Cadillac plant at 2860 Clark Street. Plymouth also has tours of what is the longest assembly line in the world — at 6700 Lynch Road.

But most tourists find the Ford River Rouge plant (*Chapter 13*) the most interesting of the industrial factories, because, being an integrated operation, it is here one can witness the entire process of auto-making — from the forging of the steel to the driving off of the completed automobile. Up to 63,000 men are employed at the River Rouge, and there are over 100 miles of railroad track on the grounds. Tours begin at 3000 Schaefer Road near the Industrial Expressway.

The Henry Ford Museum and Greenfield Village, other major attractions, are at Michigan Avenue (U.S. 112) and Southfield Road, a few miles up the River Rouge from the plant. The Museum is a gigantic repository of machinery and equipment relating to the development of the mechanical arts in the United States. There are ancient wooden reapers, row upon row of old autos, early airplanes, and obsolete steam engines. Galleries in the forward portion of the building contain displays of handicraft arts: glassware, furniture, textiles, etc.

Greenfield Village occupies about 200 acres next to the Museum, Curving roadways lead past original buildings (or authentic reproductions) where important mechanical or scientific inventions occurred: the shed in which Henry Ford finished his first car, the shop in which the Wright Brothers put together their first successful airplane, the laboratory in which Edison made important discoveries in the field of electricity. Many of the buildings contain unique exhibits, especially those in which live workmen who demonstrate almost forgotten arts of craftsmanship. Meals are served cafeteria style in the

Clinton Inn, once an important stopping place on the old Chicago Road, now U.S. 112 (see CAMBRIDGE JUNCTION for more on the Chicago Road).

**HARTWICK PINES STATE PARK**   One of the last stands of the virgin timber that once covered most of Michigan and provided the basis for the roaring lumber era (*Chapter 8*) is found in Hartwick Pines State Park. There are also reproductions of portions of a logging camp: a workshop, a kitchen, and a mess hall. The east branch of the Ausable River (from the French, meaning Sandy River) passes through the park. Fishing is allowed in this, one of Michigan's most famous trout streams. Canoes and fishing gear may be obtained in Grayling, a leading recreational area, 7 miles south.

**HOLLAND**   Few of the immigrant groups have managed to keep their Old World customs as well as the inhabitants of Holland, a town founded by Dutch folk in 1847. Probably the most famous of Midwestern ceremonies is the Holland Tulip Festival, held in mid-May each year. At this time descendants of the original pioneers don their ancestral costumes and march down scrubbed streets lined with thousands of multicolored tulips. Tours are marked out for the flood of visitors — to be taken either on foot or by car. A delightful place for a picnic, while touring tulip-beautiful Holland, is Kollen Park, on the banks of Lake Macatawa, which is actually a bay of Lake Michigan. The Netherlands Museum at Central and 12th Street contains interesting displays of Dutch living.

Holland State Park, 7 miles west of town, has an excellent beach on Lake Michigan. The tall sand dunes nearby provide exciting climbing for those interested.

**HOUSE OF DAVID**   The House of David represents one of the last of the Midwestern Utopian experiments that began with the Harmonists in 1814 (*Chapter 9*). It was started by Benjamin Purnell in 1903 when 2,000 idealistic followers gathered in the colony he laid out a few miles east of Lake Michigan (now on Michigan 139 and Britain Street in Benton Harbor), there to await the establishment of God's kingdom on earth.

The Ark, the first building constructed, still stands, as do the two large Victorian residences called Bethlehem and Jerusalem. However, Purnell died in 1926 and there have been so few new followers since then that now less than a hundred members remain. These graying Believers gain most of their income from an amusement park which was built in 1908 and which still attracts rather large crowds. Some of the men run a miniature train that circles the park, their hair, which has never been cut, streaming in the wind. The women cook and serve good vegetarian meals at the park restaurant.

But time is running out for the members of the House of David and when the aging survivors die — as they soon will — an era in Midwestern history will have come to an end.

**IRISH HILLS** In 1848 Irish immigrants, fleeing a terrible potato famine, found a pretty region of blue lakes and green hills about 60 miles west of Detroit. Delighted with its similarity to their beloved Emerald Isle, they settled there, building in 1854 a pleasing little church, dedicated to St. Joseph. Life was happy here for the Irish, especially when they found a colony of Englishmen only a few miles away at Cambridge Junction. Periodic fisticuffs with their neighbors made them feel right at home.

St. Joseph's Church still stands beside U.S. 112, and next to the church is an old cemetery where crumbling stones reveal the names of the original Irish settlers. A mile east of the church are twin observation towers where tourists can gain a wide vista of the Irish Hills, which were formed by a glacial moraine. Just north of the towers is W. J. Hayes State Park, which has a half-mile sandy beach on Wamplers Lake. Boats are for rent and fishing is allowed.

**ISLE ROYALE NATIONAL PARK** Isle Royale is one of the most isolated of all national parks, being accessible only during the summer and only by launch from Houghton or Copper Harbor, Michigan and Grand Portage, Minnesota. The 45-mile-long island was discovered by the French in 1669 and was named in honor of King Louis XIV. The American Fur Company established fisheries at Washington Harbor, Siskiwit Bay and Belle Isle. Copper deposits were mined by the Indians in prehistoric times and by Americans from 1843 to 1899 — ruins of the mines appearing at Siskiwit, Todd Harbor, Washington Harbor and other places. There are over 30 inland lakes, and shore fishing is permitted. In addition, there are many miles of well-marked hiking trails leading to secluded lakes, abandoned mines, and lookout towers. Rock Harbor Lodge and Windigo Inn take tourists from around June 25 to Labor Day.

**LUDINGTON** A large cross opposite the Pere Marquette River from the town of Ludington marks the site where Father Marquette was buried in 1675 (*Chapter 4*). The monument may be reached by a marked road which runs toward Lake Michigan from U.S. 31 4 miles south of Ludington. The site is almost entirely undeveloped, which is fortunate, for it gives an undisturbed, primeval aura about the scene:

the tree-topped dunes stretching southward as far as the eye can see, the lake water breaking soothingly against a beach free from all the debris of civilization, the sinuous, unspoiled dune plants swaying in the slightest breeze — the same vista Marquette must have seen his last day on earth. (In 1677 Marquette's remains were taken to St. Ignace.)

Car ferries make regular, 7-hour runs across Lake Michigan from Ludington. This trip is most pleasant, providing the weather is calm, and though the boats dock at Milwaukee, Manitowoc, or Kewaunee (in Wisconsin), many tourists take a round trip merely to enjoy the exhilaration of the lake cruise.

Ludington State Park, 8½ miles north of town, has facilities for swimming, camping, and hiking.

**MACKINAC ISLAND**    Mackinac (pronounced "Mackinaw") Island became one of the most important locations in the entire Northwest when the British, abandoning the wooden, mainland post they had taken earlier from the French (see MICHILIMACKINAC STATE PARK), built a massive limestone fortification on the more secure island in 1780. Fort Mackinac, the largest eighteenth century fort in the Midwest, is open to visitors who find fascination in the view from the original blockhouses and in the military displays in the old barracks.

American troops occupied Fort Mackinac, according to treaty, in 1796, but were driven out by a surprise attack during the War of 1812 when Canadian militia and Indians fired on them from a height overlooking the fort. The victors built Fort Holmes on the heights to prevent a similar strategy by Americans — a reconstruction of which may be reached by a wooded, quarter-mile trail from Fort Mackinac. There is a good view of much of the island from this, the highest point on Mackinac (325 feet above the Straits, 168 feet above Fort Mackinac).

After the war the island was returned to American rule. John Jacob Astor then established the main headquarters of the powerful American Fur Company (*Chapter 8*) on Mackinac, constructing a long row of warehouses, clerks' quarters, and residences along Market Street. Many of these structures still stand and are among the few authentic Midwestern remains of the fur era.

With the decline of the fur trade after 1830, Mackinac fell into a lethargy which was not broken until the Grand Hotel was constructed in 1887. This huge building became a luxurious refuge for the very rich and socially prominent. It is still excellently maintained and the view of the Straits of Mackinac from its spacious front porch, which is claimed to be the longest in the world, is spectacular.

Mackinac Island is now a favorite vacation place for tourists who enjoy the mile after mile of roadways ideal for hiking, bicycling, or taking the horse-drawn carriages, but over which no cars travel, for they are prohibited on the island. Regular boats leave St. Ignace and Mackinaw City for Mackinac Island, the trip taking about 40 minutes from either town.

**MICHILIMACKINAC STATE PARK** Michilimackinac, which means "Great Turtle" in Indian, was built by the French in 1715. This location, on the southern side of the Straits of Mackinac, offered better control of the waterway than could be secured from old Ft. de Buade at St. Ignace across the water. Michilimackinac State Park, which is immediately north of Mackinaw City, consists of a large wooden palisade built along the original fort wall as revealed by careful excavations. Two bastion towers now look out over the chilly waters of the Strait and the breathtaking span of the famous Mackinac Bridge. The fort was abandoned in 1780 when the British, who had won it from the French, built a new, much stronger fortification on Mackinac Island.

**MONROE** The town of Monroe is on the site of an old village called Frenchtown, built along a river named by the French the River Raisin, or River of Grapes, after the profusion of grapevines which blanketed its banks. The French church, St. Antoine aux Rivière Raisin, was founded in 1788, and St. Mary of the Immaculate Conception at Elm and N. Monroe (U.S. 25) claims to be its immediate successor.

A British detachment occupied Frenchtown at the end of the French and Indian War, but abandoned it after the victory of Anthony Wayne at Fallen Timbers (*Chapter 6*). In 1796 one of Wayne's captains raised the first American flag to fly in Michigan from a blockhouse whose location is now indicated by a plaque on the grounds of St. Mary's church.

During the War of 1812 an American army marching on Detroit was surprised while encamped at Frenchtown, and partly massacred by Indians whom the British were unable to control. News of this massacre shocked the nation and soon "Remember the River Raisin" became a rallying cry that immeasurably aided William Henry Harrison (*Chapter 7*) in recruiting the new army that ultimated defeated Tecumseh and General Proctor. A plaque to the massacre is at the corner of Elm and N. Monroe.

Near the massacre plaque is a large statue of General George Custer, who made his home in Monroe for many years. One of the strange ironies of history found Custer, who had grown up hearing stories about River Raisin, leading his men to a similar massacre on the distant Little Big Horn in 1876.

**MUNISING**    There is no better place to enjoy the setting of Longfellow's *Song of Hiawatha* (*Chapter 3*) than at Munising, whose very name is Chippewa for "the place of the big island" — referring to Grand Island which faces the town and was long a camp of the Chippewa, Hiawatha's tribe. Three-hour boat trips take the visitor along vivid Pictured Rocks, described by Longfellow. Here, in an unspoiled setting of sculptured sandstone cliffs, soft evergreen forests, tumbling waterfalls, and the limitless blue water of Lake Superior one can, momentarily at least, relive the days when the buoyant birchbark canoe and bronzed Chippewa brave rode the waves along the coast of the lake that was Longfellow's Gitche Gumee.

For those without time to make the boat trip, a portion of the 27-mile Pictured Rock formation can be reached by taking Michigan 94 6 miles east from Munising to Federal Forest Highway 41, which then goes 6 miles north to Miner's Falls at the cliff's edge.

**SAINT IGNACE**    St. Ignace, founded as a mission in 1671 by Father Marquette, is the second oldest settlement in Michigan (the oldest being Sault Ste. Marie). Marquette left the mission in 1673 to make his epic journey to the Mississippi with Louis Joliet (*Chapter 4*). Two years later Marquette died amid the lonely dunes near Ludington and in 1677 his remains were removed from the dune to be interred in the mission graveyard. This grave is now marked by an unimposing stone cross at the corner of Marquette and State Streets (U.S. 2).

A plaque in front of the Municipal Building on U.S. 2 indicates the approximate location of Fort de Buade, built a few years later than Marquette's mission. This bastion, which overlooked a portion of the Mackinac Straits, was the main French fort in the Northwest until the founding of Detroit in 1701. The fort and the mission were abandoned in 1706, as a result of a change in French foreign policy, and when the French soldiers returned to the Straits nine years later, they erected a new fort on the more strategically located south shore (see MICHILIMACKINAC STATE PARK).

The best view of the Mackinac Straits is from Straits State Park, which adjoins the town of St. Ignace on the south. Lookout Point views the Mackinac Bridge — whose 5-mile span makes it the second longest suspension bridge in the world — and Mackinac Island in the far distance.

**SAINT JOSEPH**    Certainly anyone interested in the saga of LaSalle should visit St. Joseph, where he erected Fort Miami in November 1679 (*Chapter 4*). Named after a moderately powerful Algonquin tribe, it was to have served him as his supply base between Montreal and the stronghold he intended to establish among the Illini (see FORT CREVE COEUR and STARVED ROCK STATE PARK, Illinois). It was also from Fort Miami that LaSalle set out down the St. Joseph River to discover the mouth of the Mississippi. The fort was on the crest of a long ridge that begins at the St. Joseph River and continues south to overlook the wide beach of Lake Michigan. A park has been built along Lake Bluff Street from which an expansive view may be gained of the lake and the river. The Whitcomb Hotel, directly across the street from the monument which marks the fort site, offers fine lodging, complete with hot sulphur baths.

A good time to visit St. Joseph is during the annual Blossom Festival (in late April or early May) when the surrounding countryside is a mass of pink and white as the fruit trees burst into flower. This portion of Michigan is famous for its peaches, apples, and cherries, neighboring Benton Harbor boasting the world's largest non-citrus fruit market, at 12th and Bond Streets.

**SAUGATUCK** Of all the Midwestern lumber towns, little Saugatuck probably has more of the old time flavor than any other. It is not that the town ballyhoos its lumberjack past, as does, for instance, Bemidji, Minnesota. But there is an undeniable tang in Saugatuck that appeals to almost every visitor.

To the Potawatomi Indians, calm Kalamazoo Lake, formed by an almost land-locked arm of Lake Michigan, was a favorite camping area. The Kalamazoo River, which empties into the lake, was called the "boiling water," referring to its rapids, and the Indian camping ground was named "saugatuck," or the "mouth of the river."

When the lumber era began, it quickly became obvious that the Kalamazoo River was ideal for floating logs from the forest-rich interior. Kalamazoo Lake, too, was perfect for the storage of the logs — free as it was from the storms and rough weather that made Lake Michigan totally unsuitable. Therefore, Saugatuck became a thriving sawmill town. And at this time another mill town was built at the mouth of Lake Kalamazoo, 2 miles northwest of Saugatuck, the rapidly growing settlement being presumptuously named Singapore (after the giant Far Eastern *entrepôt*) by the New York speculators who founded it. Soon the roaring sawmills at Saugatuck and Singapore were furnishing huge quantities of lumber for Chicago and hundreds of towns in northern Illinois and Indiana.

But the boom did not last. and when by the 1890's the lumber from the interior had all been felled, Singapore was deserted; it became one of Michigan's most famous ghost towns — until the shifting sand and scavengers from Saugatuck had completely demolished it. But Saugatuck, taking advantage of its lovely location, bounced back as a tourist center. Now fine lodges and motels abound; paddlewheel pleasure boats take tourists up the river and then down the channel (past the Singapore site) to Lake Michigan; dune schooners offer thrilling rides over the high sand hills; and a summer stock theater presents good plays to enthusiastic audiences.

**SAULT STE. MARIE**　Long before French fur traders named the churning rapids, which connected Lake Superior with Lake Huron, the Sault (or "Falls"), the Chippewa tribe had found the place ideal for spearing whitefish and sturgeon. Father Marquette erected a stockaded mission among the Indians in 1668 — the site of which is indicated by a bronze plaque at the foot of Bingham Avenue. This was the first white settlement in Michigan.

Later, Henry Schoolcraft, American Indian agent at the Sault (pronounced "soo"), wrote his observations of the Chippewa in books that provided Longfellow with the facts around which he wrote his *Song of Hiawatha (Chapter 3)*. The Schoolcraft House, built in 1826, is on the grounds of the Union Carbide Company near the East Portage Avenue bridge.

Almost from the very beginning it was seen that a canal and a lock were necessary if boats were to pass between the two lakes (Lake Superior is 22 feet higher than Lake Huron, making the St. Mary's River, which connects them, a series of wild rapids). Canoe passage was aided by a small canal and lock built in 1797, and larger locks were built in 1855 and 1881. However, the opening of the Vermilion and Mesabi Iron Ranges (*Chapter 13*) so increased the need for large locks to handle the ever increasing length of ore boats, that in 1887 work was begun on the first of the four present locks, named after General Orlando M. Poe, the Army engineer in charge. As traffic increased, another lock was begun, the Davis Lock, which was completed in 1914. Five years later the Sabin Lock was opened and when the Second World War increased the demand for Mesabi iron ore, the last lock, named for General Douglas MacArthur, American commander in the Pacific, was rushed to completion.

At this time Sault Ste. Marie, astride the most important canal in the world (the locks handled more traffic than the Panama and Suez canals combined), was among the most heavily guarded places anywhere: with anti-aircraft guns spotted in every available location, huge captive balloons dangling thick cables to engage possible enemy aircraft, and diligent troops constantly on lookout for sabotage.

The security regulations have since been greatly reduced, and tourists may now view the locks close range from an observation platform beside the MacArthur Lock in Government Park. However, the best way to see the famous "Soo" locks is on the sightseeing boats which make regular 2-hour trips through the locks and across the foot of the now diminished rapids.

**SLEEPING BEAR DUNE**  Sleeping Bear Dune is the most spectacular of the thousands of dunes which make the eastern coast of Lake Michigan a unique and appealing region. These dunes were formed from rocks powdered by the lake waves and deposited here by the prevailing westerly winds. Most of the sand mountains, including Sleeping Bear, are called "living dunes," referring to the fact that they are not stable but constantly rolling eastward, moved by the winds, burying as they go all barriers in their paths, including even trees and houses.

Climbing Sleeping Bear is 10 or 15 minutes of arduous exercise, for the soft sand offers no firm footing. But the view from the top is most rewarding: to the east is Glen Lake lying calm as a pool of jade between its forested shores; to the north is the distant blue of Lake Michigan curling around Pyramid Point; to the west and south is mile after mile of glistening, living dunes, a Sahara of constantly shifting sand, topped here and there by tufts of coarse grass, completely uninhabited.

For those who wish to see more of the dunes, a tour along Michigan 22 is recommended. It runs north from Traverse City for 27 miles along Grand Traverse Bay, then turns abruptly southwest to skirt Sleeping Bear and other dunes for 82 more scenic miles.

D. H. Day State Park on Sleeping Bear Bay, a mile east of the dune, offers an excellent bathing beach.

**TAHQUAMENON FALLS STATE PARK**  Tahquamenon Falls State Park is built around a 200-foot wide, golden-tinted waterfall which, in its 40-foot plunge, is the largest waterfall outside of Niagara east of the Mississippi. The Tahquamenon River was loved by Hiawatha (*Chapter 3*) who "sailed through all its bends and windings, sailed through all its deeps and shallows."

Excursion boats from Hulbert make the round trip to the Falls in about 4½ hours; boats from Soo Junction extend the enjoyable river trip to 7 hours. Michigan 117 from Newberry and Michigan 123 from Eckerman also lead to the park, passing through areas that still contain stands of virgin timber too remote for the axe of the lumberjack.

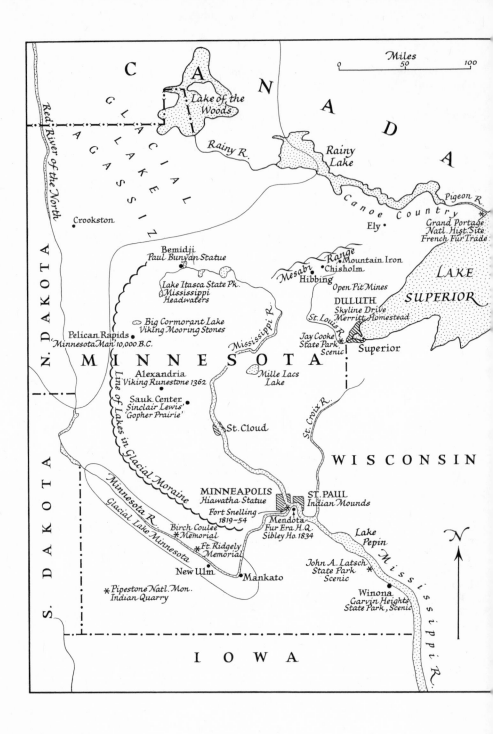

Miles
0    50    100

**C A N A D A**

Red River of the North

Lake of the Woods

GLACIAL LAKE AGASSIZ

Rainy R.

Rainy Lake

Canoe Country

Pigeon R.

Crookston

Ely

Grand Portage
Natl. Hist. Site
French Fur Trade

Bemidji
Paul Bunyan Statue

Mesabi Range

Mountain Iron

Chisholm

Hibbing

Open Pit Mines

LAKE
SUPERIOR

Lake Itasca State Pk.
Mississippi
Headwaters

DULUTH
Skyline Drive
Merritt Homestead

St. Louis R.

Big Cormorant Lake
Viking Mooring Stones

Mississippi R.

Jay Cooke
State Park
Scenic

Pelican Rapids
Minnesota Man 10,000 B.C.

Superior

**N. DAKOTA**

**M I N N E S O T A**

Mille Lacs
Lake

Alexandria
Viking Runestone 1362

Line of Lakes in Glacial Moraine

St. Croix R.

Sauk Center
Sinclair Lewis'
'Gopher Prairie'

St. Cloud

**W I S C O N S I N**

Minnesota R.

Glacial Lake Minnesota

MINNEAPOLIS
Hiawatha Statue

ST. PAUL
Indian Mounds

**S. DAKOTA**

Fort Snelling
1819-54

Birch Coulee
Memorial

Mendota
Fur Era H.Q.
Sibley Ho. 1834

Lake
Pepin

Ft. Ridgely
Memorial

New Ulm

Mankato

John A. Latsch
State Park
Scenic

Mississippi R.

N

Pipestone Natl. Mon.
Indian Quarry

Winona
Carvin Heights
State Park, Scenic

**I O W A**

# Minnesota

**ALEXANDRIA**   One of the greatest mysteries in Midwestern history began in 1898 after a farmer near Kensington, Minnesota, unearthed an oddly carved stone while plowing his fields. The farmer, unable to decipher the inscriptions, gave it to experts who subsequently discovered that the writing was ancient runic. The message was translated, and an astounding story was told:

> We are 8 Goth (Swedes) and 22 Norwegians on an exploration journey from Vinland through the west. We had camp . . . one day's journey north from this stone. We were out and fished one day. After we came home we found 10 men red with blood and dead. A V M Save us from evil.

233

Vikings in Minnesota! The experts could not believe it. But what startled them even more was the date on the stone: 1362 — 130 years before Columbus!

Soon cries of "hoax" were heard. Some scholars objected because there were minor errors in the runic writing; but this was answered by the assertion that no one knew for certain exactly what runic writing of the 1300's was like. Others objected that Kensington was too far inland to be on the route of sea-faring explorers. The believers contended that the interior of Minnesota was still partially flooded at that time by undrained waters of the glacial period and that a direct waterway then existed from Hudson Bay up the Red River and across lands now dry. This view was strengthened by the discovery of so called "mooring stones" (rocks with deep, narrow holes drilled into them) onto which the Vikings supposedly placed iron rings to fasten the lines of their ship. These mooring stones were found beside a series of lakes in northwestern Minnesota and some authorities even went so far as to pinpoint Big Cormorant Lake, where there are several mooring stones, as the site of the massacre described on the runestone.

Although there is no way of being certain of the authenticity of the Kensington runestone, officials at Alexandria (the county seat, 17 miles northeast of the hamlet of Kensington), where the 2½-foot tablet is on display in a museum at 206 Broadway, are convinced that it is absolutely authentic. But whether or not Vikings were actually in Minnesota in 1362, the mysterious runestone has cast an intriguing aura over this portion of the northern lakelands. As one stands before the tablet in the museum or the huge replica erected beside U.S. 52 on Alexandria's eastern outskirt, an unusual vision seems to overtake him — a vision of gliding, dragon-headed ships, of burly, whiskered Norsemen with horned helmets, and of sulking Indians waiting to ambush the strange giants who had invaded their homeland.

**BEMIDJI**    The isolated location of Bemidji made it one of the last places in the Midwest to become a lumber base. Logs were floated down the Mississippi, which here is only a rapid little stream, to the saw mill that was located to the southeast of the present town. (The large cement pylons that once supported the mill are still visible at the municipal beach of Nymore.) Lake Irving, a half-mile upstream, was the assembly place for the logs; and the tracks and roundhouse of the old railroad which carried the wood south can still be seen.

Bemidji has called attention to its lumber past by erecting large colorful statues to Paul Bunyan, his Blue Ox, and his famous rifle beside Lake Bemidji. These statues, while adding to the memory of Bemidji's timber era, are actually anomalies, for the stories of Paul Bunyan were begun long after the lumberjacks left the area.

Lake Bemidji State Park, 6 miles northeast of the town, contains virgin pine forests similar to those felled by the lumberjacks. There are facilities for camping and hiking.

**BIG CORMORANT LAKE** One of the most important sites relating to the Vikings, who possibly explored northern Minnesota around 1362, was Big Cormorant Lake. Here, as related by the famous runestone (see ALEXANDRIA), ten of their thirty members were massacred by Indians, probably Sioux. The mooring lines of the Viking ship were fastened to small holes drilled into the granite rocks which are found beside the lake (a quarter-mile south of the congregation of summer homes around Viking Bay). In the heavy stillness and wooded seclusion of Big Cormorant Lake, it is even now possible to imagine the thoughts of the Norsemen, frightened as they were by the danger of Indians, lonely as they must have been for their homelands which were so far away.

**BIRCH COULEE STATE MEMORIAL PARK** One of the decisive battles fought during the great Sioux uprising of 1862 (see NEW ULM for an account) took place on a grassy plateau overlooking the Minnesota River. When a detachment of soldiers was ambushed by a superior number of Sioux, the Americans quickly killed their horses and, by piling earth over their bodies, made a low barricade which offered them only the barest protection. (The outline of these bone-filled mounds can still be discerned.) Birch Coulee, a ravine that cuts through the valley side immediately east of the mounds, was used by the Indians to conceal their movements. The ferocious battle lasted 24 hours, during which time the surrounded soldiers fought without water, and ended in an American victory when reinforcements from Fort Ridgely arrived.

**CHISHOLM** The famous Mesabi Iron Range (see also HIBBING) borders Chisholm on the north. Many of the buildings and roadways on the town's outskirts are ruddy with the iron ore dust. There is an interesting open air museum at the western entrance to Chisholm on U.S. 169, in which are displayed several ore cars, a steam shovel, ore drills, and other implements of the iron era (*Chapter 13*).

**JAY COOKE STATE PARK** The area around Duluth was once smouldering with active volcanoes — although this was millions of years ago. The volcanic lava, which gushed over much of the land, has been exposed by the St. Louis River, and a scenic, 10-mile drive now takes the tourist through a deep gorge cut into this dusky-colored rock. The roadway, which connects with Duluth's Skyline Drive, is part of the Jay Cooke State Park, named in honor of an eastern financier who helped secure Lincoln's Civil War loans and was an early promoter of the possibilities of Duluth as a major port. At the park center there is a swinging foot bridge which spans the river, picnicking areas, and facilities for fishing and nature study.

**DULUTH**    Duluth occupies one of the most interesting geologic sites in the Midwest. At the end of the Glacial Age (*Chapter 2*) the weight of the huge ice masses, which still covered the land north of Duluth, caused the northern land to sink. This tilted the northern shore of Lake Superior downward. Then, as the ice gradually melted and the land slowly rose, the waves of Lake Superior broke on successively lower portions of the rising bluff. These Glacial Age beach lines still appear as distinct ribbons on the bluffs along the lake. And the land is still rising too! — although only .42 feet per century.

One of the best views of Duluth and its active harbor is from the site of the Merritt homestead (*Chapter 13*), which is now occupied by the Oneota Cemetery on Skyline Drive. From this grassy slope the seven brothers once watched the procession of ore barges making their way to the loading area — sorrowing, perhaps, for the wealth that could have been theirs. The graves of the Merritts are in the cemetery.

The fabulous Skyline Drive, which clings to the side of the Duluth bluff for 25 miles, provides a series of fine panoramas of the ore port and Lake Superior. One of the best lookouts is Enger Tower, from which one can see the coal docks and iron ore loading trestles to the southwest, giant grain elevators directly below, and the twin peninsulas of Minnesota and Wisconsin Point forming the harbor to the northeast. It was on Minnesota Points, now a sandy area of wind-swept cottages and public beaches, that George Stuntz built his trading post in 1852 (*Chapter 13*) — Duluth's first permanent settlement. (Excursion boats leave from the Aerial Bridge, which connects Minnesota Point with the mainland, providing a fine, 1½-hour trip through the harbor.)

The Skyline Drive connects on the southwest with Minnesota 39 and the Jay Cooke State Park, and on the northeast with U.S 61 and the beautiful North Shore Drive, which continues up the shore of Lake Superior 151 miles to Canada.

**FORT RIDGELY STATE MEMORIAL PARK**    Fort Ridgely was one of the main objects of the Sioux during the uprising of 1862 (see NEW ULM for an account). The fort, built in 1853, was the only American post guarding the Sioux Reservation, yet the government had so misjudged the warlike propensities of the Indians that the garrison consisted of only 100 men and 6 rusty, scarcely serviceable cannons.

On August 20th, at one in the morning, the Indians dashed up the gully southwest of the fort. The 250 women and children who had been driven from their farms by the hostilities prayed for their lives as the ancient, unpredictable cannons were aimed. To their great relief the cannons fired, and, after 2½ days of hard fighting, the Sioux left to attack what they regarded as an easier target, the community of New Ulm 20 miles east.

One of the old cannons still stands in the midst of the lush meadow that was once the fort parade ground, pointing toward the southwest ravine. The wide valley of the Minnesota River sweeps by immediately south. One of the fort buildings has been reconstructed and contains an interesting museum. The park also has foot trails, a picnic area, and a nine-hole golf course.

**FORT SNELLING**   Fort Snelling, named after its able commander, Josiah Snelling, was begun in 1819, at a time when the surrounding area was inhabited only by marauding Indians and wild animals. Snelling, who had served under General Hull at the disgraceful surrender of Detroit during the War of 1812 (*Chapter 7*), was determined to make his new fort absolutely impregnable. He therefore not only built it on the apex of a steep bluff that overhung the junction of the Mississippi and Minnesota Rivers, but constructed its walls and four imposing bastion towers of solid stone, not timber as had been the custom. So capably did Snelling build his fort that no enemy ever dared attack, and it was peacefully abandoned in 1854 when the frontier had moved west.

A visit to Fort Snelling, now used by the Veterans Administration, is very much worthwhile. The well-known Round Tower, called "the most venerated symbol of Minnesota's early history," is open to the public. Nearby is the Hexagonal Tower, which guarded the fort gateway and sprouted from the uppermost of its three stories the snouts of 12-pound cannons, Fort Snelling's heaviest armament. Still standing, too, are the Officers' Quarters (used by the VA) and the commander's residence, which is in as good repair as the day Colonel Snelling left it. Excavations show the outlines of most of the other eleven buildings of the fort.

**ITASCA STATE PARK**   Itasca State Park, centered around Lake Itasca, the source of the Mississippi, gives a tourist the unusual opportunity of stepping across the tiny river as it emerges newly born from the cool, northern lake. A sign beside the creek-river reads: "Here 1475 feet above the ocean the mighty Mississippi begins its flow on its winding way 2552 miles to the Gulf of Mexico."

The source of the Mississippi was important historically, for when the British turned the Midwest over to the United States at the conclusion of the Revolutionary War, the source was made one of the northern boundary points between the two countries. However, the exact location of the headwaters remained a mystery until 1832 when Henry Schoolcraft, Indian Agent from Sault Ste. Marie, Michigan, finally discovered it. Schoolcraft named the lake "Itasca," by combining the Latin words "veritas" (true) with "caput" (head).

Itasca State Park offers fine camping facilities along the many small lakes that abound within its borders. Fishing, swimming, and hiking are the main recreations, but for those with less time there is a 15-mile dirt road which leads through birch and pine forests and past lovely hidden lakes where wild animals abound. There is also a lodge for those who desire less primitive accommodations than camping.

**HIBBING**    Hibbing, located in the western portion of the Mesabi Iron Range (*Chapter 13*), is the unofficial capital of the region. During the halcyon iron days, the town was known far and wide for its notorious houses of entertainment. However, when in 1922 it was discovered that this metropolis of 15,000 was itself located on a rich vein of ore, the entire town was torn down and the modern one of bright, friendly homes was built a half-mile south.

**LAKE AGASSIZ**    The bed of glacial Lake Agassiz, once a body of water larger than all of the Great Lakes combined (*Chapter 2*), is one of the most fertile of Midwestern farmlands. The traveler going north on U.S. 75 from Crookstone will find himself in an extremely flat region very much different from the morainic hills to the east. This is the bottom of the gigantic lake that existed for only 1,000 years, between the receding of the glacier which covered it and the melting of the ice which blocked the natural outlet at Hudson Bay. The beaches of the lake are clearly indicated by low, sandy ridges that parallel the highway on the east.

Oddly enough, the lake bed is now so completely dry that farmers must haul water from the Red River — not even trees will grow unless they are artificially watered!

**JOHN A. LATSCH STATE PARK**    U.S. 61, as it ascends the Mississippi Valley between La Crosse, Wisconsin, and Red Wing, Minnesota, is often acclaimed one of America's most scenic highways. The gorge of the Mississippi, carved by meltwater torrents during the Glacial Age (*Chapter 2*), is marvelous to see during the entire 93-mile trip;

but the view is even more enhanced from several panoramic lookout points. John A. Latsch State Park is one of these.

The Park is situated on the top of three limestone bluffs, named Faith, Hope, and Charity, which were long-time landmarks to canoeing Indians and rafting lumbermen. There is a wide view of the valley and of the Whitman Dam below. Hiking trails lead along the bluff, and camping and picnic sites are available.

**MANKATO**   Mankato is the location of the greatest mass execution in American history. Thirty-eight Sioux warriors, who had partaken in the uprising which had thrown the entire state into an uproar (see NEW ULM) and had ultimately resulted in the deaths of 640 white settlers, were hung on specially constructed gallows on December 26, 1862. The military tribunal at Fort Snelling had originally sentenced 303 Indians to death, but President Lincoln, personally reviewing the case, excused all but the 38. An inconspicuous stone marker just north of the corner of N. Front and E. Main (U.S. 14) indicates the hanging site.

**MENDOTA**   The village of Mendota. on the southern outskirts of Minneapolis-St. Paul, is older than either of its larger neighbors. Situated at the confluence of the Mississippi and Minnesota Rivers, it was long an important meeting place between the Sioux and Chippewa tribes and the fur traders. In 1834 Henry Hastings Sibley, later governor and commonly acknowledged the "father of his state," came to Mendota as the agent of the American Fur Company (*Chapter 8*). He built a substantial stone house here, which was the first private residence in the entire state. The home has been restored and is open to the public.

**MINNEAPOLIS**   Minneapolis, Minnesota's largest city. was built around St. Anthony's Falls, then and still today the head of navigation on the Mississippi. At first saw mills, then grain mills, located close to the river where the churning water provided cheap power. The once wild Falls have now been "civilized" by a series of breakwaters, but the huge grain mills remain, producing a significant portion of the city's wealth. The view of the river and its numerous breakwaters is best seen from the campus of the University of Minnesota on the eastern bank of the river.

Minnehaha State Park, on the southern bluffs above the Mississippi, is built around Minnehaha Falls. Although the Falls are now ofttimes dry. in Indian days it was a pretty place where lived, according to legend, the beautiful Minnehaha, daughter of a Sioux arrow-maker and later wife of Hiawatha (*Chapter 3*). A fine statue shows Hiawatha holding the girl in his arms as, in the words of Longfellow:

"Over wide and rushing river
In his arms he bore the maiden."

Minnehaha Parkway, a tree-lined road running beside the long, graceful gully carved by Minnehaha Creek, connects the park with Lake Nokomis (named after Hiawatha's moon-goddess grandmother) and several of the other numerous lakes which nestle in glacial hollows on the city's western edge.

**MOUNTAIN IRON**    The first mine to be opened in the fabulous Mesabi Iron Range was at Mountain Iron (*Chapter 13*), the exact site being three-quarters of a mile north of a plaque in front of the high school on U.S. 169. There is a statue of Leonidas Merritt, "Number One of the Seven Iron Men: 1844-1926," on the library grounds. The locomotive which carried the first load of ore down the Duluth, Missabe, & Northern Railroad in 1892 can be seen in a small park beside U.S. 169. There is something quite appealing about this town, the birthplace of one of the most important industrial events in American history.

**NEW ULM**    During the summer of 1862, the small German community of New Ulm was very nearly the site of the greatest Indian massacre in American history. At this time, about 350 white men were called upon to defend over 1000 women, children, and wounded men from an attack by more than 650 war-crazed Sioux. Charles Eugene Flandrau, judge in the State Supreme Court and leader of the white force, later wrote that if the Indians had boldly charged into the town at the beginning of the fight, they would have won the day.

The Sioux uprising began early in the summer, when the promised government allotment of food did not arrive on schedule, forcing the starving Indians to begin eating their horses and dogs. On August 17, a small band of Indian hunters massacred a farm family. When Captain John S. Marsh, commander of the army garrison at nearby Fort Ridgely, set out to punish the Indians, he and his 46 men were ambushed by 200 Sioux, and Marsh and 25 men were killed (a marker on Minnesota 19, 3 miles below Morton. indicates the site). On August 20 the Indians, led by Chief Little Crow, fell upon Fort Ridgely itself where, after sharp fighting, they saw the futility of attacking against cannons and turned upon the exposed community of New Ulm.

The people at New Ulm, hearing the firing at Fort Ridgely, had in the meantime frantically prepared for the anticipated attack. By boarding up the buildings along 3 blocks of Minnesota Street between Center and Third North Streets and by destroying all the surrounding buildings they had turned the village into a somewhat effective fort. The attack lasted two days, and although the issue was sometimes in doubt, Little Crow was at last forced to admit that he could not penetrate the town's makeshift defense. The Indians then contented themselves with ravaging the outlying farms.

However, forces were being gathered in the north, and, after the Indians were demoralized by a battle at Birch Coulee, it was only a matter of time until they were brought to justice. At the trial at Fort Snelling 303 Sioux were sentenced to death and, after President Lincoln's intercession, 38 were finally hanged at Mankato.

A monument in front of the Court House is dedicated to the first settlers of 1854 and the heroes of 1862. On the parkway to the north is a column to Flandrau, on the sides of which is a brief history of New Ulm and the Sioux war.

Probably the best view of New Ulm and the picturesque Minnesota Valley in which it is located is from the top of the Sons of Herrmann monument immediately west of the town. This monument was given to the townsfolk in 1897 by Kaiser Wilhelm, German Emperor. The huge statue, 102 feet in total height and the largest bronze statue in the United States, was intended to solidify the bonds which tied the German immigrants to the old country, yet, the Sons of Herrmann clubs which once were so strong in the upper Midwest have all but died out, leaving the towering Germanic figure alone, like a forgotten god in a strange land.

Flandrau State Park, just south of New Ulm, is on the bank of a large, artificial lake which gives a pleasant setting for canoeing, swimming (with a good sand beach), fishing, and picnicking.

**THE NORTH SHORE DRIVE**   U.S. 61, as it proceeds northeast along the shore of Lake Superior from Duluth to the Canadian border, is known as the North Shore Drive. These 151 miles were replanted and beautified by the Civilian Conservation Corps during the 1930's (after they had been left an ugly area of rotting tree stumps by the lumber companies) so that now the highway travels through a land of fragrant, second growth pine, cascading rivers, and towering bluffs — all made more beautiful by the boundless blue backdrop of Lake Superior. Dozens of parks and scenic turnouts add to the pleasure of the trip. Gooseberry Falls, Split Rock, and Temperance River are among the most frequented of the state parks.

Grand Portage National Historical Monument, on a spur near the northern end of the Drive, consists of a replica of an important old fur post which supplied food and gear to the trappers who took their canoes up the Pigeon River into the Rainy Lakes country — still some of the best canoe country in the nation.

**PELICAN RAPIDS**    The oldest skeleton ever found in the Midwest was that of an Indian girl who died at the bottom of a glacial lake near the town of Pelican Rapids about 10,000 B.C. One can only imagine the terrifying circumstances that must have surrounded the watery death (*Chapter* 3). A marker beside U.S. 59, 2 miles north of Pelican Rapids, designates the location where a road building crew unearthed her skeleton — which, in the strange terminology of anthropologists, has been named "Minnesota Man."

**PIPESTONE NATIONAL MONUMENT**    During Indian days no place in North America was held in such reverence as the sacred Pipestone quarry of southwestern Minnesota. Indians from dozens of tribes often gathered here to fashion the soft stone into the bowls of the peace pipes which were the universal symbol of friendship and goodwill. Bowls from the Pipestone quarry were greatly prized and traded from tribe to tribe across the entire continent. Longfellow used this location as the setting for his opening verses of *Hiawatha* (*Chapter* 3), basing his descriptions on the authentic reports of Henry School-craft (see SAULT STE. MARIE. Michigan).

The low, pinkish bluff along which the stone was taken has been incorporated into a half-mile walk, which includes a secluded waterfall and pits where the Indians still fashion the ruddy stone into ceremonial peacepipes. The modern museum not only has many elaborately carved pipestones for sale, but contains good displays and historical descriptions relating to the quarry.

**SAINT PAUL**    Although Minneapolis and St. Paul are known today as the Twin Cities, they began separately and very differently. Minneapolis was a milling town centered at the Falls of St. Anthony. St. Paul, on the other hand, was primarily a commercial settlement, built immediately below the junction of the Mississippi and Minnesota River to take advantage of the trade from both routes. The first inhabitants of St. Paul were somewhat disreputable French-Canadian fur traders who located around Fort Snelling almost as soon as the fort was built in 1819. Colonel Snelling eventually became so put out with the practices of the Canadians that he ran them off the government ground. One Pierre "Pig's Eye" Parrant moved slightly down the river to set up a shanty where he sold liquor to the Indians. This was in 1837. Thus did Parrant become the first inhabitant of the settlement called Pig's Eye — later St. Paul.

The real founding, however, came in 1841, when Father Lucian

Galtier built a much needed chapel, which was dedicated to St. Paul. The location of this log building is indicated by a boulder on Kellogg Boulevard at the bluff end of Minnesota Street, overlooking the Mississippi and the southern shore where Parrant's liquor shack once stood. The First National Bank, one of the city's tallest skyscrapers, is a block north — its observation deck, open during the summer months, presents a grand vista.

Another good view of St. Paul, the arc of the Misissippi and the thick sandstone ledge upon which the city is built can be gained from Indian Mounds Park. Plaques in the park, which is on the east side of the city, point out the burial mounds of Sioux chieftains and describe the conditions under which the Mississippi carved out the deep gorge some 12,000 years ago.

St. Paul is the capital of Minnesota, but that honor did not come easily. When the fight with Minneapolis became deadlocked, St. Paul was made the capital, but her sister city was given the state university. The capitol building is on University Avenue between Wabash and Cedar Streets.

**SAUK CENTRE**    Sauk Centre was the home of Sinclair Lewis, whose devastating portrayal of it in his book, *Main Street*, brought it an unasked for renown which almost half a century has not completely erased. Lewis, who published *Main Street* in 1920, was probably influenced by Sherwood Anderson's *Winesburg, Ohio* (*Chapter 12*), although Lewis was more concerned with the town itself (its drab life, meaningless social clubs, exaltation of mediocrity) than the psychological quirks of its inhabitants, as was Anderson.

Sauk Centre is filled with scenes from *Main Street*. There is the colorless railroad station where the heroine, Carol Kennicott, got off the train to begin her unhappy life as the wife of the local doctor. There is the Palmer Hotel at Main and Sinclair Lewis Avenue which bears a striking resemblance to the Minniemashie House — site of a heart-rending scene between Carol and her only real friend. the rejected schoolteacher, Fern Mullins. There are the buildings along Main Street, so acidly described by Lewis, complete with the modern version of the old Rosebud Movie Palace where the inhabitants of Lewis' Gopher Prairie could gain intellectual stimulation by seeing pictures like "Fatty in Love." And there is the house where Lewis himself lived at 812 West Third (now Sinclair Lewis Avenue) which is surely the fictional home where Carol Kennicott spent many years trying not to become submerged in the spiteful purposelessness of village life.

Lewis knew well the town of which he wrote. His own father was a doctor, just as was the fictional Dr. Kennicott, and occupied an office above the corner drugstore down the street from his home. The high school Lewis attended is on Oak Street behind the Public Library, although the old building has been replaced. The Library, often used by Lewis, has a small display concerning the author, which includes the urn in which his ashes were carried from Italy. Lewis' remains lie in the town cemetery.

**WINONA**    Winona, named after the goddess mother of Hiawatha, was once a favorite spot for the Sioux and is now enjoyed by the thousands of tourists who travel the 93-mile portion of the Mississippi canyon between Red Wing and La Crosse, which is called the Hiawatha Valley. Modern visitors are impressed by the oddly shaped limestone dome called the Sugar Loaf, to the top of which a footpath leads. Almost as good a view is gained from Garvin Heights State Park, accessible by roadway. For those who wish to ride on the Mississippi, there is a small paddlewheel boat offering regular trips.

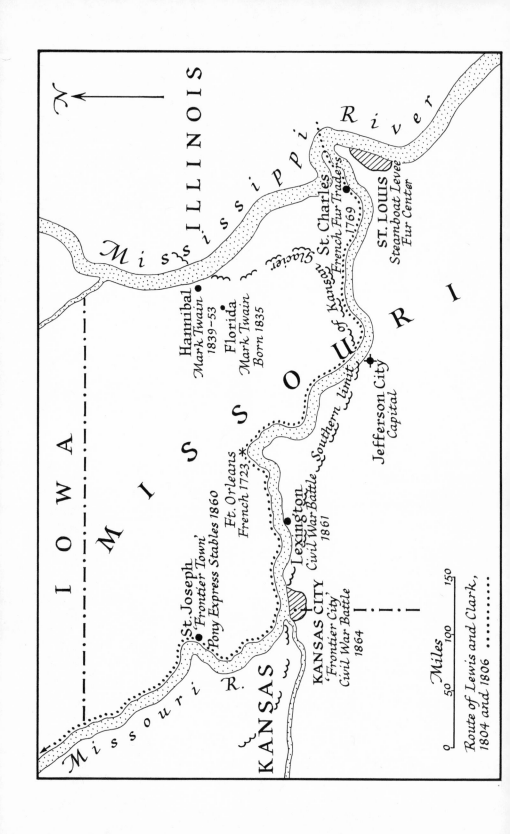

**IOWA**

**ILLINOIS**

*Mississippi River*

*Mississippi*

**MISSOURI**

*Missouri R.*

*Glacier*

Hannibal
*Mark Twain
1839–53*

Florida
*Mark Twain
Born 1835*

St. Charles
*French Fur Traders*
.1769

ST. LOUIS
*Steamboat Levee
Fur Center*

of Kansas

*Southern limit*

Jefferson City
*Capital*

Ft. Orleans
*French 1723* ✳

St. Joseph
*'Frontier Town',
Pony Express Stables 1860*

Lexington
*Civil War Battle
1861*

KANSAS CITY
*'Frontier City',
Civil War Battle
1864*

**KANSAS**

*Miles*

0    50    100    150

Route of Lewis and Clark,
1804 and 1806 ............

# Missouri

FLORIDA
FORT ORLEANS
HANNIBAL
KANSAS CITY

LEXINGTON
ST. CHARLES
ST. JOSEPH
ST. LOUIS

**FLORIDA**  Activity in the hamlet of Florida centers mainly around the Mark Twain Birthplace Memorial Shrine, a surprisingly modern, $300,000 building, which incongruously contains as its central attraction the dilapidated shanty in which the famous author was born November 30, 1835. This house originally stood on the east side of Mill Street between Walnut and Main, and was lived in by Twain for only the first six months of his life. Twain's memories of Florida actually concentrated on the farmhouse of his Uncle John Quarles, in which he spent the first four years of his life and to which he returned each summer until he was twelve or thirteen. It is said that nothing remains of the farmhouse (which stood beside Missouri 107 about 3 miles

247

north of Florida) except a few foundation stones, a concrete storm cellar, and two rock cisterns.

When Mark Twain's father arrived in Florida in 1835, he opened a general store, which is thought to have been on the south side of Main Street between Front and Water. But the boom for which John Clemens had hoped never came, and a few years later the dour man led his family 39 miles east to Hannibal.

In Mark Twain State Park, encompassing the area around the Memorial Shrine, there are housekeeping cabins for those lucky enough to secure advance reservations. The trails which wind along the bluffs overlooking Salt Creek offer grand views of the forested gorge and rugged hills. The vista from Buzzard's Roost, a rocky promontory that juts out over the creek, is especially appealing.

**FORT ORLEANS**    The marker which indicates the site of Fort Orleans (*Chapter 4*) is on the U.S. 24, 5 miles west of Brunswick. The location has been turned into a small roadside park. Once the Missouri passed close by, but the river has since changed course and a railroad embankment now prevents the visitor from viewing the distant water. Nevertheless the site is important, for it was the first European post in the Missouri Valley and represented a daring effort on the part of the French to counterbalance Spanish expansion from the southwest.

The fort was built in 1723, and was staffed by forty men who undoubtedly felt themselves to be in one of the most remote places on the face of the earth — which indeed they were. The French remained here only a few years, but when they abandoned the fort they took with them a pretty Indian girl, called by them the Princess of the Missouri. She accompanied the Frenchmen to France, was baptized in Paris, and eventually married a French army man.

**HANNIBAL**    When Mark Twain, a puny, redheaded lad of four-and-a-half arrived in Hannibal in 1839, the town was a small but active river port with about sixty families. The Clemenses settled in the Virginia Hotel, a rickety building once located at the northwest corner of Hill and Main. John Clemens opened a general store on the first floor, but was no more successful than he had been in Florida.

Hard times forced Mark's father to give up the little hotel which he had unwisely purchased, and from 1842 to 1844 the family made their residence in several other locations, none of which are known. However, in 1844 a brief flurry of prosperity enabled John to build a small frame house at 208 Hill. Mark Twain lived here (except for two years when the family moved across the street to the building now known as the House of the Pilasters) until he left Hannibal at the age of eighteen. This building has become known as the Boyhood

Home and is Hannibal's chief tourist attraction. Much of *The Adventures of Tom Sawyer* takes place in a house obviously based on this. Outside is a reconstruction of what must be the most famous fence in the Midwest — the one Tom Sawyer whitewashed. A museum adjoining the Boyhood Home contains many personal items of the author, including the cherry desk upon which he composed *Tom Sawyer.*

As a small boy, Mark Twain attended a little log school at the southern end of Main Street. It was here that he met the boys that would later become part of the fictionalized Tom Sawyer gang. Here, too, he met his childhood sweetheart, Laura Hawkins — the Becky Thatcher of his writings. Blond, blue-eyed, and winsome, Laura lived across the street from the Clemenses, and her home, known as the Becky Thatcher House, is also open to the public. On the second floor is the small bedroom in which Laura slept. It is furnished so convincingly in period pieces that one would almost expect a little girl in clothing of the 1840's to be sitting on the bed watching for Sam Clemens to come bolting out the door of his house opposite her window.

During the early 1840's John Clemens became Justice of the Peace and rented the first floor of a building on Bird Street near Main. This building has been moved to a location beside the Becky Thatcher House. When Mark was a lad of only thirteen, he came across a corpse on the law office floor. One of his favorite stories later concerned how he turned in fright and dove through the window — glass and all.

Mark's best friend was Tom Blankenship, son of the town drunkard. With little parental guidance or restrictions, Tom was free to roam as he pleased, and so became Mark's ideal — and the prototype of Huckleberry Finn. An alley ran in back of the Clemenses' home to the shanty in which the Blankenships lived a half block away on North Street. This "Huckleberry Finn Home" has long since disappeared, but its site is indicated by a plaque.

Immediately north of the Boyhood Home is Holliday's Hill, the Cardiff Hill upon which lived the Widow Douglas, who was in so much danger in *The Adventures of Tom Sawyer*. The short climb to the top presents a rewarding view of the town.

No one should fail to visit the Mark Twain Cave, reached by following Main Street south to River Road (Route A) and then a mile further south on River Road to the sign indicating the cave entrance. Half-hour guided tours are available and are highly recommended. As the visitor walks through the narrow passageways, his thoughts are certain to turn back to that chilling section of *Tom Sawyer* where Tom and Becky are lost for three days in the labyrinth with Injun Joe, a ruthless killer, somewhere nearby. The terror became even greater when their only candle began to sputter, and they saw "the feeble flame rise and fall, climb the thin column of smoke, linger at its top a moment, and then — the horror of utter darkness reigned!" Mark wrote the incident from a personal recollection, for he himself was lost in the cave with Laura Hawkins — although only for a few hours, not days.

But after the houses and hills and caves have been visited, the majestic Mississippi still remains the life-blood of both Hannibal and of Mark Twain. One should certainly not fail to go to the municipal wharf at the foot of Broadway — the town center during the heyday of the steamboat. A portion of the old brick levee recalls the days when "a Negro drayman... lifts up the cry, 'S-t-e-a-m-boat...' and all in a twinkling the dead town is alive and moving. Drays, carts, men, boys, all go hurrying from many quarters to the common center, the wharf."

One can sip the past as he takes a boat ride from Nipper Park, immediately south of the levee. Much of the river bank is still as wild and uninhabited as in the days when Mark Twain guided the trim steamboats down to New Orleans. The river, too, seethes and foams, just as when Huckleberry Finn and Jim, the fleeing Negro slave, began their adventuresome flatboat journey. And Jackson's Island can still be seen just south of Hannibal, clothed in a tangle of trees and driftwood, just as it was when Tom Sawyer's pirates made it their headquarters.

For a final view of the Mississippi, go to Riverview Park, a mile or two north of Hannibal. Here, amid 250 acres of beautifully landscaped grounds, one can gaze down on the Mississippi, and can even see the spires of Quincy, Illinois, over 20 miles away. The river will be bluish or olive colored, as the light of day commands; the foliage along its fretted shore will be verdant or golden or winter-brown, as the season dictates; but the Mississippi will always be the titan that it is: massive, overpowering, and rich with stories of the past.

**KANSAS CITY** The name "kansas" is an Indian word meaning "smoky wind" and refers to the prairie fire haze that often drifts over the land from the great grasslands to the west. Although Lewis and Clark camped on the site of Kansas City during their trip to the Pacific in 1804, the first permanent settlement was not begun until 1821 when St. Louis traders constructed a post to be used as a collection point for furs gathered in the west. As the steamboats began using the river after 1832, the old fur post and camping ground became a thriving levee, with Grand Street leading up the bluff to the new stores and homes that were being built there.

Kansas City, as a Midwestern "frontier town," is able to draw its wealth not only from the corn belt of Iowa, but from the cattle country to the west and the cotton and oil fields to the south. The best place to gain a good visual picture of the strategic location of Kansas

City on the edge of the western plains is either from Lookout Point, high on the clifftop at the end of West Tenth and Summit Streets, or from the observation deck on the 217-foot Liberty Memorial Tower on Main Street. From these places one can look far off into the hazy western distance, imagining the almost endless troops of pioneers, traders, soldiers, and Indian warriors who once made their way along the sinuous Kansas River. The river route is still used by the western railroad lines to bring long train loads of cattle to the vast pens which are at the base of Lookout Point.

The importance of Kansas City to the South is best indicated by the fact that it was the only major Midwestern city attacked by Confederate forces during the Civil War. The Battle of Westport was fought from October 22 to 24, 1864, and the victory of the Union forces virtually took Missouri out of the war. A monument to the battle is on Meyer Boulevard at 63rd Street. Much of the fighting occurred in Swope Park, a rugged, forested area now one of the city's favorite places for recreation.

**LEXINGTON**   Missouri, as the only Midwestern state to permit slavery, was the scene of many battles between Confederate and Union forces during the Civil War. A state park has been set aside at the location of the Battle of Lexington, won by the Confederates September 20. 1861. The outline of the Union trenches is still visible. and the old Anderson House, which was used as a hospital during the fighting, has been restored and is open to the public. The Courthouse likewise survived the battle. In the east column of this pleasing Greek Revival structure (which is the oldest courthouse still in use in the state) is a small cannonball fired during the battle. Lexington boasts many beautiful ante-bellum houses, especially along Dover Road — U.S. 24. As a town established in 1819 on a ferry route across the Missouri, Lexington's history dates back to the early days of western river travel.

**ST. CHARLES**   St. Charles is one of Missouri's oldest towns, having been settled in 1769 by French-Canadian fur men. Lewis and Clark made it their last stop before stepping off into the wilderness in 1804. As the Missouri River opened to the fur trade, St. Charles became one of the most important of the riverports — rivaling even St. Louis. Main Street, which borders the flatlands leading to the Missouri River, is still lined with scores of buildings dating back to those days, many with plaques giving their date of construction and a brief description of their history.

Between 1821 and 1826, St. Charles was the state capital. The modest, 2-story brick building used as the seat of government is on Main just west of Madison. Although the importance of St. Charles may have been largely forgotten, the past still lingers there amid the aged buildings along Main Street.

**ST. JOSEPH**   The rolling, glaciated land that makes up the Midwest ends at the pancake-flat Great Plains just beyond the Missouri River. For many years the Great Plains were seen, not as the rich wheatfields which they eventually became, but merely as an undesirable, Indian-infested barrier restricting communication with the developing California settlements. In order to bridge this wasteland, a mail express was established with St. Joseph, located on the Midwestern frontier, as its base.

Daring riders of the Pony Express, as the organization was called, would leave the stables at 912 South Penn Street, dash up Eighth Street, pick up the mail at the Olive Street railroad station, and then load their horses on the ferry at the foot of Jules Street. After they reached the western shore of the Missouri, they would gallop to the first of the 190 relay stations that were spaced about ten miles apart all the way to California, and after obtaining a fresh horse, they would continue west at breakneck speed. Ten days later the mail would arrive in Sacramento, 1975 miles away. It was truly a remarkable achievement.

There are a few buildings remaining in St. Joseph which were used by the Pony Express. The stables still stand and have become a museum. Patee Park, directly opposite the stables, was the location from which the very first Pony Express left on April 3, 1860. The Express riders and the many distinguished guests who came to St. Joseph inevitably stayed in the luxurious Patee House, which now is in use as a factory at Penn and 12th Streets, 3 blocks east of the stables. At one time the Patee House was the second largest hotel in the nation.

**ST. LOUIS**   Ever since 1935 St. Louis has been in the throes of clearing nearly 40 city blocks along the riverfront for conversion into the Jefferson National Expansion Memorial, which will commemorate the purchase of the Louisiana Territory by President Jefferson in 1803. This area comprises the original village of St. Louis as founded by Pierre Laclede Liguest and Auguste Chouteau in 1784. This area, the heart of the city during the fur and steamboat eras, was swept by a disastrous fire in 1849, which consumed almost all the French homes so vividly described by Charles Dickens (*Chapter 8*). Then, when the Eads Bridge was erected in 1874, the center of the city moved westward, leaving the waterfront a backward section of drab warehouses and saloons. The Memorial, scheduled for completion by 1966, will replace these buildings, which have already been torn down, with a beautifully landscaped plaza, a museum of early St. Louis history, and a gigantic, stainless steel arch which will be taller than the Washington Monument and will contain at its top an observatory capable of accommodating over 200 persons.

On the grounds of the Memorial will be the two buildings that escaped the fire of 1849. The larger of these is the Old Cathedral, built in 1831 on land originally set aside by Laclede. This church is still in use by its Roman Catholic parish. The other building, the Lisa Warehouse, or Old Rock House, goes back to 1818 when it was a riverfront storage place for Manuel Lisa, one of the foremost fur traders of that day. Though currently dismantled, the Lisa Warehouse will eventually be reconstructed on or near its original site.

William Clark had two homes within the Memorial area. The first of these was at the corner of Pine and First (then called Main). Clark later moved to a second home on the northwest corner of First and Vine — which would put the home at the northern base of the great arch. It was to this house that young Kennerly came to see the famous Council Room filled with Clark's Indian relics (*Chapter 8*). Auguste Chouteau, one of the city's founders, lived 2 blocks south of Clark at the corner of First and Market Streets — or near the southern base of the arch.

The headquarters of the National Park Service is in the Old Courthouse, which borders the Memorial at Fourth Street between Market and Chestnut. The Courthouse, begun in 1839, was for many years a focal point in the civic and political affairs of the town. It is an excellent example of the Italianate style of architecture that captivated the designers of many public buildings during the nineteenth century. For those who think a building must be new to be beautiful, let him stand beneath the artistic dome and view the tier after tier of murals painted on each projecting dome drum.

The site of the home of William Kennerly's French grandparents was just south of the Memorial area, occupying the block bounded by Second, Third, Lombard, and Gratiot Streets. Here, in a location now filled with dingy warehouses, was a charming Old World garden of herbs and flowers brought from France and raised with loving care. The Kennerly home, Persimmon Hill, was 5 miles northwest of the waterfront at the streets now called Taylor and Kennerly, currently an area of lower income residences.

About a mile north of Persimmon Hill is Bellefontaine Cemetery, named for the "beautiful fountain" which spouted here. William Clark is buried at the bend in Meadow Avenue. On the extreme northern end of the city is Chain of Rocks Park, which offers a good view of the Mississippi from its lofty bluff.

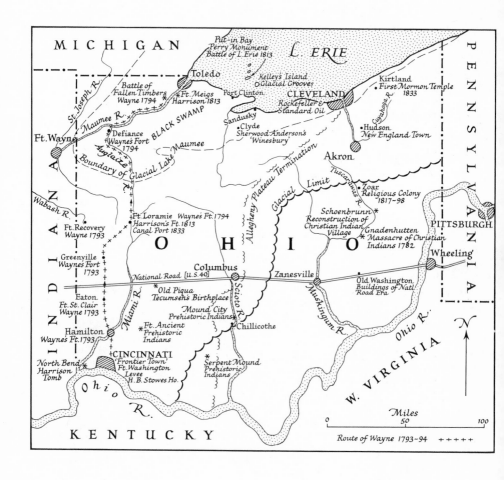

MICHIGAN

PENNSYLVANIA

*L. ERIE*

Put-in Bay
Perry Monument
Battle of L. Erie 1813

Toledo

Kelleys Island
Glacial Grooves

Kirtland
First Mormon Temple
1833

Battle of
Fallen Timbers
Wayne 1794

*St. Joseph R.*

Port Clinton

Ft. Meigs
Harrison 1813

CLEVELAND

Rockefeller &
Standard Oil

*Cuyahoga R.*

*Maumee R.*

BLACK SWAMP

Sandusky

Clyde
Sherwood Anderson's
'Winesbury'

Hudson
New England Town

Ft. Wayne

Defiance
Waynes Fort
1794

*Maumee*

*Auglaize R.*

Boundary of Glacial Lake

Akron

Allegheny Plateau Termination

Glacial Limit

*Tuscarawas R.*

Zoar
Religious Colony
1817-98

*Wabash R.*

Ft. Recovery
Wayne 1793

Ft. Loramie  Waynes Ft. 1794
Harrison's Ft. 1813
Canal Port 1833

OHIO

Schoenbrunn
Reconstruction of
Christian Indian
Village

Gnadenhutten
Massacre of Christian
Indians 1782

PITTSBURGH

Greenville
Waynes Fort
1793

Wheeling

Columbus

Zanesville

Old Washington
Buildings of Natl.
Road Era

National Road [U.S.40]

Eaton
Ft. St. Clair
Wayne 1793

Old Piqua
Tecumseh's Birthplace

*Miami R.*

*Scioto R.*

*Muskingum R.*

*Ohio R.*

Mound City
Prehistoric Indians

Hamilton
Waynes Ft. 1793

Ft. Ancient
Prehistoric
Indians

Chillicothe

North Bend
Harrison
Tomb

CINCINNATI
'Frontier Town'
Ft. Washington
Levee
H. B. Stowes Ho.

Serpent Mound
Prehistoric
Indians

W. VIRGINIA

*Ohio R.*

N

Miles

KENTUCKY

0       50       100

Route of Wayne 1793-94  +++++

# Ohio

**CINCINNATI**  The best place to gain an overall view of Cincinnati is from Eden Park, high on the city's eastern bluffs. Seeing Cincinnati sprawling along the barge-filled Ohio River, it is difficult to believe that before the arrival of Anthony Wayne (*Chapter 6*) it was only Fort Washington which prevented a few thousand Shawnees from completely wiping out the then tiny settlement.

Fort Washington, the main American military base west of Pittsburgh during the 1790's, was situated on a low, flood-free ridge about a half-mile behind the river landing. Little has been done at the present time to commemorate this establishment: there is only a small plaque on the side of a modern, six-story parking building at Third and Broadway and another on the front of Guilford Public School at

255

Fourth and Ludlow — although there are plans for a worthy monument in the future. William Henry Harrison was the commander of Fort Washington shortly before the Territorial Legislature elected him to Congress in 1799 (*Chapter 7*).

When "Mad" Anthony Wayne and his Legionaires arrived in Cincinnati in 1793, they encamped just northwest of the fort; a marker at Fountain Square in the heart of the city (Fifth Street between Vine and Walnut) indicates the site. There is a fine fountain in the square imported from Germany. Across from the Square is Carew Tower, Cincinnati's tallest skyscraper (49 stories), which offers visitors a breathtaking vista from its observation deck.

The old steamboat levee is at the foot of Broadway, a few blocks south of the fort site. The granite blocks still support huge iron chains that anchor the riverside wharves, from one of which Greene Line steamers take tourists as far as St. Louis and New Orleans. In the summer the levee is crowded with sports enthusiasts who find the gradual slope ideal for launching their pleasure craft. Charles Dickens once stepped ashore on this very levee (*Chapter 8*).

Small portions of the Cincinnati of Dickens' day still exist. Many of the quaint, red brick homes that the author saw beneath the "amphitheatre of hills" are in use today as residences on the city's west side. And the Taft Museum, a graceful, Greek Revival mansion built in 1820, still stands at its original location on Fourth and Pike Streets, a representative of the luxury enjoyed by Cincinnati's wealthy class during those early days.

During the decades leading up to the Civil War, Cincinnati became a Midwestern "frontier town" (*Chapter 1*) directly across the Ohio River from the slave plantations of Kentucky. Harriet Beecher Stowe — who gathered most of the material for her disturbing novel on slavery, *Uncle Tom's Cabin*, while living in Cincinnati — spent much of her time in the home of her father, whose house at 2950 Gilbert Avenue (U.S. 22) is now a museum.

**CLEVELAND**    In 1796 Moses Cleaveland and his surveying party of about half a hundred landed at a point near St. Clair and West Ninth Streets. One of their first acts was to pace off a 10-acre New England village green — which is today, at Superior Avenue and Ontario Street, the focal place of the city. Most of the party returned to New England that winter, but Job Stiles and his wife remained in a rustic log cabin (on what later became Superior Avenue) a little west of the village green — to become Cleveland's first permanent white inhabitants. A replica of this first building in Cleveland is in the Western Reserve Historical Society Museum at 10825 East Boulevard.

Cleveland languished for many years after its founding, its real awakening not coming until the completion of the Ohio and Erie Canal in 1833. This canal, by giving Cleveland access to markets as far inland as the Ohio River, eventually enabled the city to surpass its cross-state rival, Cincinnati, in population. Portions of the picturesque old canal may still be followed as it wends its quiet way along the east side of the Cuyahoga River from Cleveland, through Akron, through the Portage Lakes, and at last into the Muskingum River system. It is of value even today for the water that it channels to the industries of Cleveland and Akron.

Although the Rockefeller produce firm (*Chapter 13*) was at 32 River Street, of far greater interest is the gigantic Standard Oil Refinery at 735 Broadway — still bordering the now inconspicuous Kingsbury Run. The company operates under the brand name of "Sohio" since the original Standard Oil trust was broken into regional parts by government action in 1911. Tours of the refinery are available to groups who make arrangements in advance.

Rockefeller's mansion occupied the entire block between Euclid, Case, Prospect and 40th Streets. Each morning he would drive his prancing horses — his pride and joy — down Euclid to his office at 43 Euclid on the Public Square. The home unfortunately was demolished in 1938; but long before, this once fashionable portion of Cleveland had declined to a district of low-income rooming houses.

Any account of Cleveland must mention the Terminal Tower, built in 1928 and still today one of the tallest and most spectacular skyscrapers in the Midwest. It was designed to crown the fantastic and flimsy railroad empire created by Oris and Mantis Van Sweringen, and is still the terminal for a dozen lines. The Van Sweringen brothers went bankrupt during the Depression and so derived little use from their hundred million dollar monument. The view of Cleveland and Lake Erie from the 42nd-story observation area is magnificent.

**CLYDE**  In many ways life at Clyde has changed a great deal since the 1880's and 90's when Sherwood Anderson (*Chapter 12*) was living with his parents at 19 Spring Avenue or 14 Race Street (both houses still stand.) The railroad depot, then the most active place in town — where Anderson was called "Jobby" and sold newspapers — has now been demolished. Main Street, which during Anderson's youth was a dirt roadway where farmers sometimes raced their horses, is now paved. The open fields which surrounded Clyde — to which Anderson drove the townsfolks' cows to pasture for 5 cents a cow per week — are now largely fenced in.

But in many more ways Clyde is still the Winesburg so vividly portrayed by her most famous, though disenchanted son. To wander down Main Street after reading *Winesburg, Ohio,* is to relive parts of one of America's most famous books. Start at the northern end of town, the portion across the railroad tracks, which was called "Canada" in Anderson's time. Here was the home of some of Winesburg's misfits, such as Louise Trunnion, free with sexual favors, and her father, the original, rustic settler in the area. Just south of "Canada" was the railroad station where the telegraph operator, Wash Williams, told the young reporter, George Willard, the strange story of his life. Across from the station was the New Willard House (actually the Empire House and still partially standing) run by Tom Willard, unloving husband to his emotional wife, Elizabeth, and father of George, the book's central figure.

On Main Street near the hotel was the Heffner Block, a building which still stands on the west side of the street where lonely Enoch Robinson had a room. Here too was the office in which Dr. Reefy treated, and silently loved, the dying yet pathetically flirtatious Elizabeth Willard. Next down Main Street was the office of the Winesburg *Eagle* (fictionally located at the northwest corner of Buckeye Street), the newspaper for which George Willard worked, and into which the stories of all of Winesburg's happenings eventually made their way. The Presbyterian Church is also on Main Street, at West Forest, complete with the bell tower from which the distraught Reverend Curtis Hartman fought with his soul while watching the teacher, pretty Kate Swift, alone in her bedroom.

Just beyond the Town Hall was Anderson's Buckeye Street, actually West Cherry Street, which led past the home of Banker White. Here lived sophisticated Helen White, in love with George Willard, yet afraid to express her feelings. West Cherry continues out to the Waterworks where George Willard was beaten by Ed Handby, violent bartender at Griffith's saloon. A remnant of the Fair Ground — the site of the emotional rendezvous between George and Helen White the evening before the reporter left for a new job in the Big City, is just southwest of South Main and Fair Streets.

Thus does fictional Winesburg live in the quiet streets of the sleepy country town.

**DEFIANCE**   The modern town of Defiance, at the confluence of the Maumee and Auglaize Rivers, takes its name from the fort General Wayne built there in 1794 — which itself occupied land long used for Indian councils (*Chapter 6*). The earthworks of Wayne's fort are faintly visible in the park which occupies the prow of land pointing down the Maumee. Fort Defiance was Wayne's last major resting point before he and his iron-disciplined army marched eastward to meet the savage foe.

**FALLEN TIMBERS STATE MONUMENT** The Battle of Fallen Timbers, where "Mad" Anthony Wayne defeated the Indians on August 20, 1794 (*Chapter 6*), is marked by a handsome statue of the General with an Indian and a pioneer on each side. The blufftop location of the monument gives the visitor a good view of the long valley down which the Americans marched. The Indians were massed behind a breastwork of hurricane-tossed trees which extended along the base of the bluff and the Legionaires charged them with the river at their backs. When the Indians broke, they dashed for the supposed safety of the British Fort Miami 2 miles east. The earthworks of this fort, which the British closed to their Indian allies, can still be seen on River Road in the town of Maumee.

**FORT ANCIENT STATE MEMORIAL** There is no more impressive monument to the vigor of the Hopewellian Indians (*Chapter 3*) than the huge, hilltop construction known as Fort Ancient. This structure, built around 1300 A.D., consists of two large walled-in areas (the North Fort and the South Fort) connected by a narrow ridge, likewise walled (the Middle Fort). There are 3½ miles of these earthen embankments, which reach their most massive size at the East Gateway where they are 70 feet wide and 23 feet high. The North Lookout Point, at the end of the park road in the South Fort, offers an excellent view of the valley of the Little Miami River far below.

The word "fort" is probably incorrect in referring to Fort Ancient, for the fact that the walls are broken by 70 openings suggests the structure was used for purposes other than military. It is now generally believed that Fort Ancient was a religious shrine; a view that is enhanced by the fact that 200 Indians were buried in massive limestone coffins near the North Lookout Point — suggesting ceremonial interment of high priests, rather than a military mass burial.

An Indian village has been discovered at the base of the North Fort, and the quantities of pottery shards, arrowheads, and other artifacts found there have been incorporated in exhibits in the park museum.

**FORT LORAMIE** On their way to battle the Indians in the Maumee valley, Anthony Wayne and his Legionaires paused to construct a small fort on the site of an old trading post built by a French trader, Peter Loramie. The Treaty of Fort Greenville subsequently made Fort Loramie the northern boundary of white settlement. Twenty years later William Henry Harrison used this strategic location for an important fort to guard his supply route to Fort Meigs. A marker in the village center indicates the site of these old forts.

On the other side of the marker is a notation relating to the Miami and Erie Canal, completed in 1833, which flowed directly through town on a bed that is now a long, grassy park. Fort Loramie, on the low height of land that divided the waters flowing into the Ohio from those flowing into Lake Erie, was one of the most important locations on the canal. There are still dozens of buildings in the village, especially on the east side of Ohio 66, which were built during the old canal days — their brick exteriors setting them off from the usual white frame structures of rural Ohio. A stone bridge, which formerly spanned the canal, leads across the park to the west side of town.

In order to carry the canal over the rolling land between the Maumee and Ohio rivers, 103 locks, 19 aqueducts, and 3 reservoirs were built. One of these reservoirs can be seen from Loramie Lake State Park 1½ miles east of the village. Visitors will have no difficulty in walking along the top of the dam which impounds the lake to examine the iron wheels that enabled the keeper to regulate the water flow from the lake into the canal. There are also facilities for swimming, fishing, or picnicking in the park.

The 14-mile drive along Ohio 66 between Fort Loramie and St. Mary's reveals many more of the old canal buildings; and the canal itself, here filled with water, is outlined by a long row of trees that grows along its border immediately west of the highway.

**FORT MEIGS STATE MEMORIAL**    Fort Meigs, constructed in 1813 (*Chapter* 7) on the edge of the bluff which dominated the important portage path around the rapids of the Maumee River, contained high earthen walls topped with razor sharp timbers projecting outward. A circular roadway now takes visitors along the partially disintegrated ramparts where markers indicate the locations of the underground magazines and the positions of Harrison's batteries. The outlines of the two deep trenches that the General dug to protect his men from the fire of the British across the river are still clearly visible. The state has made ample provision for picnickers, even erecting a glassed-in shelter complete with a large, flagstone fireplace.

**FORT RECOVERY STATE MEMORIAL**    The state has constructed two blockhouses and a sturdy palisade on the site where a detachment of General Wayne's men built Fort Recovery during the dismal Christmas season in 1793 (*Chapter* 6). One can well imagine the disquietude of the soldiers as they found themselves 23 miles from the main encampment at Greenville amid the bleached bones and grimacing skulls of General Arthur St. Clair's massacred army. There is a small museum in one of the blockhouses.

**GNADENHUTTEN**   Between 1772 and 1782 a group of Christian Indians occupied a settlement called Gnadenhutten, which was immediately north of the modern village of the same name. Nothing remains of the Indian encampment, for it was wiped out by white frontiersmen (*Chapter 5*), and now a tall pylon on the village site contains an inscription that will forever bear a terrible indictment of the pioneers: "Here Triumphed in Death Ninety Christian Indians, March 8, 1782." The Tuscarawas River flows peacefully by on the west, and just east of the pylon is an ancient Indian graveyard with tombstones bearing dates as early as 1775 — before the United States had been formed.

**GREENVILLE**   Fort Greenville was "Mad" Anthony Wayne's principal base and winter quarters in 1793-94 (*Chapter 6*). U.S. 127, which follows the old military supply road from Cincinnati, turns abruptly west at the point where it once passed through the gates of the fort. As one entered the fort, he would have seen the troops' barracks on his left and the council house and Wayne's headquarters on his right.

The traffic circle where U.S. 127 meets Ohio 49, 71, 118, 121, and 502 was once the parade grounds, and it was from here that the fearful, yet strangely confident 2,500 legionaires set out for the Indian stronghold in the Maumee valley. Notice the plaque on highway 127 where it crosses Greenville Creek (a short distance north of the circle), which commemorates the bridge built here by Wayne in 1794.

After the victory at Fallen Timbers, Wayne returned to Fort Greenville to await the defeated chiefs. In June 1795 they signed the Treaty of Fort Greenville, one of the most important documents in Midwestern history, which made most of Ohio entirely American and gave the United States the sites of Chicago, Detroit, Toledo, and Vincennes. The defeated Indians camped beside Greenville Creek just west of the parade grounds, now a large, well-kept park.

**HAMILTON**   The bustling city of Hamilton now occupies the site of a fort built by the ill-fated army of General Arthur St. Clair in 1791, and named by St. Clair after his admired friend, Alexander Hamilton. Anthony Wayne enlarged and strengthened the fort two years later (*Chapter 6*) and it then became a major supply point on the military road (now U.S. 127) leading from Cincinnati to Fort Greenville. A blockhouse and a portion of the palisades have been reconstructed on the original location beside the Miami River. Ohio 129 crosses the Miami at this point on a site once used by a covered bridge.

**HUDSON**   Hudson, a quiet college town of a few thousand inhabitants, is replete with reminders of the days when this portion of Ohio was Connecticut's Western Reserve — and in reality was part of New England. Almost all the homes are white frame, trimmed with green, and having none of the spacious front porches seen in other Midwestern country towns. The Hudson Library and the Episcopal Church, both fronting the typical New England village green, are superb examples of eastern architecture. The entire town contains a relaxed atmosphere, as if it knew it were different from the rest of the Midwest, as if it felt itself to be alien, even superior, to the active world that cannot destroy its green and white tranquillity. No one visiting Hudson would have any doubt that he was on a Midwestern frontier (*Chapter 1*).

**KELLEY'S ISLAND**   This peaceful, wine-growing island is about 45 minutes by car ferry from Sandusky and is only a short distance from Put-In Bay where Commodore Perry set out to meet the British in the Battle of Lake Erie (*Chapter 7*). The main interest at Kelley's Island centers on the knee-high grooves scoured in solid limestone by the glaciers that ground across its surface. These glacial grooves, found on the northern side of the island (close to a fine swimming beach) are among the best in the Midwest.

The limestone bedrock of Kelley's Island is part of the Niagarian formation that comprises the basin of the Great Lakes (*Chapter 2*). This limestone was once quarried here and taken by ship wherever good building stone was needed. (Portions of the locks at Sault Ste. Marie, Michigan, were constructed from this limestone.) However, more accessible stone was gradually found on the mainland, and by the 1940's most of the quarrying operations on the island had stopped. There is an abandoned pit immediately west of Glacial Grooves Park, and crumbling stone-loading platforms still protrude into the lake near the ferry dock.

With its aging, weather-worn homes, picturesque ruins of quarrying days, and miles of lake-lovely roads and pathways, Kelley's Island is a far-away paradise for those who wish to escape the frantic living of modern America.

**KIRTLAND**   Kirtland, as the site of Mormon beginnings, occupies a special place in their feelings (*Chapter 9*). The temple, which Joseph Smith commanded to be built in 1833, still stands and is kept in excellent condition. Dedicated Mormon guides point out the very place where Smith saw the Lord gazing upon the congregation, His eyes flaming brighter than the equatorial sun. Smith directed many meetings from the Melchisedec pulpit at the head of the church and used a room on the third floor for his office. Visitors are usually impressed by the pink and white church interior, which gives it a cheery aspect seldom found in religious buildings, and by the original, hand-blown glass, which, with its irregular surface, transforms the exterior world into an unreal, ethereal landscape.

A plaque over the church entrance reminds us that the Mormon Church split during the 1870's, the eastern, less numerous segment becoming known as the Reorganized Church of Jesus Christ of Latter-day Saints (it is they who own the Kirtland shrine) to distinguish it from the Mormons who followed Brigham Young to Utah. (See also NAUVOO, Illinois)

**MOUND CITY GROUP NATIONAL MONUMENT**  Mound City, a 13-acre Hopewellian graveyard (*Chapter 3*), is enclosed by an ancient earthen wall which sets off the sacred burial mounds. There are 24 of these mounds, and their lack of number seems to indicate that the Hopewellians interred here were the highest officials in the nation — deemed man-gods, perhaps, by their followers. The dead dignitaries were placed in wooden mausoleums and, after what must have been impressive, magic-tinted ceremonies, the coffins were burned and earth piled up around the ashes. The largest mound was described by early visitors as being 17 feet high and 90 feet wide.

Some of the finest implements made in pre-historic America have been found in the mounds. A few are on exhibit in the Monument headquarters; others are in the Ross County Historical Society museum in nearby Chillicothe.

**THE NATIONAL ROAD**  The old National Road (*Chapter 8*) is still very much in use today, although the original gravel roadbed has been replaced by concrete and the name changed to U.S. 40. Much of the former color remains, however, expecially in eastern Ohio where scores of ancient inns still line the highway, their gray-stone exteriors, squat, rectangular shapes, and gable roofs with chimneys at either end clearly announcing their early vintage. There are, in addition, frequent stone bridges, easily seen from the modern highway, that were once used by the old conestoga wagons as they rumbled westward. One of the best examples of these bridges will be found beside U.S. 40 2 miles west of Middlebourne — where it is used today by a county road.

The original milestones will also be seen along U.S. 40, announcing on one side the distance to the next town and on the other the mileage from Cumberland, Maryland, the starting point. At Springfield, Ohio, Richmond, Indiana, and Vandalia, Illinois, statues known as the Madonna of the Trail have been erected in honor of the courageous women who followed their men down the dusty, rockstrewn roadway.

For those who wish to capture more of the old-time National Road atmosphere than can be gained amid the throb of interstate traffic, we recommend a visit to Old Washington, a village now off the modern highway.

**NORTH BEND**    The village of North Bend, located on a northerly turning of the Ohio River, was the site of the home to which William Henry Harrison retired in 1829 when he imagined his public life over. However in 1840 the Whig Party, searching for a presidential candidate who would capture the public fancy, settled upon the aging victor of Tippecanoe (*Chapter 7*). Under a campaign slogan of "Tippecanoe and Tyler too" (John Tyler was his running mate), Harrison won the presidency. But the rigors of Washington proved too much for the sixty-eight-year-old frontiersman, and he died on April 4, 1841 — only 31 days after taking office.

Harrison was buried near his North Bend home in a small, brick mausoleum. Although in the following years the grave of this man who did so much to win the Midwest was greatly neglected, in 1919 the mausoleum was at last renovated and five years later a tall shaft erected to Harrison's memory. The magnificent view of the Ohio from the grave hill must be much the same as the old man saw from his front porch as he sat, longing, perhaps, for the heroic days of his youth.

**OLD PIQUA**    The site of the Shawnee capital of Old Piqua (*Chapter 7*) was about 5 miles west of modern Springfield. A monument beside Interstate 70 is dedicated to George Rogers Clark, who defeated the Shawnee in the Battle of Piqua, fought here in 1780 — a year after Clark had driven the British from Vincennes (*Chapter 5*).

Although some authorities claim Tecumseh was born near modern Piqua, 30 miles to the northwest, it seems more probable that this site along the Mad River was his actual birthplace. There is a recreational area at the Old Piqua location where one may partially recapture the river scene that was so well known and loved by the Shawnees.

**OLD WASHINGTON**    The little village of Old Washington, fortunately bypassed by the modern highway, gives the tourist one of the few authentic views of a National Road town as it once appeared to the westward-bound immigrants. The main street — quiet, shaded by tall, aged maples, lined by many of the sturdy, brick buildings that were built when the town was on the National Road — presents a scene right out of the 1830's. It is as if the town has been caught in an eddy of time. One can almost see the heavily laden conestoga wagons making their way down the street to the Colonial Inn (built in 1805 and one of the most commodious inns on the Road,) which still commands the western end of the village — although it is now a nursing home.

**PUT-IN BAY** Put-In Bay on South Bass Island, the place from which Commodore Oliver Hazard Perry sailed on September 10, 1813, to meet and defeat the British fleet (*Chapter* 7), is the site of the Perry's Victory and International Peace Memorial — a 20-story, white granite column. The view from the top of this tower is most spectacular: the linear vineyards of South Bass Island spread out below; the hump of Gibraltar Island nearby (upon which Perry's lookout first sighted the emerging British fleet); the green plateau of Middle Bass Island in the distance; and, in a line extending northwest from Rattlesnake Island, the area in which the two fleets met.

Put-In Bay is accessible either by an hour ferry ride from Catawba Point, or from Sandusky, from where a leisurely full day round trip can be made — the boat stopping at Kelley's Island and some of the other picturesque wine ports.

**SCHOENBRUNN VILLAGE STATE MEMORIAL** Schoenbrunn (*Chapter* 5), named by the German missionary, David Zeisberger, for the bubbling spring that flowed nearby, was the chief village of the Christian Moravian Indians whose compatriots at Gnadenhutten were massacred during the Revolutionary War. When Schoenbrunn was built in 1772, it was the first Christian settlement in Ohio. Although the village was abandoned in 1777 (when Zeisberger, apprehensive of the violence of the war, moved his converts to what he deemed a safer location to the north), much of it has now been carefully reconstructed.

The visitor can see the hand-hewn schoolhouse where Delaware Indian children studied spelling, using a book Zeisberger himself had written in their language. Here, too, is the reconstructed church where Zeisberger conducted daily services. The barren log building where the missionary lived adjoins the church.

After the terrors of the Indian-white warfare had diminished, Zeisberger led his now-diminished Moravian followers back to the Tuscarawas valley, where they built in 1798, a village opposite the destroyed Schoenbrunn. It was in this village, called Goshen, that the aged and disillusioned missionary died in 1808 — with only 20 Indian converts remaining to represent a lifetime of the most arduous work. Zeisberger's grave will be found at modern Goshen in a neglected cemetery which occupies a tiny patch of ground next to the grade school.

**SERPENT MOUND STATE MEMORIAL** Serpent Mound is well

known to archeologists as one of the largest effigy earthworks in the world. The mound is in the form of a gigantic snake, which slithers along the top of a bluff for nearly a quarter of a mile, its jaws enclosing an oval object and its coiled tail appearing almost ready to fall down the precipice into the sycamore-studded stream below. The purpose of the effigy is not known, but it could hardly have been other than religious. It piques one's fancy to imagine the mysterious Hopewellian ceremonies that might have occurred here: weird chanting, rhythmic dances, human sacrifices.

There is a small museum on the grounds which has displays relating to the Serpent and other mounds found on the blufftop. Visitors will also enjoy the picnic areas and hiking trails which abound.

**ZOAR** One of the idealistic colonies established in the Midwest during the early nineteenth century was that called Zoar, after the Biblical town where Lot sought sanctuary. A religious colony existed here from 1817 to 1898, its German-speaking inhabitants keeping carefully aloof from their American neighbors. Life at Zoar would have been very dull to moderns for the Zoarite beliefs included the refusal to observe any holidays, including Christmas, and the disdain of any sort of color or gay ornaments in personal dress. Individuals were suppose to concern themselves with love of God only, and for a time family life itself was totally discontinued. However these stern views could not withstand the more easygoing life of the ever-encroaching Americans, and as the fervent first and second generations died out, the colony began to change — so radically in fact that it was finally abandoned after 81 long, uneventful years.

The first thing to catch the eye of the tourist entering the village from the north is the colorful, block square garden which has been restored to its original beauty. The Zoarites intended the garden to be symbolic: the central spruce representing God; the encircling junipers, the 12 disciples; the radiating walks, the paths to heaven. The large beds of multi-colored flowers which the Zoarites grew between the paths were locally famed and their seeds brought good prices in Cleveland.

South of the garden is the baronial, red brick Number One House, home of the Zoar leader, Joseph Baumeler. It is now a museum containing important materials concerning the life and crafts of the Zoarites. A short distance south of Baumeler's house is the hotel, which, by permitting the influx of strangers with disrupting, materialistic ideas, was one of the main reasons for the downfall of Zoar. Also to be found in the environs is the dilapidated mill, the calaboose, the cabin in which Baumeler preached his first sermon, and many of the original Zoar homes.

**Miles**
0  50  100

Route of Joliet and Marquette 1673 -----

LAKE SUPERIOR

DULUTH

Superior

U P P E R

M I C H I G A N

M I N N E S O T A

St. Croix R.

ST. PAUL

OLD TIMBER LANDS
1830 ~ 1890

W I S C O N S I N

Eau Claire
Paul Bunyan
Camp

Chippewa R.

Lake Pepin

Green Bay
Nicolet Landing 1634
Marquette 1673

Door Pen.

Perrot State Park
French Fort
*1685

West Salem
Garland Ho.

Mill Bluff State Pk.
Sandstone Buttes

Glacial Lake Wisconsin

Wisconsin R.

Fox R.

Ripon
Ceresco 1844
Birthplace of
Republican Party
1854

Old Wade Ho.
*Inn 1852

*Parnell
Tower

M I S S I S S I P P I

D R I F T L E S S

A R E A

Wisconsin
Dells
Scenic Waterway

Portage
Marquette 1673
Kinzie Ho. 1834

Kettle Moraine

Prairie du Chien
Fur Era
Villa Louis 1843

Baraboo
Range

Devil's Lake State Pk.
Mountain Stub

Holy Hill
Highest Moraine
Point

M I C H I G A N

Tower Hill State Pk.
Tunnel

Madison

MILWAUKEE

Wyalusing
State Pk.
Marquette 1673

Mineral Point
Old Cornish Mining
Center

Aztalan State Pk.
Prehistoric Indians
Reconstr. Pallisades

N

I O W A

Dubuque

I L L I N O I S

# Wisconsin

**AZTALAN STATE PARK** Archeologists who first discovered the eroded earthen pyramids along the Crawfish River believed they had found the city from which it was rumored the Aztecs of Mexico had come. The ruins were, correspondingly, named "Aztalan," after that legendary Aztec land. However, later investigations revealed that the site had been inhabited by Indians of the Mississippian culture (*Chapter 3*), and it is now surmised that the people of Aztalan migrated up the Rock River (of which the Crawfish is a subsidiary) from the Mississippian centers around Cahokia.

The people of Aztalan were quite different from the more primitive tribes who then inhabited Wisconsin, and, either because of their aggressive, warlike tendencies or fearful cannibalism (there are cracked human bones in the areas once Aztalan refuse dumps), the Aztalanians found themselves besieged by the hostile natives. To protect themselves, they constructed a tremendous wall around not only their entire village but their fields as well. But Aztalan was doomed. In what must have been a most viciously fought battle, the walls were breached, the village burned, and the inhabitants killed or carried off as slaves.

One cannot help but feel that the past is very close as he visits Aztalan State Park. The Crawfish River, flecked with white as it cascades over the rapids, is much the same as when the Mississippian men and women fished in its waters 700 or 800 years ago. The pyramids — the tallest two probably dedicated to the sun and the moon — still rise along the river bank, mutely recalling the days when painted priests offered incantations on their tops. Even portions of the walls have been reconstructed and again stand out proudly against the surrounding hills.

**DEVIL'S LAKE STATE PARK**    Possibly no Midwestern area presents a more unique and picturesque location for swimming or hiking than Devil's Lake State Park. The lake is enclosed by 500 foot bluffs of lavender quartzite that sparkle brightly in the sunlight. This quartzite is known as a mountain stub, for it was once deep in the interior of an Alpine-like range and was exposed to the surface only when, after eons of time, the thick overlaying rock was eroded away. Thus the visitors to Devil's Lake have the unusual opportunity of swimming in the heart of an ancient mountain.

During the Ice Age (*Chapter 2*) the quartzite hills, which are known as the Baraboo Range, underwent another great transformation. As the gigantic glacier ground through the northern pass, it rounded the mountain edges to their present smoothness; and when the glacier melted, it left a huge pile of gravel in the pass which impounded the meltwater to form Devil's Lake. The Wisconsin River, which formerly flowed directly through the Baraboo Range, therefore was forced to skirt its eastern edge before it could resume its westward flow to the Mississippi. This means that not only is Devil's Lake encircled by a mountain stub, but its bed was once part of the Wisconsin River.

**EAU CLAIRE**    Some of the finest stands of timber on the continent were found along the Chippewa River — and the chief sawmill town was Eau Claire, the "clear water" of French voyageurs. The mills at Eau Claire cut the rough logs into planks, which were then formed into rafts to be floated down the river to the finishing mills at Dubuque or St. Louis. Although the peak of the lumber business came in 1892, the forests were being felled at such a rapid rate that by 1910 the logging operations at Eau Claire were over.

The city has built a replica lumber camp as a monument to the days of the timber frontier (*Chapter 8*). This camp, consisting of a long bunkhouse, a blacksmith shop, a horse barn, and a tool shed, is in Carson Park on the west end of Grand Avenue. Although the display is not as complete as one might wish, there is no question of its authenticity. From the quiet, wooded hill overlooking Half Moon Lake (in which there is swimming and fishing) it is hard to realize that in only 60 years teams of men working from small camps such as this were able to topple the almost interminable forest that covered Wisconsin, Michigan, and Minnesota.

**GREEN BAY** Green Bay, as Wisconsin's oldest city, holds a special place in state history. The name is the literal translation of the French "La Baye Verte," which was given at first to the bay itself, then thought to be the fabled northwest passage to the orient.

The best historical approach to Green Bay is from the northeast on Wisconsin 57, a highway which parallels the route of Jean Nicolet, the first white man to penetrate the Midwestern heartland (*Chapter 4*). About 12 miles from Green Bay is a fine statue to Nicolet, which overlooks the bay near the place where the explorer first set foot on Wisconsin soil in 1634. Interested tourists should take the country road just north of the statue and proceed a mile or two down the low bluff to the bay shore, where a marker indicates the exact landing site. From there follow county road A the rest of the way into Green Bay — it is a most pleasant, waterside drive.

Once in town, stand for a while on the Main Street bridge (U.S. 141) and let history swirl around you. In 1673 Joliet and Marquette made their way past this spot as they headed up the Fox River into the Great Unknown. In the years that followed, a French stockade rose beside the river a few hundred foot north of the bridge on a location now occupied by the Chicago and Northwestern railroad depot. During these days of the fur frontier the bark wigwams of a Sauk village was opposite the fort on the east side of the river. In 1733 the French garrison, determined to avenge the death of their commandant at the hands of the capricious Sauk, crossed the river, ferociously attacked the Indians, and completely wiped out their village. The Beaumont Hotel now occupies the Sauk village site and a plaque on the corner of Washington and Main describes the battle.

Around 1745 a French village of traders, trappers, and voyageurs began to grow along the eastern river's edge 5 blocks south of the Main Street bridge. The home of Green Bay's first permanent settler, Augustin De Langlades, is indicated by a marker at 308 S. Washington Street. As the years passed, the village spread across the river where the home built in 1776 by Joseph Roi, a voyageur, still stands at Fifth Street and Tenth Avenue — the oldest house in Wisconsin (now known as the Tank Cottage after a later occupant).

After the Midwest passed to the Americans, John Jacob Astor and his powerful American Fur Company branched out from their headquarters on Mackinac Island to establish an important post at Green Bay, choosing as their post site the centrally located graveyard of the old French settlement. A series of plaques at the eastern end of the Mason Avenue bridge (route 54) describes the American Fur post and the luxurious Astor House, one of the finest hotels in the old Northwest.

In 1816, at the insistence of the Astorians, the American government built Fort Howard on the location of the decayed French (and later British) fort. The old fort hospital still can be visited at N. Chestnut and Kellogg Streets.


**KETTLE MORAINE**   During the Glacial Age (*Chapter 2*) two huge lobes of ice rumbled down upon eastern Wisconsin — one glacier plowing out the bed of Lake Michigan, the other the bed of Green Bay. Where the edges of these two lobes met, extra high masses of debris were piled, remaining today as the Kettle Moraine — a mile wide ridge running from Elkhart Lake in the north to Whitewater Lake in the south. The State of Wisconsin, which has incorporated existing state and local roads into the Kettle Moraine Drive, has constructed a great many scenic picnic sites along the 120-mile way.

There are few better locations to observe the effects of the glaciers than along the Kettle Moraine Drive. Probably the best place to gain an overall view is from the Parnell Tower near the northern end of the Drive (4 miles north of Dundee). Atop the high lookout, one can see the twisting ridge coursing off on both sides, its tree-covered surface causing it to stand out like a mighty river from the agricultural fields on each side. Another excellent view is from the spire of the Holy Hill Cathedral, on State 167 at the highest portion of the moraine.

As you take the Drive, watch for the oddly shaped kettle holes which were once isolated blocks of ice beneath the glacial drift (*Chapter 2*). You will also see circular kames (mounds that were gravel lake bottoms on the glaciers' surface). And strangest of all are the narrow, winding eskers (formerly beds of glacial streams). One of the longest eskers is immediately south of the Parnell Tower.

At the northern end of the Drive is the Old Wade House, only a few miles above the Parnell Tower. This excellently restored stage coach house is interesting historically, for it is well over a hundred years old and was one of the earliest inns in this portion of the state.


**LAKE PEPIN**   The formation of Lake Pepin, actually part of the Mississippi, occurred during the end of the Glacial Age when the Chippewa River, flooded with meltwater torrents, churned into the larger stream with such great and continuing force that it laid a long ridge of sediment across the Mississippi, thereby damming its waters and forming Lake Pepin. Anyone crossing the now-diminished Chippewa would hardly dream that it had once challenged and conquered the Father of Waters.

Lake Pepin is certainly one of the most beautiful bodies of water in the Midwest. Although U.S. 61 follows it closely on the Minnesota side, Wisconsin 35 is somewhat more scenic. Shortly after Route 35 crosses the Chippewa going north, it comes to a turnout where a marker indicates the site of Fort St. Antoine, a French post built here in 1686 — only 13 years after Joliet and Marquette had discovered the upper Mississippi. In 1689 the commandant, Nicolas Perrot, gathered about him representatives of the local tribes and held an impressive ceremony on the spectacular bluffside where he took possession of the entire upper Mississippi region in the name of the King of France. About this time the French named the lake after the Pepin brothers, colleagues of Sieur Du Luth, discoverer of Lake Superior.

The American raftsmen of the timber frontier regarded Lake Pepin unfavorably, for treacherous squalls often drove their unwieldy crafts on the rocks. But at other times the lumbermen would revel in the beauty of the lake, calling one of their favorite landmarks Maiden Rock (now on Route 35 just south of the entrance to the modern village of the same name).

The beauty of Lake Pepin has impressed many famous travelers. A turnout plaque a few miles north of Maiden Rock quotes William Cullen Bryant as stating that the lake "ought to be visited in the summer by every painter and poet in the land." And we agree.

**MILL BLUFF STATE PARK**    One of the most unusual portions of the Midwest is in Wisconsin's Driftless Area around Mill Bluff, where a number of tall, flat-topped buttes remind one of Arizona, not the rounded Midwestern lands. These buttes, composed of the most ancient sandstone, were once part of a great plain that was level with their tops but which was largely eroded away over the ages. Now only Mill Bluff and a few other buttes remain — like massive monuments to an age long past.

During the melting phase of the Ice Age, the triangular area bounded by Baraboo, Tomah, and Stevens Point became a vast body of floodwater, known as Lake Wisconsin. At this time Mill Bluff was transformed into a foam-ringed island. During the lumber era, a saw mill was located near the bluff, giving it its name. Two hundred steps now lead to the blufftop, where there is a good view of the interesting and unusual countryside.

**MINERAL POINT**    One of Wisconsin's most historic, yet least known towns, is Mineral Point, located in what was once the center of an important lead mining region and the most populous portion of the state. The lead deposits were discovered in 1828 on a long, narrow ridge which, because it was part of the Driftless Area and free from the covering of glacial deposits, was close to the surface. Mineral Point, taking its name from the metallic ridge, was soon a boom town, and so great was its fame that over 8,000 miners from distant Cornwall in the British Isles migrated there. When Wisconsin became a Territory in 1836, Henry Dodge, the first governor, took his oath of office in Mineral Point, the most important place in Wisconsin. The town nearly became the permanent capital, but the legislature chose a more central location: the beautiful, though uninhabited, isthmus between Lakes Mendota and Monona, now the city of Madison.

Even though the lead gave out in the 1860's many buildings of the old era still stand. There is the Walker Hotel, now in dilapidated condition across from the Chicago, Milwaukee, & St. Paul railroad depot — built in 1836 and the oldest building in town. There is the brewery on the north side of town, a still-operating-relic of the 1830's. And, most interesting of all, there are the original Cornish houses which line one side of a lane called Shake Rag Street.

Shake Rag Street, opposite the Mineral Point Ridge, is an authentic piece of transposed Cornwall — for many of the quaint, little homes have been restored. In one home, Pendarvis by name, authentic Cornish meals are served. In another, Polperro, visitors can browse through the low-ceilinged rooms (the Cornish were short people), ascend the narrow staircase to the even tinier second floor rooms, or gaze through the minute windows made when glass was expensive. And as evening falls, perhaps one will even hear again the shrill voices of the long dead Cornish wives and see the rags they are shaking in the air to call their men home from the digging on Mineral Point.

**PERROT STATE PARK**   One of the central landmarks on the upper Mississippi is the massive hump of the mountain, which, with its bulk detached from the canyon wall, was called by the French Mont-trempe-l'eau, or the mountain-with-its-feet-in-the-water. Nicolas Perrot, the dynamic French Commandant of the West, built a fort on the flat-lands beside Trempealeau in 1685. The fort site has been located and a plaque indicates where the hearthstone was found. However the post was only temporary, and the following year Perrot moved his main base to a ridge overlooking Lake Pepin 50 miles upriver.

Park trails lead up the bluff where there are good views of the Mississippi and Trempealeau Mountain. The park also contains swimming, camping, and picnicking facilities.

**PORTAGE**   One of the most significant events in Midwestern history occurred at the Fox River just east of Portage on route 33. This was the exact place, as markers point out, where Joliet and Marquette began the 1¼-mile portage which would lead them to the Wisconsin River, a branch of their long-sought-for-Mississippi (*Chapter 4*). If any date can be given for the birth of the Midwest as a region, it is June 14, 1673, for then the two men discovered the Mississippi system and thereby found that the area west of the St. Lawrence was not merely a narrow neck of land obstructing access to the orient, but was a subcontinent itself. On this day the Midwest began to exist.

The route taken by Joliet and Marquette (along an Indian trail) was utilized by Americans in 1840 for a canal to connect the Fox with the Wisconsin. Thus the explorers' path is now clearly indicated by the old canal, now fallen into disuse, which skirts the town of Portage to the south. Large locks open into the Wisconsin at what is probably the identical place where the excited Frenchmen dipped their canoes into the water.

In 1828 a fort was built at the Fox end of the portage, partly at the instigation of John Jacob Astor who was irritated with the Winnebagoes for charging his trappers tolls to use the path. The surgeon's quarters, used from 1834 until 1845, still stands near the Fox River bridge.

On the west side of the Fox, and slightly to the north of the fort, was the old Indian Agency house, residence of the Federal official in charge of distributing the treaty annuities to the Indians. The handsome home, now restored and open to the public, was built in 1832 under the supervision of Lieutenant Jefferson Davis, later President of the Confederate States. Juliette Kinzie, young and pretty wife of the Indian Agent, living in the house during the terrible uncertainties of the Black Hawk War ( see ROCK ISLAND, Illinois), slept with loaded pistols beside her pillow.

**PRAIRIE DU CHIEN**   Prairie du Chien, named by the French for the Fox chief, Le Chien (or "the Dog"), was an important fur center during the early days. The first settlements were on St. Friol Island, where the home of the trader, Brisbois, built in 1808, will still be found. A succession of French, British, and American forts were likewise located on the island, and a blockhouse has been reconstructed on the site of the American Fort Crawford, built in 1816. The island Fort Crawford was abandoned in 1831 and a new fort constructed on a nearby mainland bluffside where it had a more expansive command of the countryside. The hospital of the newer Fort Crawford may still be visited.

At the time the army abandoned St. Friol Island, young Hercules Dousman, agent of the American Fur Company, purchased much of the government land, where he built 12 years later the town's most magnificent mansion, the Villa Louis. When the fur man married, he brought his bride home to the mansion where, to the young woman's surprise and delight, more than 500 candles were blazing on the glassed-in porch. Today the Villa Louis — with its graceful facade, calm reflecting pool, period furnishings, and souvenirs of the fur trade — is a major tourist attraction.

**RIPON**    On March 20, 1854, an event occurred in Ripon which eventually changed the entire fabric of early America. At this time a group of men held a meeting in a little frame schoolhouse which, although it originally was intended to be merely a protest against the pro-slavery actions of the Democratic and Whig parties, resulted ultimately in the founding of a new party, the Republican, and thus insured a split in the country which could only be closed by a civil war. The schoolhouse still stands on Routes 44 and 49 just east of the center of town.

Ripon was also the site of an interesting Utopian settlement along the lines of New Harmony (*Chapter 9*). In 1844 a small group of pioneers began a village which they called Ceresco, after the Roman goddess of grain. The village was a kind of community corporation where everyone worked for the common good with property held jointly but at wages which were commensurate with one's skill. At the end of the year the profits were divided among the members according to the amount of money which they had invested in the enterprise.

In 1849 Ceresco reached its highwater mark, when 200 persons were members. At this time it was deemed necessary to build a large, communal dwelling, called the Long House. However shortly thereafter, discontent with the wage scale and community property caused the dissolution of the enterprise and the eventual absorption of the settlement by Ripon. All that now remains of Ceresco are the odd angle streets which differentiate it from Ripon, the park at Union Street (formerly the central meeting place for the Utopians) and the Long House, across from the park, which now is used for private residences.

**TOWER HILL STATE PARK**    Tower Hill is a most interesting remnant of the lead mining era — which was so important in early Wisconsin history that the numerous, Badger-like lead excavations gave Wisconsin its nick-name: the Badger State. At Tower Hill, sometime around 1829, a 200-foot well was dug into the sandstone, at the bottom of which a large vat of water was placed. Molten lead was dropped down the deep well, and, as it hit the water, it solidified into balls ideal for cannon shot. A 100-foot tunnel ran from the bottom of the well to Mill Creek, where the shot was placed aboard boats headed for St. Louis. Although the shot making stopped in 1861, visitors can still walk through the dark tunnel where the original pick marks can be seen. In the vibrating darkness the twentieth century seems far away; one almost expects to hear the creak of lead wagons and the cackle of old miners.

**WEST SALEM** West Salem, an agricultural community of only 1,400 persons, has probably changed but little from the days when Hamlin Garland brought his father back to it around the turn of the century (*Chapter* 8). The Garland house stands surrounded by elms at 357 W. Garland Street (City U.S. 16) — though it is a private residence and not open to tourists. Here, indeed, was the sad end of the "sunset trail" for one of the pioneers who had entered the Midwest with such high hopes.

The old Garland farm was on the side of Green's Coulee, a canyon rounded by glaciers, which ended at the sawmills on Onalaska two miles west. Hamlin was born on the farm in 1860 and attended school in Onalaska before the family moved into Iowa when he was eight. The driver who travels the seven miles between West Salem and Onalaska will see some of the beautiful, yet harsh land that Garland described in his most popular fiction book, *Main-travelled Roads*:

> "The Main-travelled road is hot and dusty in summer, and desolate and drear with mud in the fall . . . and in the winter the winds sweep the snow across it; but it does sometimes cross a rich meadow where the songs of larks and bobolinks . . . are tangled."

**WISCONSIN DELLS** The town of Wisconsin Dells is located at the dam which divides the Wisconsin River gorge into upper and lower portions. The Upper Dells (or Dalles as the French traders called them, from the layers of stone through which the river cut) contains the narrows, the most treacherous portion of the river for the lumbermen who once guided their awkward rafts southward from the timberlands (*Chapter* 8). The excursion boats which now ply the Upper Dells take the tourist through the narrows, although, due to the construction of the dam in 1909, the water level is 20 feet higher than formerly and much of the vertical grandeur of the twisted canyon walls has been lost. After the raftsmen passed through the narrows, they enjoyed the exuberant hospitality of the Dell House, a three-story hotel built in 1838. The site of this old hostel, which burned to the ground in 1899, is pointed out on the three-hour excursions.

While the Lower Dells are not as primitive as the Upper Dells, nor as honeycombed with hidden and beautiful glade-canyons, the water of the dam has not hidden the pristine exotic forms that the glacial-fed river carved in multi-layers of sandstone. There are several resorts along this part of the river with most scenic vistas and facilities for boating or swimming.

A small group of Winnebago Indians maintains a summer village on the western river bluffs. Although this settlement may be visited, the real highlight is the superb ceremony the Indians give every summer night at the Stand Rock outdoor amphitheater. Here, amid bizarrely beautiful sandstone formations, illuminated with just the right number of colored floodlights, the Winnebagoes and representatives of other tribes again indulge in the frenzy and grace of prehistoric dances — while the Dells again echo to the rhythmic pulsations of their tom-toms.

**WYALUSING STATE PARK** It seems fitting to end this book with the description of Wyalusing State Park, for here, at least to the author, is the sentimental center of the Midwest.

Wyalusing means "The Home of the Warrior," and a half-mile series of Indian burial mounds on Sentinel Ridge attest to the reverence in which the Indians held these heights above the junction of the Mississippi and Wisconsin Rivers. Here was an unofficial Indian boundary: the domain of the plains-loving Sioux was west of the Mississippi, that of the forest-loving Algonquin tribes to the east. Prairie du Chien, 14 miles north, was long a favorite trading place between the Indians and the French, British, and Americans who established successive posts there.

Joliet and Marquette were the first white men to see the sacred bluffs of Wyalusing when they climbed its 530-foot height in 1673 to gain their first expansive view of their ardently sought for goal, the Mississippi, the Father of Waters (*Chapter 4*). A lookout has now been built on the approximate location where the elated French explorers stood.

During the fur era, the rivers below Wyalusing would often be studded with canoes heavy with beaverskins; in the lumber days huge rafts would glide downstream; and during the steamboat age, gaily painted riverboats would sputter past, streaming long trails of black smoke behind them like disintegrating ribbons. And still today the rivers are used by modern barges while their shores are lined with some of the most beautiful highways in the nation.

Wyalusing is the near-center of the upper Midwest, almost equidistant as it is between Minneapolis in the piney northlands, Council Bluffs on the great western grasslands, St. Louis on the tepid southern frontier, and Chicago in the heart of the cornbelt. Here, amid the trails and grand-vistaed lookouts, one can contemplate the splendor of the past and muse upon the mystery of the future.

# Index